*Work and Lifecourse in Japan*

*This book is sponsored by the Joint Committee on Japanese Studies of the Social Science Research Council and the American Council of Learned Societies*

*DAVID W. PLATH*, EDITOR

# *Work and Lifecourse*

# *in Japan*

*with contributions by*

SAMUEL COLEMAN, THEODORE F. COOK, JR.,
KAREN C. HOLDEN, JILL KLEINBERG,
SOLOMON B. LEVINE, JACK G. LEWIS,
SUSAN O. LONG, JAMES MCLENDON,
PAUL H. NOGUCHI, JULIUS A. ROTH,
AND KENNETH A. SKINNER

*State University of New York Press*

ALBANY

Published by
State University of New York Press, Albany

©1983 State University of New York

For information, address State University of New York
Press, State University Plaza, Albany, N.Y., 12246

**Library of Congress Cataloging in Publication Data**
Main entry under title:
Work and lifecourse in Japan.

  Includes index.
  Contents: Life is just a job resume? / David W. Plath
— Careers and mobility in Japan's labor markets /
Solomon B. Levine — Changing employment patterns of
women / Karen C. Holden — [etc.]
  1. Japan—Occupations—Social aspects—Addresses,
essays, lectures. I. Plath, David W. II. Coleman,
Samuel.
HD6957.J3W67  1983      305.9′00952      82-10481
ISBN 0-87395-704-0
ISBN 0-87395-705-9 (pbk.)

10  9  8  7  6  5

# Contents

# CONTENTS

# List of Tables

vii

# List of Figures

# Acknowledgments

Many people helped and encouraged me through the uncertain career of this study project. It's good to be able to thank them in print.

My colleagues on the Joint Committee on Japanese Studies indulged my ambition to direct the project. They provided funds for it on two occasions, and they often provided the hard-hitting criticism that a project godfather needs to keep him honest. Membership on the Committee has varied during the period of the project but has included the following:

Karen Brazell, Cornell University; Robert E. Cole, University of Michigan; Haruhiro Fukui, University of California, Santa Barbara; G. Cameron Hurst III, University of Kansas; Ellis S. Krauss, Western Washington University; Earl R. Miner, Princeton University; Masao Miyoshi, University of Chicago; Tetsuo Najita, University of Chicago; Hugh D. Patrick, Yale University; T. J. Pempel, Cornell University; Kenneth Pyle, University of Washington; J. Thomas Rimer, Washington University, St. Louis; Barbara Ruch, University of Pennsylvania; Satō Seizaburō, University of Tokyo; and Ronald Aqua, staff.

In addition to the contributors to this volume, the following colleagues also prepared working papers for the project: L. Keith Brown, University of Pittsburgh; Liza Crihfield Dalby, University of Chicago; Inoue Shun, Osaka National University; Christie W. Kiefer, University of California, San Francisco; Kōhara Yukinari, Rikkyō University; Bernard Silberman, University of Chicago; and Wakabayashi Mitsuru, Keiō University.

Others who participated in one or more of the project's meetings are John B. Grossberg, University of Illinois at Urbana-Champaign; Ishihara Kunio, Japan National Institute of Mental Health; Masuda Kōkichi, Kōnan University; Susan J. Pharr, University of Wisconsin — Madison; and Ronald Aqua, staff.

The Research Board, University of Illinois at Urbana-Champaign, paid for the services of a part-time assistant who helped me with a bibliographic search while I was planning the project. And I am grateful to Ikeda Keiko for taking on that assignment. The University's School of Social Sciences and its Center for Asian Studies helped defray local expenses for two project sessions held on campus. And from beginning to end I have been able to count on the Center's office staff for secretarial help of many kinds.

*Work and Lifecourse in Japan*

INTRODUCTION

# Life Is
# Just a Job Résumé?

David W. Plath

As citizens of high-technology societies, we know from common experience what it means to be commuters. The commuter is one of the great archetypes of the industrial lifestyle. His master tempo of activity revolves around a daily shuttle from home to workplace and back again. (Or in the years when he is adapting to the commuter tempo, a shuttle between home and school.) Each of these two centers of activity is ordered by its own rhythm of long-term conduct: work and home each involve us in different, often contradictory, career timetables. Our commuter fate obliges us to exert ourselves continually in order to reconcile quick ripples of productive effort with slower waves of promotions and rewards, and with long tides of turnover as generation follows generation in the household. We have to syncopate our motions, and this can grow difficult when we become too caught up in just one career line, become homebodies or workaholics. To sustain personal integrity, to go on reaching for the promise of maturity, we need to cultivate a healthy measure of self-centering, a balanced attachment to distant goals and detachment from present roles.

Those who study career continuities in the West readily make a distinction between objective and subjective careers — between the norms of an organization on the one hand and the long-range perspectives of its members on the other. But this distinction remains blurred in much of what is being said lately about the nature of human conduct in modern Japanese society. A group model of Japanese life has dominated the mental landscape for the past generation — though the model is beginning to be much mooted.

1

By positing a basic Japanese personality that is born fused (versus being born free, as is supposed to happen in Euro-America), by assuming a self that is congenitally over-attached to society, the group model has obfuscated the dynamics of lifecourse self-preservation. Personal indentity is dissolved into a property of group solidarity. Self-indentity is said to be weak in Japan when compared with the ruggedly individualistic self that is thought to grow in cultures of Western extraction. Psychologically, Japanese are said to have uncommonly high "need affiliation," a special "craving for closeness" called *amae* in Japanese parlance (Doi 1973). Sociologically, they are regarded as over-socialized or "sociocentric." Listening to the current rhetoric about lifetime employment in Japan, for example, we might infer that on his retirement day the typical Japanese worker would not be able to write an autobiography: his life would consist of a job résumé. In short, the group model assumes that cultural differences in the style of social involvement will overpower all that Japan and the West have in common as systems of human action that pulsate to the same basic rhythms of industrialism.

## Careers and Lifecourse

A lifecourse approach to careers in Japan, a vision of adulthood as a cluster of concurrent timetables for personal conduct, is the point of departure for the book you now hold. The other contributors and I will try to show persons as well as organizations in Japan, the subjective shaping of careers as well as the objective structuring of them. We will try to bring out the biographical slippages and conflicts, between tempos of action in the workplace and tempos in settings where people are not being paid to act, that are as much a feature of human fate in today's Japan as in any other high-technology milieu.

Career outcomes, we maintain, are not any more patently assured for those who happen to have been born Japanese. Some Japanese will end up with work histories written in chapters of continuing success. But many, like the railway workers in Chapter Four who are sidetracked at Shiranai Station, will find that work ends in a routine that leads to who-knows-where; that brings only another day of punching tickets and of sweeping the platform clean of gum wrappers, cigarette stubs, and dried vomit. To even begin to comprehend what career insecurity can mean for the tempo and quality

2

of adult life in Japan, one must set aside the group model and with it the narrower lenses of industrial sociology. One must reach for a wider-angle view of the human lifecourse.

In these chapters we offer you a sampler of the dimensions of career development in an array of contemporary Japanese settings. To study careers is to study society in its mode of routine, to study development is to see society in its mode of drama. The essence of a career is that it is a predictable sequence of movements, a relay of roles set up to normalize the potentially turbulent flow of persons through an organization. The essence of development, however, is that the outcomes of activity are uncertain. There is scope for change, hope for improvement, and faith that one's efforts can make a difference. People survive by routine, but live by drama. And the dramatic tensions of lifecourse choice and chance in Japan are what we are trying here to pull into the analytic spotlight.

Our view of mankind, the set of assumptions behind this line of inquiry, starts with an image of the person as an entity propelled through the years, figuratively "writing" his biography in acts of behavior. As an agent in society, the normal person is under a moral imperative to maintain continuity — a sense of identity and integrity — across time and through many different arenas of conduct. So he must regularly monitor his conduct, evaluating its probable results over longer as well as shorter intervals.

All along the way he guides himself by cultural standards that define goals, competence, and achievement; and he is guided by other persons close about him who have the power to interpret the general standards as applied to his life's particulars. The standards are articulated in an array of pathways, routes and timetables that provide for continuity in an individual's conduct. The primary group of others around the individual make up a unique convoy of consociates — those who grow older with him, whose lives run parallel to his; they provide for continuity in his human relationships. (Plath 1980)

Every society has its quota of loners, individuals without so much as one intimate and enduring human connection. It also has its quota of flower children, those who by choice or by circumstance disregard career paths and so live, in effect, in an ongoing here-and-now. But the majority of normal adults — the topic of this book — traverse the years concurrently, moving on plural pathways and in the company of a plurality of consociates. In such a milieu, a person's movement along one pathway will shape, and be shaped by, his actions along other lines. Simultaneously, people around him

3

will be moving along their career paths. Their actions will shape his options, in ways that may be complex and often are cumulative. Or as Keith Brown reminded our study group at one of our meetings, it takes three generations to produce one grandmother.

On the academic roadmap you will find our subject at the intersection of three lines of investigation — those that look into lifecourse (or adult) development, those that examine the social organization of industrial work, and those that consider culture and behavior in modern Japan. From the lifecourse approach we draw our sense of problem: the scheduling of events across the biographical flow of the adult years. From industrial sociology we draw our chief analytic tool: the concept of careers as timetables for activities. From our training in Japanese Studies we draw an ambition to elucidate the Japanese experience for the benefit of people elsewhere. We hope that our reader will gain new awareness of the human dilemmas that are shared by all people, wherever situated, who must shape their lives to the rhythms of an industrial order.

## The Lifecourse in Japanese Studies

In scholarly reports on Japan, the dramas of career development and adult life scheduling seldom are played stage-center. So we hope that our essays will stimulate attention to these dramas on the part of our colleagues in Japanese Studies. The problem is not one of knowledge but of point of view. The specialist knows the human drama that is today's Japan in its rich and baffling detail, a diversity that our mass media fail — or even, it sometimes seems to me, perversely refuse — to communicate. When he turns to explicate that scene, however, the specialist has a tendency to lean upon the same clichés that the media purvey. For more than a generation in sociological thinking, Japan has been populated by replicas of the Organization Man and his mate, the Professional Housewife. They are shown passing through the stages of adulthood as if they were merely repeating a ritual they had practiced many times over.

Part of the difficulty may stem from the sectarian habit patterns of the social scientist, a problem not unique to Japanese Studies. The industrial sociologist, for example, may have a keen eye for career phenomena in the workplace, but not trouble himself to follow the workers out the gate and find out about their lives off the job. The family sociologist may scrupulously depict changes in the domestic cycle as if these took place behind closed doors. The per-

4

sonality psychologist may find a world of difference between the growth patterns of two-year-olds and three-year-olds, but regard adults of whatever age as undifferentiated victims of developmental burnout.

Deeper set and less tractable is the problem-style that percolates through the minds of a whole generation of scholars and almost unconsciously shapes the very way they frame their questions. I see this in the manner in which the time dimension has been posed in social science studies of Japan. To put the point abstractly, if there are three timelines along which to chart the flow of social action — the line of historical time in a whole social system, the line of structural time in its institutions, and the line of lifecourse time in its members — only the first two are used widely for framing research on Japan. The prevailing problem-styles have been the historical one of how to account for Japan's "rapid" modernization and the structural one of how to discover what is unique about Japanese ideology and organization.

History and structure end up swallowing biography. That individuals change over the years is certainly not denied or brushed aside. But it is explained, for the most part, by attributing it to adaptation: people are shown changing in response to the "impact" of modernization or to the "socialization pressures" of stages in the standard life cycle. One can always find exceptions. Whether or not Japan is the homogeneous society it is alleged to be, the fraternity of those who study Japan is anything but homogeneous. But the biographical timeline — and the problem of how a person tries to steer his life's course and make sense of its trends — have been core ideas in at most a handful of the books written about Japan since World War II.

## The Careers Project

By conflating the lifecourse timeline with those of history and of institutional structure, the prevailing mind-set lends credence to the stereotypes of Japan as a society in which over-attached selves work together in an unusual, consensual harmony. The Joint Committee on Japanese Studies (sponsored jointly by the American Council of Learned Societies and the Social Science Research Council) has been encouraging investigations that challenge groupist theories of human conduct in Japan. Committee projects have been examining topics such as social mobility and social conflict, and, in the project

5

from which I have selected these essays, careers and the lifecourse.

"Project" may be too high-sounding a word for what my collaborators and I have been doing. It may evoke an image of Big Science with its platoons of researchers, technicians, and secretaries; and with money to build costly apparatus that can probe outer space, the ocean depths, or the innards of atomic nuclei. Our "project" has had funds enough to assemble small groups of volunteers for three study sessions, and to pay for the typing, duplicating, and circulating of a score of working papers. I am not posturing about lack of resources, though like any project leader I dream about what we might do were we given them. I only want the reader to be aware of the ambience in which this book originated.

Producing a book was not, in the beginning, a project goal. The aim was to encourage new ways of thinking about contemporary Japan; the hope was that this exercise would lead, in turn, to new departures in research. Most of the project participants have, in fact, since gone ahead to address lifecourse issues in their later studies; and on this score I count the project a success.

I asked participants to prepare for our meetings by putting together case-study essays. We had neither the time nor the money that in a perfect world would have allowed us to design and execute a coordinated battery of new empirical inquiries. We had to make do with data already on hand; and that meant using data collected, for the most part, from structural and historical perspectives. In a mood of academic recycling, I had each participant reanalyze, from a lifecourse point of view, a body of information that he or she had collected or was familiar with already.

The topic of career uncertainty emerged en route. There seem to be three reasons why. All of us were bothered by the widespread distortions that have resulted from the cliche of "lifetime employment"; it made a convenient target for attack. Several of my collaborators had done field research on occupational subcultures; if their field notes offered little evidence on other lifecourse issues, the notebooks did hold ample material regarding careers. And in addition — to consider motivations that are more personal — most of the project participants are junior scholars, not yet holders of tenured positions: thoughts about career uncertainty resonate in their own human situation.

As interest in the theme began to snowball, I chose to make it the focus of one of our sessions. Only then, with draft reports on hand, did I see how persuasive these essays are when read as a set. I saw how, taken together, they outline a terrain in contemporary Japan that I hope other colleagues will help us go on to carefully map, namely, the meanings of work in adult Japanese lives. I urged my collaborators to take up the chore of revamping their reports for publication. Subsequently, in putting these together, I added essays volunteered later by Samuel Coleman and by Jack G. Lewis.

Julius A. Roth's study, *Timetables*, is for me personally one of the few books of twentieth century sociology that remain memorable. (Roth 1963) No one else has analyzed so tersely the scheduling dimensions of lifecourse conduct. Roth's ideas shaped my own thinking as I was organizing this project, and they were influential with many of the project's participants. So I am particularly happy that Roth, now Professor of Sociology in the University of California, Davis, accepted my invitation to provide reflections on this set of case studies and on the study of lifecourse scheduling in the post-industrial era.

## The Logic of Presentation

I have ordered these studies in a sequence that moves from a narrow to a wider view of work and its place in the human lifecourse. And I have grouped them as responses to four master questions — though every case study will almost always offer information pertinent to a whole array of questions.

### How uncertain are working careers?

The notion of lifetime employment assumes that workers enter paid hire once out of school and remain with the same organization until they retire thirty or more years later. If this were so, then for any one year the rate of changing jobs, and the percentage of people entering or leaving the labor force, ought to be impressively low.

Solomon B. Levine (Chapter One) casts an economist's eye at the Japanese labor force as a whole over recent decades. The average Japanese employee, Levine finds, in fact experiences several job changes during his years of hire. Annual rates of job turnover are of the same order of magnitude as in Europe. (The U. S. rate of high mobility is what seems out of line and in need of explanation.) For the great majority of Japanese adults, then, lifelong job tenure is more a dream than a reasonable expectation. If they want continuity across their adult years, they must build it into other paths of activity.

7

Women have always made up a large fraction of modern Japan's labor force, but relatively few of them have held long-term employment. The usual explanation is that (except in a few service occupations such as nursing and teaching) a woman is content to work only for a few years, and then she gladly "retires" to build lifecourse continuity into her career as mother and household manager. Karen C. Holden (Chapter Two) examines a sequence of recent female cohorts in the Japanese labor force. The trend that appears, as she contrasts each cohort with its predecessor, is for more women to take up paid employment, fewer to withdraw for childbearing, more to reenter the labor force in middle adulthood, and more to delay retiring in their older years. Perhaps there are not yet many Japanese women who can plan for their life's work to be done in paid employment. But jobs are making up an ever larger part of their life planning. This implies, in turn, that family planning must make allowance, more and more, for a wife's as well as a husband's work schedule — an issue that Samuel Coleman takes up in Chapter Nine.

Labor force data can only yield gross trends, macro-level patterns of movement in the mass. From such data, as Levine shows, we cannot pull out more than vague lines of flow in working careers. We cannot get at the operational, real-time dimensions of scheduling as they are preceived and acted upon by persons in a particular line of work. For that we must use micro-level, ethnographic styles of inquiry. We must interview people, observe them, if possible work alongside them. All the reports in Parts Two, Three, and Four are based on evidence collected by direct field investigation.

### What else goes with tenure?

Lifetime employment is a promise that one's working life will have continuity; it is not a guarantee of the working life's quality. There are obvious advantages to being able to predict, years ahead, one's general level of income. But in some portraits of it, lifetime employment is also said to entail "regular promotions." This would be a feat of managerial acumen; to assure large numbers of employees that they will routinely gain in power and prestige. The notion probably is a misperception of a practice that *is* fairly common in large Japanese organizations (though scarcely peculiar to them), that of providing annual increases in the longevity-based component of an employee's pay.

8

But Japan or elsewhere, not every Organization Man is called upon to be department head, and fewer are chosen to become president. Competition for promotions, or for assignments that offer more power or excitement, is as familiar to the lifetime employee as to his colleague overseas. He may be loyal to the organization, he may serve it with diligence. This does not mean he deposits his mind in the company safe. He must maintain a healthy detachment, sustain a sense of personal continuity amid what he is likely, in his organization role, to experience as a planless tangle of reassignments and delays.

In Chapters Three and Four we offer worker's-eye views of two settings where lifetime employment is the norm. Kenneth A. Skinner describes the subjective careers of white-collar men in a public corporation in Tokyo, and Paul H. Noguchi those of blue-collar workers on the Japanese National Railways. In the public corporation, Skinner finds "aborted careers" to be the usual fate. A national ministry supervises this corporation, and as a means to regularize its own internal promotion flow, the ministry regularly posts its own civil servants out to tours of duty in the corporation. So upper-level positions in the corporation are "colonized" by the ministry, and few men are promoted from the inside. Employees find themselves moved arbitrarily, often on short notice, to new assignments, so that they can form no clear idea of what "normal" career progress ought to be. For the railwaymen at Shiranai ("Who Knows?") Station, Noguchi paints an even more discouraging picture. Charged with keeping the trains running on time, they see themselves as side tracked and running late in their careers. If the promotion schedule is clear enough in principle, it operates ever more slowly in practice. For they are in a declining industry, in a corporation forced to cut its operations to reduce financial losses, and overpopulated with employees in the 40 to 50-year age bracket.

These are case studies. We do not offer them as representative of all Japan, the typical picture of the tenured worker. In a "growth industry," whether in the public or private sector, the promotion and assignment outlook can be very bright indeed. But we *are* suggesting that figures on lifetime employment in Japan are not very significant in the absence of figures on lifetime opportunity.

*Can you survive outside the organization?*

The men described in Part Two are in the ideal-type industrial

9

career setting; continuity in their working life is supplied by the framework of a large organization. Their problem is to reconcile their imperfect work histories with the perfect careers predicated by the organizational scheme. It is different for the men we look at next. They have a form of lifetime commitment, but it is to their profession or craft or calling rather than to a particular organization. Their career timeline is set by continuity in professional performance; to sustain performance they may have to hire out in a variety of organizations or perhaps become self-employed.

Susan O. Long (Chaper Five) examines phases in a doctor's career. She depicts three forms of employment open to a young physician — with a medical research program, on a hospital staff, or in private practice. And she shows what each of these options entails for the "intertwined careers" that a doctor may try to carry on in other domains of his life. As he moves from one "practice style" to another over the years, we see him evolving a new lifestyle in order to reconcile his professional progress with his activities at home, among colleagues, and in civic organizations.

Malpractice aside, a physician can anticipate a certain demand for his services. The prospect is otherwise for the man who aspires to a political career: he must accede to the verdict of the ballot box. Jack G. Lewis (Chapter Six) investigates evidence for continuities in the careers of local elected officials, and indicates how they must concurrently cultivate "fail-safe" lines of work that will sustain them during periods when they are out of favor with the electorate.

The ultimate extension of this type of situation occurs when an occupation has been suddenly and totally eliminated. Theodore F. Cook, Jr., asks what happened to the officers of the Imperial Japanese Army, who in 1945 saw their organization and their life's work vanish overnight, thrown into disrepute (Chapter Seven). They had to invent second lives for themselves. Through Cook's eyes we see many of them transfer military job skills to new lines of work. We also hear many of them say that they were not mere "careerists" in the Army, organization men grubbing for promotion. They had a personal calling — to serve throne and nation — and many now regard their civilian employment as a peacetime extension of that mission.

*How do you reconcile work with the family?*

The case studies in Parts Two and Three have concentrated on men and on their scheduling problems in the public arenas of employment. In Part Four we expand the view to include women and the private timelines of family life. The issue of "career versus family" is one for everyone in an industrial economy, although of course more salient for women because of warps in the job opportunity structure. The situation often is complicated, with multiple timelines to be kept in mind and the needs of multiple actors to be weighed. On the practical side there are likely to be almost daily tradeoffs and mutual adjustments. On the theoretical level, although research has addressed some topics (e.g., "women's two worlds," or dual-career families, and links between the domestic cycle and family income) there is no standard vocabulary of analytic ideas.

In Chapter Eight James McLendon shows us the Tokyo headquarters office of an international business firm as the younger employees see it — not just as a place to earn income and perhaps to launch a career, but also a place to find a spouse. Both sexes forage for a mate in the arena, but the conditions of search differ radically. A man who succeeds in the search not only will continue with the corporation but even be regarded as a more dependable member of the organization. A woman who succeeds must resign and go home. The personnel department makes a point of hiring women who it judges will cheerfully stop working and then become good company wives. McLendon traces how a young woman must balance her investments in work skills, female friendships, personal cultivation, and mate-search, as she periodically reevaluates her prospects for successfully retiring from the office and embarking on a household career instead.

What happens after that is the focus of Coleman's report (Chapter Nine). He looks particularly at the timing of marriage and at the tempo of spacing for childbirths. Such decisions are arrived at, he shows, only after due consideration has been given to long-range outcomes. And Coleman brings out again and again the many-factored social symbiosis that operates between employment opportunities and family composition.

Coleman deals mostly with families where the husband/father works for hire away from home. Work at home is an alternative pattern that has by no means vanished from modern Japan — although it is often branded "traditional" as if to imply that it is anachronistic. Family enterprise and cottage industry hold great adaptive vigor in twentieth-century Japan, and Jill Kleinberg explores the pattern in her essay (Chapter Ten). She traces the "paired trajectories" of family formation and skill development in households that produce folkcraft ceramics. Drawing a contrast among three successive cohorts of potters, she illustrates the fine-tuning that can be made between household duties and craft assignments, delicately adjusting the system to external changes in market demand for pottery and in options for other employment, while struggling to uphold internal ideals of household continuity.

## Coda

A handful of case studies cannot be extrapolated to make up a new theoretical model for analyzing the adult lifecourse in Japan — although we hope that they point to major features of such a model. Nor can these few studies capture the empirical diversity of working careers and career dilemmas in a society of 115 million people — though we think that we are able to bring out some key dimensions in that diversity.

Ours is not a campaign of iconoclasm, wanting to crush the clichés of groupism and lifetime employment. Like all stereotypes, these have their elements of truth. But we want to help our reader see them in proportion. Normal adults in Japan, as anywhere else, maintain a healthy detachment — clichés to the contary — and a subjective stance towards their careers. This does not transform them into rugged individualists, on the lines of the image that the Euro-American lies to believe he sees in his mirror. The truth, as usual, is somewhere in between the notions of "independent individual" and "submerged self" that we use to bracket it.

Claims that work behavior in Japan is excessively group-based or structurally dominated, however, need to be backed by evidence that subjectivity is in fact weak. Nowhere in our field studies does it appear so. And the idea that the subjective side of Japanese life is weak will seem as a general proposition implausible to anybody familiar with the expressive richness of Japanese literature and art.

## References

Doi Takeo
  1973　The Anatomy of Dependence. John Bestor, trans. Tokyo: Kodansha International.

Plath, David W.
  1980   Long Engagements: Maturity in Modern Japan. Stanford:
         Stanford University Press.
Roth, Julius A.
  1963   Timetables: Structuring the Passage of Time in Hospital
         Treatment and Other Careers. Indianapolis: Bobbs-Merrill.

# Part One

# CURRENTS OF EMPLOYMENT

Is it possible for a high-technology economy to provide lifetime employment for everyone who wants it? (Let's allow that some people are unemployable, some would rather be self-employed, and some would just as soon not work at all.) Perhaps an economic genius could draft a scheme that would sustain the inertia of a universal tenure system with the adaptive flexibility that is needed for a national economy caught up in a fluid world order. Current economic philosophy, however, takes for granted that there has to be some degree of labor mobility in the system, although no one knows quite how much is needed.

Over the years since 1920 — the period when most people now in the labor force have come of age — Japan's economy has done well in terms of making jobs available to its ever-expanding population. Unemployment has remained at a level that in world perspective is enviably low. This means that when making lifecourse plans, an adult today has been more certain, if Japanese, of finding a paid job of some kind. (How desirable a job, is another issue.) Chances for remaining in the job indefinitely, however, do not appear to be any greater in Japan than in some other industrial nation. The durability of Japanese products may be setting a world standard, the durability of jobs is no better than elsewhere. By Solomon B. Levine's calculations presented in Chapter One, the average Japanese worker will be re-cycled through at least three or four positions in the labor force across his years of paid employment.

Do these job changes link up, one to the next, in some sort of orderly progression or meaningful sequence? In some institutions and some occupations it will be easy to spot standarized career lines. But will the average Japanese adult, as a general rule, be able on retirement day to display a job résumé that lists anything other than a disjointed succession of posts? In my view, the great majority will have experienced uncertain careers.

That may be regarded as a working hypothesis. For now, we cannot confirm it directly by weight of evidence. Although labor force bookkeeping is carried on as energetically in Japan as anywhere else, the unit of recording is the job, not the person. From such data we can reasonably infer general currents of employment, as Levine and Karen C. Holden do in the two reports that follow. Information on work histories, however, is all but impossible to retrieve.

Not many large-scale studies of job histories have been carried out in any industrial nation; and none, so far as I can determine, in Japan as yet. But if Harold W. Wilensky's investigations are a good indication, then uncertain careers are the lot of most adults in a modern economy. Wilensky examined the job histories of nearly seven hundred white males in the United States, asking if the skills and experience a man gained in one job had some carry-over into later jobs. He reports that:

> In the middle mass — a relatively secure population, well off by American standards — only 30 percent can by any stretch of the imagination be said to act out half or more of their work histories in an orderly career. If we count the lower class, excluded from this sample, it is apparent that a vast majority of the labor force is going nowhere in an unordered way or can expect a worklife of thoroughly unpredictable ups and downs. (Wilensky 1968:325-326)

In Japan, overall rates of job-changing are somewhat lower than in the United States, though on the same level as in European economies. But the portrait of employment currents painted for us by Levine and Holden is one of considerable turbulence. If one is so inclined, one can pluck out differences and label these as "the Japanese way." The Japanese pattern seen as a whole, however, does not in our eyes add up to a different *kind* of system, one somehow insulated against "thoroughly unpredictable ups and downs."

In short, not only does the average adult in Japan today fail to win a guarantee of lifetime employment in one organization. He must also anticipate a high probability of changing jobs sometime down the line, and a high probability that his next job will be at best loosely connected to his present one. If he has any long-range goals in life, then in striving toward them he will need to give a good deal of thought and managerial effort to his career development.

16

Some readers, especially those well-informed about contemporary Japan, may regard our efforts in Part One as a harping on the obvious. I have two reasons for including these reports. First, the stereotype of lifetime employment is widely held in the United States (and for that matter, in Japan too, as a symbol of Japanese uniqueness). When I give public lectures, people in the audience often ask about it. Not only that, when Levine offered a synopsis of his chapter to a national meeting of Asian Studies specialists, some listeners expressed surprise on hearing that lifetime employment is not more widely in effect. It is important that the reader see evidence that places the stereotype in its factual context.

The second reason has to do with the sense of problem that underlies this whole book. Studies of contemporary Japan most often start by assuming that Japanese society and culture are inherently different from those in the rest of the world. The goal of such a study, then, is to discover and document the differences. But we start from the view that Japanese confront the same lifecourse problem that we do: how to adapt one's personal trajectory and tempo of biographical events to the contours and rhythms of the post-industrial world order. I think it important for the reader to be aware of these rhythms on the wider scene before he turns to the little worlds protrayed in the case study chapters that make up the rest of the book.

The authors in this part, SOLOMON B. LEVINE and KAREN C. HOLDEN, are both at the University of Wisconsin-Madison. Levine is Professor of Economics and Business Administration; Holden is Research Associate in Economics and is affiliated with the Center for Demography and Ecology.

## References

Harold W. Wilensky
  1968    Orderly Careers and Social Participation: the Impact of Work History on Social Integration in the Middle Mass. *In* Middle Age and Aging, Bernice L. Neugarten, ed., pp. 321-340. Chicago: University of Chicago Press.

# CHAPTER 1

# Careers and Mobility in Japan's Labor Markets

## Solomon B. Levine

Since the end of World War II there have been enormous changes in the level and structure of the Japanese economy, plus a remarkable elongation in life expectancy; and the result is that great new opportunities have emerged for changing one's income-producing career. In this chapter, after a brief sketch of prewar trends, I offer an overview of the aggregate evidence for changes in jobs, occupations, and employment status since the later 1940's, the period during which the majority of people in the Japanese labor force today developed their careers of paid employment. My focus is upon labor mobility, or, in the lingo of the economist, on the interplay of supply and demand in labor market behavior. In the context of the labor market I look at income-producing careers as the succession of individuals from one paid job, occupation, or employment status to another.

A few considerations need to be kept in mind when using labor market data. These are, after all, macro-level data; they do not allow us to probe very far into people's motivations or reasons for changing jobs. The key notion here is opportunity cost: the relative advantage, as measured in monetary terms, that induces the work-experienced individual to move from one job to another. It is clear from the history of most industrialized countries that only a small fraction of the employed will be induced to move to another job in any limited time period, say a month or a year. Such movement fundamentally depends on changes in the demand for and supply of workers; these changes are highly complex matters involving economic, political, technological, and social events and changes. It

18

is not likely that any one factor will predominate for long. Even then entry into jobs is likely to draw heavily upon new (inexperienced) recruits to the labor force or upon the experienced unemployed rather than upon those already in employment. Much of this represents intergenerational mobility.

No one has determined the optimum rate of labor mobility for an industrialized society. Labor stability is required as well as movement, and the degree to which each is present depends on such matters as the level of economic activity, changes in the industrial system, technological requirements, quality of labor, and the cost of labor relative to other factors of production.

Labor market analysts usually focus upon "voluntary" versus "involuntary" labor turnover among those already employed (or intragenerational mobility). At best, this is a crude distinction. Voluntary movement presumably heightens when the economy expands; involuntary when it contracts. A rough indication of the trends is seen in the rate of accessions to and separations from employment. However, in reality the two types of movements may be mixed ("You can't fire me, I quit"). Macro-analysis does not deal satisfactorily with this problem, and it is better left to the study of individual cases at the micro-level.

I am dealing here with long-run historical trends, so that millions of individual decisions are masked by net changes in the various jobs or occupational categories that make up the composition and distribution of employment. Only a small portion of the long-term changes in this distribution will be affected by the life-cycle job shifts of those already in the labor force. Most of the historical changes in categories will arise from the inflow of inexperienced entrants and immigrants and the outflow of retirees, the deceased and emigrants.

Aggregates also mask the likelihood that labor force mobility in a modern industrialized nation is "segmented" among a variety of labor markets. Mobile workers appear to be active only in selected portions of the economic structure. There is usually no single market, but a series of submarkets between which there may be only narrow channels, if any, for movement. In terms of rewards (income), the segments may form a hierarchy ("dualism") of markets for the higher and lower reward systems. Again, the lines of demarcation among the markets, while often fuzzy, depend on a host of factors; these include employee qualifications (such as education, work experience, age, and sex), rate of economic change, shifts in economic structure, technological requirements for labor, and organizational rules derived from government regulation or from collective bargining. These matters, too, are perhaps better studied at the micro-rather than macro-level. A prominent case of segmentation, which in recent years has received considerable attention, is the alleged division between "internal" and "external" labor markets, which may be explained both in terms of capital theory and of institutional theory (Shimada 1974). Basically, the distinction has to do with the degree of interfirm mobility. An "external" market provides a firm with its labor needs from outside. An "internal" market does it from within (through transfer, promotion, demotion, etc.). Presumably, with the growth of large-scale organization, internal markets become increasingly prevalent.

I will proceed as follows: First I will summarize major trends in employment and in the size and structure of the Japanese labor force over the past century. Then I will look more closely at the period since World War II, examining the evidence for labor turnover and for job changes among the employed, looking particularly at interfirm movements. And I will conclude by asking what this suggests with regard to the likelihood of changing jobs during a typical income-producing career as it has been experienced by most Japanese who are in the labor force today.

## Growth and Structure of the Japanese Labor Force, 1875-1975

As is well known, Japan has experienced vast changes in the size and distribution of its labor force since industrialization commenced more than one hundred years ago. This required new kinds of labor markets that did not exist to any appreciable degree before 1870. Hosts of new organizations, firms, occupations, and jobs were created. Especially dramatic have been the growth and shift in the years since the early 1950s.

Estimates of the size and composition of the Japanese labor force are not highly reliable prior to the first official census in 1920. Even then, it was not until 1948 that the method for labor force estimation used today was instituted, and at various times since 1948 the method has been revised and improved. Thus, there is a problem of data consistency as well as reliability over the decades since the beginning of industrialization.[1]

As best as can be estimated, employment (which is somewhat less than the labor force itself) nearly doubled from 1875 to 1940, rising from 17.5 million to 32.3 million persons. This increase almost paralleled the growth of Japan's population in that period, from 35.3 million to 71.9 million. Actually, the employment/population ratio varied annually from 45 to 57 percent; but from decade to decade, especially between 1900 and 1940, the rate of increase of employment greatly accelerated, from 4.5 percent to 9.7 percent.

After 1950 (estimates are far too poor to use for 1940-1950), growth of employment was in some respects even more dramatic than the prewar period. It rose from almost 36 million in 1950 to 53 million in 1975 — an absolute expansion in 25 years greater than that for the 65 years from 1875 to 1940. (Prior to 1955, the count included those 14 years of age and older; since 1955, 15 years and older.) Population, which received a boost in the immediate postwar years by the return of about 6 million overseas expatriate Japanese, rose from 72.2 million in 1945 (83.2 million in 1950) to 111.3 million in 1975. While the employment/population ratio became slightly lower, ranging between 43 and 50 percent, employment went up by 22.4 percent in the 1950's and then 19.1 percent in the 1960's, continuing the acceleration experienced in the prewar decades. Since 1970, the rate of climb has eased considerably, largely reflecting the sharp fall in birthrates in the 1950's. It is clear, however, that most people employed today in Japan entered the labor force during an era of rapidly expanding job opportunities.

The shift in employment composition by major economic sector has been equally dramatic. Using the broad standard categories of primary, secondary, and tertiary sectors, the ratios in 1875 were respectively, 87.4, 4.2, and 8.4 percent. One hundred years later, they were 14.0, 34.2, and 51.8 percent. In absolute numbers, primary sector employment dropped from 15.2 to 7.4 million persons; secondary rose from 0.7 to 18.1 million; and tertiary soared from 1.5 to 27.5 million. By around 1920 the majority of those employed in Japan were in the nonagricultural sectors. The urban-rural distribution of population, too, had reversed.

The most striking sectoral changes occurred between 1955 and 1975. Primary sector employment, which had actually gone back to about 50 percent of the total in the five chaotic years after the surrender in 1945, numbered about 17.5 million in 1950. With an average drop of 400,000 individuals each year (in reality, there was considerable yearly variation), almost two-thirds of these had left agriculture by 1975.

Furthermore, the net gains in the secondary and tertiary sectors by far outmatched the net losses in the primary sector. Secondary

21

sector employment grew from 8.1 million in 1950 to almost 10 million in 1955 and to 18.2 million in 1975. In this period, secondary employment was averaging a net increase of half a million persons each year. Even more explosive was the rise in tertiary sector employment, as it grew from 8.9 million in 1950 to 15.6 million in 1955 and then went on to 26.9 million by 1975. Thus, the average net gain in this sector was more than a half million persons a year across the two decades. The large growth in the secondary and tertiary sectors after 1955 drew not only upon the increasing numbers of persons first coming of working age and those shifting out of agriculture, but also upon older individuals who had not been in the labor force.

The number of men in the labor force grew steadily from about 21.9 million in 1950 to 24.6 million in 1955 and on to 32.9 million in 1975. This increase in males was about double that for females, who numbered 14.2 million in 1950, 17.4 million in 1955, and 19.8 million in 1975. The 3:2 male-female ratio in the labor force varied only slightly over these years, with females having a high point of 41.5 percent in 1955, and males rising to a high point of 62.4 percent in 1975. Note, though, that in the manufacturing sector females outnumbered males until the early 1930's.

On the other hand, labor force participation rates (percentage of the working age groups actually willing and able to work whether employed or unemployed) have been steadily declining after an upward spurt between 1950 and 1955. The overall ratio dropped from 70.8 percent in 1955 to 62.9 percent in 1975. This decline was due mostly to the fall in the female ratio. The male percentage, mainly as the result of increased years of schooling, declined only from 85.9 to 81.1 while the female, primarily because of withdrawals from agriculture, fell from 56.7 to 45.8. It should be noted that in this period almost all those of employment age who wanted and sought work obtained it. Unemployment (as defined by the Japanese survey method) between 1950 and 1975 rarely rose above one million (1955), or 2.5 percent of the labor force — in most years the percentage was half that figure or less.

An even more telling indication of the shifts in Japanese employment are the changing proportions among the self-employed, the unpaid family workers, and the wage and salary employees. The postwar changes in the economy rapidly accelerated trends that had already been under way long before 1945. In 1920, more than one-third of the people in employment were self-employed and at least another 37 percent worked as unpaid family members. Ten years later, when the oldest members of today's labor force first went to work, only slight changes in these proportions had taken place, with a small shift toward wage and salary employment. Then the expansion of heavy industry following the Manchurian Incident in 1930 brought about a dramatic change-over: by 1940, self-employment had fallen to 26.3 percent and unpaid family workers to 31.8 percent, while wage and salary employees had risen to almost 42 percent.

These trends were reversed in the aftermath of the surrender, but quickly resumed in the 1950s. Although the absolute number of self-employed fell only slightly (from more than 10 million in 1950 to 9.3 million in 1975), this represented a proportional decline to 18 percent of total employment. Similarly, family workers dropped sharply, to less than 12 percent by 1975. Note, however, that these declines in self-employment and unpaid family work are accounted for primarily by withdrawals of males. The absolute number of self-employed females has actually increased, and the number of female unpaid family workers has dropped only slightly (see ChapterTwo). Also, the drop in these two statuses has come largely in the primary sector. Their numbers have actually increased in the secondary and tertiary sectors; again, especially for females.

To look at this another way: only in the past generation has Japan become predominantly a nation of wage and salary earners. Their numbers almost tripled from 1950 (12.7 million) to 1975 (36.1 million; and their ratio to total employment almost doubled, from 35.4 to 69.8 percent. This shift into wage and salary employment was greater by far than the entire growth in employment during these 25 years. Even so, the proportion of the labor force in wage and salary jobs in Japan continues to be well below that in most other industrialized nations.

Changes in occupational categories reflect the shift toward wage and salary work. The number of professionals, managers, administrative and technical personnel, clerks, and service workers doubled from 1955 to 1975, continuing a long-term trend towards a rising proportion of white-collar employees in the labor force (today, approaching 50 percent of the total). Transport and communications workers increased in number more than three times in the same period. On the other hand, salespersons and skilled and semiskilled nonfarm manual workers numbered only a little over one-third more in 1975 than they did in 1955; while the numbers of agricultural workers, miners, and unskilled nonfarm laborers registered declines.

There were many more firms in Japan by the 1970's than in the 1950's (Japan Institute of Labour 1974: 46-51). Taking only private establishments in the nonagricultural sector, the total grew from 3.46 million in 1957 to 5.11 million in 1972. In that period, the largest (those employing 500 persons or more) grew in number from 1,821 to 3,868, altogether expanding their employment from 2.2 million to 4.5 million. The medium-sized firms (100 to 499 employees) increased from 13,389 to 35,533, with an employment rise from 2.5 million to 6.4 million. And among the small establishments (30 to 99 employees) the increase was from 60,465 to 154,429, with employment going up from 2.8 million to 7.2 million; while in the ultra-small group (1 to 29 employees), the number of firms grew from 3.39 million to 4.92 million, with an employment rise from 6.4 million to 12.5 million. Public sector employment (4.48 million in 1975) was less than 15 percent of the total nonagricultural employment in the private sector.

Thus, by the mid-1970s large-scale establishments had no more than 30 percent of all wage and salary employees outside of agriculture; ultra-small establishments had close to 40 percent. Throughout the period, about two-thirds of the total increase in employment in the private, nonagricultural sector flowed into medium, small, and ultra-small establishments.

All of the above figures support the contention that enormous ferment has characterized Japan's labor markets during the past three decades. While the bulk of the inflow and outflow involved new entrants (or reentrants after long withdrawals) and retirees, there was continuing turnover also among the experienced, with workers moving from sector to sector, firm to firm, occupation to occupation, and job to job. Unfortunately, it is difficult to estimate precisely how much of the movement is represented by those already in the labor force or in employment. The evidence is fragmentary. Karen Holden has made sample calculations for males by age group, using shifts into and out of occupational categories over the years from 1955 to 1960. For those in the 20-to-24 age cohort, for example, she estimates that 8.5 percent of all entries and exits were "interoccupational migrants." In the 55-to-59 age group, the ratio was close to 42 percent (Holden 1973:283-287). No doubt the high proportion in the older group reflected large amounts of shifting as the result of "retirement" from "regular" jobs or careers.

## Interfirm Mobility

Most of the available data on mobility among those already

24

employed in Japan show us the movement of wage and salary employees from one establishment to another. There are few official figures in this regard, and it is suspected that those that do exist are underestimates because they tend to omit transfers from "parent" firms to closely related firms such as subcontractors.

Monthly rates of quitting employees give an index of mobility among those already in employment, but they do not directly show how many of the "separations" result in "accessions." Overall, in Japan since the 1950s these rates have been fairly steady, although they vary with the business cycle (Japan Institute of Labour 1974:65; 1979, 5:5; Shimada 1980:9). Accessions to firms (number of employees) entering firms with 30 + workers, as a percentage of all employees) averaged between 2.2 and 2.4 percent per month for all industries for most years from 1955 to 1973. After the oil crisis, the accession rate in manufacturing fell to between 1.2 and 1.6 percent per month from 1974 to 1978. Separations from firms also averaged between 2.2 and 2.9 percent per month until 1973, after which they, too, dropped to between 1.4 and 1.9 percent in manufacturing.

Accessions will outpace separations as employment expands, and vice versa when it slows down or contracts. Large firms tend to have lower accession and separation rates than do smaller firms. The rates for manufacturing also tend to be slightly lower than the rates in the other nonagricultural sectors.

Roughly speaking, Japan's labor turnover rates have averaged about half those experienced in the same time period in the United States. However, especially among smaller firms, they are not at that low a level compared to Western European countries. It is the United States which has unusually high rates of labor mobility, rather than Japan having unusually low ones. As I have already mentioned, the optimum rate for any country is unknown.

In Japan as elsewhere there are various channels for obtaining employment: public employment offices, schools, relatives and friends, advertisements, and other methods such as private employment agencies and off-the-street hiring. Between 1956 and 1972, recruitment through friends and relatives appeared to be the most important, accounting for about one-third of all accessions. Public employment offices, which were greatly expanded and systematized as part of the postwar labor reforms, placed about one-fourth. Direct recruitment from school, although obscured by ties with public employment offices, varied between one-tenth and one-fifth. While advertising has grown in importance, it takes credit for less than one-tenth to about one-fifth of the placements. Other channels are of less significance (Japan Institute of Labour 1974:66).

There is a myth that Japanese firms recruit new employees almost exclusively from among young people who have just graduated from school. In fact, if we look at firms with 30 or more employees, we find that in the 1950's and 1960's only about one-third of their new entrants were recent school graduates. And since 1970, with a trend towards longer schooling plus a larger percentage of young people remaining in school, the figure has dropped to less than one-fourth of new recruits. The grain of truth in the myth is that the very largest firms have a greater fraction of recent graduates among their new recruits than do the smaller firms.

For all the expressed employer preference for new graduates, the supply just hasn't been there. Establishments with 30 or more employees have had to turn to recruitment among other inexperienced workers, such as housewives and older persons, and among the relatively few unemployed, and to attracting experienced workers away from other firms and occupations. Between 1956 and 1965, inexperienced recruits other than new school graduates provided 10 to 15 percent of all new employees. Since 1965, their proportion has risen to 20 percent. However, by far the largest group of new recruits have been experienced workers — ranging from 45 percent to 55 percent of the total of new hires each year from 1956 to 1972 (Japan Institute of Labour 1974:68-69). As mentioned, these are probably underestimates, because they omit transfers of workers among related firms. One survey found that about 80 percent of the firms covered recruited some experienced workers (Evans 1971:77).

The above figures fit well with data for "voluntary" and "involuntary" separations from establishments with 30 or more workers each. Quitting for "personal" reasons accounted for four-fifths of all separations from 1956 to 1972. Presumably these are mainly "voluntary" moves to other establishments. Far less important were separations of a more purely "involuntary" kind. Failures to renew fixed-term contracts of individual employment averaged about 10 percent of all separations in the late 1950s, but dropped to about half that in the 1960s and early 1970s as labor supplies tightened. Discharges for economic or disciplinary reasons also declined in similar proportion. Given the youthfulness of the labor force in the postwar period, "retirement," too, has been a comparatively minor reason for separation: from as high as 3.3 percent in 1957 to as little as one percent in 1967. Likewise, separations due to illness or injury rarely rose above 2.5 percent per year from 1956 to 1972 (Japan Institute of Labour 1974:67).

By using such turnover data, we can calculate for the average worker in Japan during the past generation a rough estimate of the number of moves from firm to firm. If we assume that accessions are evenly distributed among experienced employees, at a rate of 2 percent per month, then close to one-fourth of Japanese workers will have moved from one employer to another during a given year. Most likely the actual figure is not that high, since mobility is concentrated in selected groups such as seasonal and temporary laborers. Nevertheless it is unlikely that firms draw only upon these groups in recruiting the roughly one out of two new employees who are experienced workers.

In general, the tendency is for experienced workers to move from large firms to small ones, and from small firms to other small ones, but not from small to large or from large to large. Also, since the 1950s, exit from the larger firms has tended to increase more rapidly than exit from the smaller firms (Evans 1971:76). This would indicate that a sizable share of the mobility of experienced workers has occurred among those permanently in the labor market, rather than among temporary workers. Japan Ministry of Labor data for 1970 indicate that more than one-eighth of all workers hired that year had had previous occupational experience (Shimada 1980).

Further, as in the United States, although at a lower rate, interfirm mobility in Japan tends to be highest among younger workers. For example, in 1965, 10.2 percent of all male employees aged 18 to 19 changed jobs (presumably employers, too) at least once; and 7.5 percent aged 20 to 24 also did so. In contrast, only 2.8 percent in the 40-to-54 age group changed jobs that year (Evans 1971:78). Evans estimates that, overall, 4.6 percent of the nonagricultural labor force changed jobs (and presumably employers) in 1965, and that on the basis of probabilities half of the labor force made such a change at least once every 10 years (Evans 1971:81). This would mean that the average wage and salary earner makes at least two or three changes of employer during his or her working career.

This estimate squares with the figures for interfirm mobility among experienced workers. Assuming that regular workers account for only a one percent accession rate per month, or 12 percent a year, the typical employee career would see a change in employer every eight or nine years — or again three times or more over a 30-to-40-year working lifetime. While highly speculative, this does not seem to be an unreasonable minimum estimate, given the vast changes in labor force size and composition during the postwar period.

27

SOLOMON B. LEVINE

## Longitudinal Studies of Career Mobility

Among the few investigations of aggregate labor mobility on a
longitudinal basis in postwar Japan are those by Taira (1970) and
Cole (1979). Their findings further support the likelihood of several
job changes during the careers of most Japanese wage earners.

Taira was among the first to conclude that worker mobility in
Japan has been substantial over much of the century since the beginning of Japanese industrialization. His approach was to focus on
evidence for length of service of workers who had a single employer.
First, from samples of workers in factory employment in various
years from 1900 to 1957, he found that length of employment indeed increased over the long term. In 1900, for example, less than
10 percent had served five or more years; but by 1957 (the only year
he uses that might include many present-day labor force members)
more than 21 percent had served 5 to 10 years, and almost 16 percent, 10 years or more. Similarly, in 1900, close to 45 percent had
been employed one year or less, while by 1957 the figure was down
to 22 percent. In the sampled years (1900, 1918, 1924, 1933, 1939,
and 1957) there was considerable fluctuation in these ratios, ap-
parently closely related to the state of the economy. The percentage
distribution of workers by length of employment was remarkably
alike in the depressed years of 1924 and 1957 but quite different
from the more prosperous years of 1900 and 1939, which also were
similar (Taira 1970:153-154).

Although it deals only with the prewar era, more germane to the
issues here is Taira's analysis of workers who remained with the same
employer from 1924 to 1933. In a sample of those first employed in
1924, less than 20 percent were with their initial employer nine years
later; that is, on the average almost 10 percent a year had left. Even
among those who in 1924 had already been employed in the same
company for 11 to 16 years, only about half were still there by 1933.
Of those who had served from two to 10 years in 1924, the rates of
retention nine years later were merely one-fifth to two-fifths (Taira
1970:157). Certainly in those years, movement from employer to
employer was the common experience for workers.

Unfortunately, no parallel analysis exists for a post-World War II
period. However, even if we assume that the turnover rate fell by
half after the war, the movement from employer to employer would
have remained substantial, say in the neighborhood of 5 percent per
year. At that rate, a worker typically would change companies at
least two or three times in the course of a working career. A sizeable

28

proportion would have made more changes than that, especially it would seem those employed by small- and medium-sized firms.

Cole is virtually the only investigator who has examined the careers of a large sample of Japanese workers and compared their mobility with that of American workers. His analysis is based on data from closely matched representative groups of male employees between the ages of 16 and 60 in 1970 and 1971 in Yokohama and Detroit. For each respondent (583 in Yokohama and 638 in Detroit) Cole compiled a complete work history, based on the respondent's recollection, running back to 1945 where applicable, including periods of unemployment and withdrawals from the labor force. In cases of those whose work experience dated from before 1945 (the earliest was about 1930), only the first full-time prewar job was recorded. (For an explanation of his method, see Cole 1979:47-56).

One of Cole's most significant findings for our purposes is that in the Yokohama sample about 35 percent reported that they had not as yet changed from their initial employer. In Detroit, it was 13.5 percent. But the longer the number of years since initial full-time employment, the higher the percentage of those who had left their first employer. Among those who initially became employed during 1966 — 1970, about three-fourths had not as yet moved; but among those who began during 1961 — 1965, about half had already done so. Thereafter, the percentage who had not transferred employment dwindled as the number of years since full-time employment increased. Of those who were first hired between 1946 and 1960, about two-thirds had moved from their initial full-time employment.

While Cole does not give a detailed tabulation, he does report that, among those who actually changed jobs, the total mean number of such changes, adjusted for the amount of labor force exposure, was 2.16 in Yokohama and 3.26 in Detroit (Cole 1979:64). The total mean number of employer changes was 0.08 per person per years of employment in Yokohama, and 0.16 in Detroit. Cole also calculates annual rates of interfirm job changes for a series of cohorts defined by age at the time of change. In both cities the rate is higher for younger than the older workers. Education level and size of firm seemed to make little difference for interfirm experience. (Cole 1979:68-87). No data are given as to whether rates of movement change with the ups and downs of the business cycle.

Confirming Evans' observations on the reasons given for job separations from employing firms, Cole found that at least 15 percent of those who had changed employers in Yokohama reported they had been "involuntarily dismissed" and that another 10 percent said that they had left because of "threat to job and security" (probably in anticipation of dismissal). Surprisingly, the total of these two types of separation was about the same in Detroit. Thus about three-fourths who reported changing jobs in Yokohama, as in Detroit, said they did so for "voluntary" reasons. One other surprising finding was that involuntary discharge was more often given as a major reason for leaving large firms than for small (Cole 1979: 88-90).

Still other evidence on interfirm mobility can be culled from Koshirō's study of labor turnover in 1975 in four factories (auto assembly, steel, shipbuilding, and textiles), (Koshirō 1983). Note that 1975 was a recession year. At the beginning of the year the shipyard had had about 4,000 regular manual workers; by December, 7.5 percent had terminated, about half of them for supposedly "voluntary" reasons. (The 1975 average for the shipbuilding industry as a whole was 18 percent termination). Koshirō estimates that about one-third of these voluntary quits actually were discharges stemming from previous disciplinary warnings or other employer pressure. Furthermore, a majority of the rest of the "voluntary" quits were really retirements. The turnover rates had been a good bit higher before 1975, in the boom years of the 1960's and early 1970's. With regard to separations within one's first five years after being hired, Koshirō found that in the steel mill about 25 percent had left — a figure similar to Cole's. However, in the shipyard the figure was 50 percent, in the auto assembly plant 60 percent, and in the textile mill 80 percent.

Interfirm mobility is, of course, only one form of change in income-producing activity. Other forms probably are every bit as significant — e.g., from self-employed to paid employment, or from one status or occupation to another within the same company — but reliable, systematic data on such phenomena are few and far between. And even where data can be found, we encounter major difficulties when we want to use them for standardized international comparisons. For example, it is often alleged that interfirm mobility is higher in Japan than in the United States, because of lifetime employment. Job changes within the firm, that is, are supposed to compensate the worker for lower opportunities for finding employment in other firms. But Cole does not find this to be so when he compares workers in Yokohama and Detroit. One explanation for this, says Cole, may be that jobs and tasks are demarcated more precisely in Detroit, so that American workers are more aware of job shifts than are Japanese ones.

## Conclusion

For all the gaps in the evidence as to labor market mobility — elsewhere as well as in Japan — there is ample evidence to indicate that the concept of lifetime employment does not describe the career of a typical Japanese worker. Even the oft-heard claim that one-third or so of Japanese wage and salary workers "enjoy" lifetime employment is much in need of proof. Perhaps the typical worker in Japan does not change jobs as many times across a working life as does his or her American counterpart, but relatively few will remain with the same employer from first to last career payday. (A recent study of continuous employment among American workers estimates that the typical employee averages eight years in one firm. Hall 1982).

It is not clear why the concept of Japanese lifetime employment has had so much credence. During the 1940's and 1950's there was a growing body of investigation of labor market mobility in Japan (Ujihara and Takanashi 1971; Rōdō Chōsaron Kenkyūkai 1970). Then, paradoxically, just as mobility rates took off on a sustained rise, the lifetime employment idea captured and dominated the intellectual arena.

Lifetime employment may well be the dream of many, even most, Japanese (and perhaps Americans). But to the extent that the notion describes actualities rather than ideals, it is valid only for a limited fraction of the labor force — some of those employed in the public sector, and some of those employed by large-scale private corporations. Career change and uncertainty has been the experience of the vast majority of gainfully employed Japanese. They shuttle among the smaller firms, try self-employment, serve in family enterprises — showing no great reluctance to quit in order to pursue new opportunities. Their career patterns and mobility pathways appear to differ radically from what is implied by the notion of lifetime employment (Okamoto 1967; Koike 1979, 1983a, 1983b).

It is astonishing how little we know about the labor market behavior of these, the vast majority of Japanese workers. Four-fifths of our research energy seems to have been put into investigating the careers of one-fifth of the labor force. A change of direction seems more than overdue.

## Notes

1. For statistical estimates for this period, along with a review of

31

methodological problems, see Shirai and Shimada (1979), especially pages 284-310. In this section of the chapter I am drawing data from their study except where noted otherwise.

# References

Cole, Robert E.
  1979  Work, Mobility, and Participation:  A Comparative Study of American and Japanese Industry.  Berkeley and Los Angeles: University of California Press.
Evans, Robert, Jr.
  1971  The Labor Economies of Japan and the United States. New York: Praeger.
Hall, Robert E.
  1982  The Importance of Lifetime Jobs in the U.S. Economy. American Economic Review 72 (4, September): 716-724.
Holden, Karen C.
  1973  A Comparative Study of Labor Force change:  Japan 1920-60 and the United States, 1890-1955. Ph.D. dissertation, University of Pennsylvania.
Japan Institute of Labour
  1974  Japan Labor Statistics. Tokyo.
  1979  Labor Turnover Rates, Accessions and Separations. Japan Labor Bulletin 18 (5, May):5.
Koike Kazuo
  1979  Employment in Japan, a "Superdeveloped Country". Japan Echo 6, (2, Summer): 34-47.
  1983a  Internal Labor Markets:  Workers in Large Firms. In Contemporary Industrial Relations in Japan, Shirai Taishirō, ed., Chap. 2.  Madison: University of Wisconsin Press.
  1983b  Workers in Small Firms and Women in Industry. In Contemporary Industrial Relations in Japan, Shirai Taishirō, ed., Chap. 4. Madison: University of Wisconsin Press.
Koshirō Kazutoshi
  1983  The Quality of Working Life in Japanese Factories. In Contemporary Industrial Relations in Japan, Shirai Taishirō, ed., Chap. 3.  Madison: University of Wisconsin Press.
Okamoto Hideaki
  1967  Enterprises in Japan: A Sociological Perspective.  Japan Labor Bulletin 6 (7, July): 4-8.
Rōdō Chōsaron Kenkyūkai (Hen)
  1970  Sengo Nihon no rōdō chōsa [Labor Surveys in Postwar Japan]. Tokyo:  Tokyo University Press.

Shimada Haruo
  1974  The Structure of Earnings and Investments in Human Resources:
        A Comparison Between the United States and Japan. Ph.D. dis-
        sertation, University of Wisconsin — Madison.
  1980  The Japanese Employment System. Tokyo: The Japan Institute
        of Labour, Japanese Industrial Relations Series, No. 6.
Shirai Taishirō and Shimada Haruo
  1979  Japan. *In* Labor in the Twentieth Century, Walter Galenson
        and John T. Dunlop, eds. New York: Academic Press.
Taira Koji
  1970  Economic Development and the Labor Market in Japan. New
        York: Columbia University Press.
Ujihara Shōjirō and Takanashi Akira (eds.)
  1971  Nihon rōdō shijō bunseki. [Analysis of Japan's Labor Markets]
        Two vols. Tokyo: University of Tokyo Press.

CHAPTER 2

# Changing Employment
# Patterns of Women

KAREN C. HOLDEN

Women have made up a substantial segment of Japan's labor
force throughout the modern century. During the postwar period,
however, educational and employment opportunities have grown
and changed, making a wider range of choices available to them
and leading to major changes in the timing and continuity of work
over the lifecourse. Furthermore, it is now more readily accepted
that women will work. Nonetheless, the stereotype still holds that a
woman typically works for a few years after leaving school and that,
outside of a few occupations such as nursing, teaching, or beauty
care, she exits from the labor force at marriage.

Data on women workers in Japan counter this stereotype. The key
findings presented in this chapter are that women of all ages and
family status have responded rapidly and in large number to growing employment opportunities outside family farms and business;
that this response has led them to increase their participation in
paid work and to continue to work during marriage and childbearing — the years during which previous generations ceased work; and
that these changes have altered the character of the Japanese work
force from one heavily male and young to one in which growth in
the number of older female employees is a major component of
employee growth. In this chapter I measure the changing trends in
women's labor force participation in Japan in recent years by looking at the behavior from 1960 to 1975 of a succession of birth cohorts
of women. Change is defined as the difference between a cohort's
actual pattern of labor force participation and the pattern one
might have predicted from the behavior of earlier cohorts.

34

The major limitation of this inquiry is that changes in labor force patterns are being inferred mainly from census data: Such aggregate data can only reflect net changes. By themselves, such macro-level data can at best only partly capture one of the most crucial changes, that of mobility among various subgroups in the labor force.

In what follows I first look at the general trends by birth cohorts in women's labor force participation since 1960. Next I examine changes in the proportions of women who are in agricultural jobs, in nonagricultural ones, and in unpaid family work. Third, I examine shifts in the kinds of jobs held by women as paid workers in the nonagricultural sector.

## General Trends in Participation

Table 2.1 presents the age-specific labor force participation rates for each birth cohort. The rate is simply the percentage of each age group that reported itself as working during the census reference week. We can use the table to follow changes in one particular cohort as it ages or to check for trends in employment of women in a specific age bracket. For example, the figures in bold type follow the cohort of women who are aged 20 to 24 in 1950 up to 1975, when they were aged 45 to 49. Over this 25-year period the percentage of those women in the cohort who were working declined to 51.3 (in 1965, when they were aged 30 to 34), rose again to 63.6 percent in 1970, and then began to drop off once more. To find trends in age-specific participation rates, one must read Table 2.1 along a diagonal from lower left to upper right. Thus if we look at the age group 20 to 24, for each census year we see its members have participated in the labor force at about the same rate — around 68 percent — since 1955.

Table 2.1 indicates that the life-cycle curve of labor force participation for Japanese women has been stable from cohort to cohort across the past generation, except for a marked decline in employment of women under 20 and over 70. The intertwining of work and family events is also apparent from the table. Labor force participation peaks for all cohorts at 20 to 24 years of age, followed by a sharp drop, with then a later but always lower peak between 45 and 54 years of age. Because these are aggregate data, they do not tell us whether the women at work during the 45 to 54 age interval are the same ones who were working during the 20 to 24 age interval. But the pattern and high rate of participation at all ages make it plausible to assert that few older women workers in Japan are in the labor force for the first time in their lives (Evans 1971).

*Table 2.1.* Female Labor Force Participation Rates in Japan, 1950–1975

| Age in 1950 | Year | | | | | |
|---|---|---|---|---|---|---|
| | 1950 | 1955 | 1960 | 1965 | 1970 | 1975 |
| 10- 6 | | | | | | 22.6 |
| 5- 1 | | | | | 35.9 | *66.6* |
| 0- 4 | | | | 37.6 | *70.8* | 43.5 |
| 5- 9 | | | 48.0 | *69.7* | 44.9 | 42.9 |
| 10–14 | | 50.1 | *69.4* | 46.4 | 47.1 | 52.9 |
| 15–19 | 57.4 | *68.2* | 50.1 | 48.0 | 56.3 | 59.2 |
| 20–24 | *63.0* | **51.8** | 51.3 | **58.3** | **63.6** | **62.2** |
| 25–29 | 47.9 | 49.6 | 55.1 | 62.1 | 64.7 | 58.6 |
| 30–34 | 48.6 | 53.4 | 56.7 | 62.6 | 60.8 | 50.7 |
| 35–39 | 51.8 | 55.5 | 56.8 | 57.3 | 53.8 | 38.9 |
| 40–44 | 54.3 | 54.4 | 51.7 | 50.1 | 43.2 | 25.9 |
| 45–49 | 53.7 | 51.3 | 46.7 | 39.3 | 31.0 | 14.0 |
| 50–54 | 52.3 | 45.7 | 39.1 | 28.2 | 18.9 | 7.5 |
| 55–59 | 46.5 | 38.4 | 30.6 | 16.6 | 9.9 | |
| 60–64 | 39.4 | 29.5 | 21.1 | 8.2 | | |

Notes: Percentage refers to women in each birth cohort reported to be in labor force during census reference period. Bold figures refer to same selected age cohort over different years. Italics refer to cohorts of the same selected age in different years.

Sources: Japan Bureau of Statistics (n.d., 1960, 1962, 1967, 1973, 1978).

## Trends in Types of Employment

The stability across cohorts of the life-cycle curve of employment that is apparent in Table 2.1 is misleading; these data, for women in all types of jobs and industries, mask major changes in the type of work in which Japanese women are engaged, and the continuity of their labor force participation. In 1960 just under half of all working women (43.5 percent) were in agriculture, with a comparable 40.4 percent as nonagricultural paid employees. By 1975 this distribution had altered substantially, with only 18.4 percent of working women in agriculture and 59.6 percent in paid nonagricultural jobs. This shift, indicating the flow of workers out of agriculture in response in part to technological innovations, economic growth, and employment opportunities in other sectors, occurred despite little change in total labor force participation rates of women.

Thus, only by looking at the expansion of nonagricultural employment can one capture the impact of postwar economic changes on the diversity of jobs open to women and in turn on their participation in paid jobs. These changes in paid employment are comparable in magnitude to the better documented changes among United States women (Cain 1966; Oppenheimer 1970; Sweet 1973). Their scope in Japan is evident only when agricultural and nonagricultural employment are distinguished and when changes in participation in the nonagricultural sector are compared across cohorts of women.

The analysis used in this chapter to examine changes in nonagricultural labor force participation by cohort reflects the assumptions and techniques of both conventional cross-sectional and cohort analysis. Cohort analysis assumes that each cohort goes through a series of life events that will shape for it a unique pattern of behavior; I assume here that each cohort's reaction to external change will also be affected by the norms set by earlier cohorts. The significant change identified is not just the increase or decrease in participation which is observed over time for each cohort, but the difference between this change and that which might have been expected based on the pattern set by earlier cohorts. Thus, the following analysis focuses on changes in work behavior that depart from a presumed standard of behavior. That standard is hardly self-evident; for purposes of analysis I have established it by looking at the behavior of previous cohorts at a similar life-cycle stage. "Change" is said to occur if the work behavior of a cohort differs from that of the cohort five years older when the latter was at the same life-cycle stage.

Table 2.2 offers an example of the technique, applied to an analysis of changes in the work participation of women aged 40 to 44 in 1970 and 45 to 49 in 1975. Between these two years, this cohort declined in their total labor force participation from 63.6 to 62.2 percent — an actual decline of 1.3 percentage points (column 4). Had this cohort acted precisely as did the cohort of women five years older, however, their labor force participation would have risen by 1.1 percentage points (column 3). Thus, one can say that, compared to previous cohorts, this cohort's propensity to work had actually declined by − 2.4 percentage points (column 5). It is this change that is discussed throughout the rest of this chapter — the change in

*Table 2.2.* Patterns of Participation Rate Changes for One Birth Cohort, Japan, 1970–1975

| | Year | | Participation Rate Change | | |
|---|---|---|---|---|---|
| Age | 1970 (1) 40–44 | 1975 (2) 45–49 | Expected[1] (3) | Actual (4) | "Change" from Previous Cohort (5) (3–4) |
| Overall Partici- pation Rate | 63.6 | 62.2 | 1.1 | -1.3 | -2.4 |
| Nonagricultural Participation Rate[2] | 42.7 | 46.2 | -0.7 | 3.5 | 4.2 |
| Employees | 28.2 | 32.5 | -1.4 | 4.3 | 5.8 |
| Self-employed[3] | 6.5 | 6.0 | .5 | - .6 | -1.0 |
| Unpaid Family Workers[4] | 8.0 | 7.7 | .3 | - .3 | - .6 |
| Agricultural Participation Rate[5] | 20.8 | 16.0 | 1.8 | -4.8 | -6.6 |
| Employees | 0.4 | 0.4 | 0.0 | 0.0 | 0.0 |
| Self-employed[3] | 4.0 | 2.6 | 1.0 | -1.4 | -2.3 |
| Unpaid Family Workers[4] | 16.4 | 13.0 | 0.8 | -3.4 | -4.2 |

Participation Rate: The percentage of women in the five-year birth cohort reported in the labor force.
[1] The actual change for the preceding birth cohort between 1965 and 1970.
[2] Participation rate for nonagricultural labor force only.
[3] Includes workers on own account without employees.
[4] Family workers in household business.
[5] Participation rate for agricultural labor force; includes forestry, hunting, fishing and aquaculture; but these four account for only 11% of the women in agriculture in 1975.
Sources: See Table 2.1.

a cohort's probability of working compared to the probability suggested by the experience of the cohort born five years earlier.

Table 2.2 demonstrates the already indicated importance of disaggregating work participation rates by industry and employment status in order to understand the types of changes in the employment of women that occurred in response to postwar industrial growth. Both nonagricultural and agricultural employment are divided into three types: (1) *paid employees,* "persons employed by a person, company, corporation, or government office"; (2) *self-employed* persons, proprietors with or without employees; and (3) *unpaid family workers,* "persons who work in the business, farm, trade, or professional enterprise operated by a member of the household in which they live." (Definitions from Japan, Bureau of Statistics, *Population of Japan 1975* 5, Part I, Division 1:xv.)

The decline in labor force participation by this cohort of women aged 40 to 44 in 1970, between 1970 and 1975 documented in Table 2.2 is the net effect of rapid employment growth in nonagriculture and declines in agricultural employment. The shift out of agriculture and into nonagriculture was more rapid for this cohort than it was for the next older group. The marked increase in the percentage of women in paid jobs in the nonagricultural sector (the employee group) contrasts sharply with the larger than expected declines in agricultural employment and in the percentage self-employed or working as unpaid family workers in nonagriculture. The actual increase of 4.3 percentage points is even more impressive when compared with the decrease expected (-1.4%) from looking at the preceding cohort. Looking across all cohorts in this comparative way demonstrates the magnitude of growth in paid employment of Japanese women since 1975. This is shown in Table 2.3. The left-hand panel gives actual rates of paid employment outside of agriculture for each cohort; the center panel gives the amount of "change" where the change is defined above (i.e., as in Table 2.2, column 5). Because output growth in nonagriculture may also be expected to increase employment of family workers in small businesses, changes in this employment status are presented in the right-hand panel. Sharp declines in this status confirm that the primary impact of postwar economic change on employment has been on opportunities in *paid* work.

Table 2.3 captures each cohort at a different stage in the life cycle, and we can see how labor force participation varies both within and across cohorts as they respond to various life-cycle events. For example, women aged 25 to 29 in 1960 were beginning to withdraw from the labor force in part due to marriage and childbearing, but by 1975 were starting to return to paid employment. Older cohorts were starting to withdraw permanently. But regardless of these variations by life-cycle stage, each successive period found that in every cohort a larger percentage of women were in paid employment outside of agriculture than we would have expected from the behavior of previous cohorts. There is only one significant exception: Women under age 20 were less likely to hold paid jobs, a change which reflects the increase in the percentage of women enrolled in higher education.

*Table 2.3.* Participation Rates and Changes in Nonagricultural Employment and Unpaid Family Work between Adjacent Female Birth Cohorts at Comparable Ages, Japan, 1960-1975

| Age in 1960 | Participation Rate as Employees[1] | | | | Change in Participation Rate of Employees[2] | | | Change in Participation Rate in Family Work[2] | | |
|---|---|---|---|---|---|---|---|---|---|---|
| | 1960 | 1965 | 1970 | 1975 | 1960-1965 | 1965-1970 | 1970-1975 | 1960-1965 | 1965-1970 | 1970-1975 |
| | % | % | % | % | % | % | % | % | % | % |
| 0-4 | | | | 21.7 | | | -11.3 | | | -1.8 |
| 5-9 | | | 32.9 | 60.7 | | -0.9 | 0.3 | | -0.9 | -3.9 |
| 10-14 | | 33.8 | 60.4 | 31.9 | - 5.8 | 3.8 | 4.8 | -6.1 | -2.8 | -4.5 |
| 15-19 | 39.6 | 56.6 | 27.2 | 24.7 | 10.1 | 2.4 | 3.5 | -8.6 | -4.8 | -5.7 |
| 20-24 | 46.5 | 24.7 | 21.2 | 29.1 | 2.9 | 2.2 | 4.1 | -5.9 | -4.8 | -5.0 |
| 25-29 | 21.8 | 19.1 | 25.0 | 32.8 | 2.8 | 2.2 | 4.6 | -5.0 | -1.8 | -6.0 |
| 30-34 | 16.2 | 22.8 | 28.2 | 32.5 | 6.9 | 5.0 | 5.7 | -1.6 | -4.0 | -4.8 |
| 35-39 | 15.9 | 23.1 | 26.7 | 28.0 | 7.8 | 5.5 | 5.3 | -0.9 | -2.8 | -3.3 |
| 40-44 | 15.3 | 21.3 | 22.7 | 21.7 | 7.4 | 5.5 | 4.9 | 0.3 | -2.8 | -5.5 |
| 45-49 | 13.9 | 17.2 | 16.9 | 14.2 | 6.7 | 4.6 | 3.8 | -0.4 | -2.5 | -6.5 |
| 50-54 | 10.6 | 12.3 | 10.4 | 7.2 | 5.3 | 1.4 | 1.6 | -1.7 | -2.3 | -5.4 |
| 55-59 | 7.0 | 9.1 | 5.6 | 3.0 | 4.8 | 0.2 | .4 | -1.6 | -1.1 | -4.5 |
| 60-64 | 4.3 | 5.4 | 2.6 | | 2.7 | 0.6 | | -1.6 | -0.3 | |
| 65-69 | 2.7 | 2.0 | | | 0.8 | | | -3.3 | -1.2 | |
| 70-74 | 1.2 | | | | | | | -4.8 | | |

[1] Nonagricultural employees as a proportion of population.
[2] Rate change: Percentage point difference from participation rate of next older birth cohort at same ages.
Sources: See Table 2.1.

*The Life-Cycle Pattern*

Thus, while the labor force participation of Japanese women continues to dip sharply at those ages during which women are most likely to marry and bear children, the rate of withdrawal has dropped with each successive cohort. Similarly, looking at larger stages of the life-cycle, we see that the rate of reentry into paid employment has been increasing for each later cohort. In general, the change has been as significant in the later as well as the earlier stages of the life cycle.

We arrive, then, at the following picture of changes in Japanese women's labor force participation across the life cycle. Each new female cohort, when compared with earlier cohorts, is (1) more likely to take up paid work, although beginning at a slightly later age; (2) less likely to stop working during the early years of marriage and parenthood, (3) more likely to return to the labor force in the middle years, and (4) more likely to delay retirement. There also is a marked shift from unpaid work in a family business to employment away from home, for wages, supervised by employers who are not kin. A common stereotype about social change and women's labor force participation holds that it is younger women who primarily respond to shifting opportunities. What we see in Japan is that there are significant shifts in the labor force behavior of women at all stages of the life cycle.

Furthermore, these changes in nonagricultural employment of women have resulted in important changes in the sex and age composition of the total nonagricultural work force. Since 1955 the growth in the number of women employed in the nonagricultural sector has been more rapid than that of men employed in this sector.

With few exceptions, this is true for virtually all occupational categories. What is particularly interesting is an apparent trend towards greater utilization of older women (35 years old and above) in paid employment (Table 2.4). For example, during the 1970-75 period, when female employment was growing at a relatively slow rate, almost 30 percent of women entering the labor force were over 35.

It seems safe to predict that this trend will continue, if only because of the diminishing absolute size of younger birth cohorts of the population. The pool of younger potential female workers is shrinking. For example, in 1975 there were 14.6 percent fewer women aged 15 to 24 than there were in 1970. As these smaller birth cohorts move through the life cycle they will influence the labor pool at all age stages. Thus even if age-specific *rates* of

Table 2.4. Components of Percentage Changes in Nonagricultural Female
Employment, Japan, 1960-1975

|  | 1960-1965 | 1965-1970 | 1970-1975 |
|---|---|---|---|
|  | % | % | % |
| Total Growth[1] | 28.4 | 17.0 | 9.7 |
| Retirements[2] | -0.2 | -5.3 | -2.1 |
| Withdrawals[3] | -12.6 | -14.6 | -13.8 |
| Entries | 41.1 | 33.7 | 25.6 |
| Percentage aged 35 or above | 22.8 | 15.9 | 28.9 |

[1] Percentage change between census years in average number of female employees.
[2] Percentage change between census years in birth cohort above age 50 at first census.
[3] Percentage change between census years in birth cohort between ages 20 and 35 at first census.
Sources: See Table 2.1.

employment remain unchanged, the absolute numbers of women in the future entering the labor force at early ages will fall.

Smaller birth cohorts alone would tend to result in a rise in the average age of women in the labor force in Japan. The trend is further spurred by changes in the rates of employment for different age groups. As we see in Table 2.3, women under age 20 are more likely to stay in school. And although women aged 20 to 24 are taking paid jobs in the nonagricultural sector at a slightly higher rate than before, this increase is not enough to compensate for the decline in the absolute numbers of women in this age group. In addition, a growing percentage of older women are in paid jobs. In 1960, only 24.5 percent of employed women were between the ages of 35 and 64 years; by 1975 the percentage had almost doubled to 45.5 percent. In short, Japan's female labor force is aging—i.e., the average age of employed women is rising—much more swiftly than one would predict from looking only at the aging of the population as a whole.

## Occupational Trends

In all industrial economies the percentage of workers employed in crafts has declined while those in white-collar occupations has increased — a demonstration of the shift in output and employment from manufacturing to service. Solomon Levine (Chapter One) notes this for Japan; it is well documented elsewhere (Fuchs 1968; Sorrentino 1971; Singelmann 1978). Table 2.5 documents this shift for Japanese women by presenting data on the occupational distribution of women in two separate years, and by giving rates of growth in the number of women employed in each occupation between 1970 and 1975. The only occupations in which the absolute number of women employees increased were professional, managerial, clerical, sales, and nondomestic service. By 1975, 69.9 percent of all female employees were in these white-collar jobs.

This shift towards white-collar jobs, shown for all female workers in Table 2.5, appears as well when cohort-specific changes by occupation are analyzed — each successive cohort is more likely to find employment in professional, clerical, and service jobs.[1] Some cohort differences do appear when changes in occupational employment are analyzed by the cohort technique described above. It is primarily younger women for whom participation in the work force as professionals has grown. For women over 30 the probability of employment in these occupations did not increase — a fact that may reflect higher educational levels and longer training periods demanded for entry into many professional jobs. The higher employment of young women in professional jobs is accompanied by their lower-than-expected employment in craft occupation, even as women 35 and older continued to have higher than expected employment in nontextile craft jobs. All cohorts have been rapidly leaving domestic service jobs., although in nondomestic service work we find, as with crafts, declining participation by younger women but higher-than-expected participation by older women.

## Discussion

I have outlined some of the major trends in paid employment for women in Japan across the past generation. To bring out the connections between careers and the life cycle, I have focused on changing *rates* of labor force participation among successive cohorts rather than on changes in absolute numbers.

As in all industrial economies, the broad shift is away from farming occupations and from unpaid family work to employment in paid jobs outside the agrarian sector. In Japan the number of women holding paid jobs outside of agriculture grew by 74 percent from 1960 to 1975. A large portion of this increase had to be recruited from women over 35 — since younger women of working age are staying in school longer and so enter the labor force later. Over 70 percent of these "new" employees came from "unexpected" increases in participation (unexpected in the sense that we would not have predicted them from the behavior of earlier cohorts); and 79.4 percent of that total increase as accounted for by women over 35. To put the point more generally, work experiences have changed as much for older as for younger Japanese women in response to postwar educational advancement, to expanding employment opportunities, and, perhaps, to rising standards of living expected by families and to price increases which may have induced women to search for outside employment. Futhermore, all cohorts, old and young, have responded to the growth of jobs in white collar occupations. Clerical work has become a more prevalent and acceptable job choice for Japanese women, although younger women have also sought employment in the professions and older women in crafts and nondomestic services.

*Table 2.5.* Occupational Distribution Changes, in Percentages, of Female Nonagricultural Employees Aged 15 to 59, Japan, 1970–1975

| Occupational Category | Percentage of Female Employees | | Percentage Change in Number of Women Employed 1970-1975 |
|---|---|---|---|
| | 1970 | 1975 | |
| | % | % | % |
| Professional and Technical | 10.0 | 12.0 | 27.0 |
| Managerial | 0.8 | 0.8 | 25.1 |
| Clerical | 31.0 | 34.0 | 17.6 |
| Sales | 10.7 | 10.7 | 9.2 |
| Transportation and Communication | 2.1 | 1.4 | -26.9 |
| Crafts | 30.9 | 26.0 | - 7.1 |
| Textiles | 8.7 | 6.8 | -15.5 |
| Other | 22.2 | 19.3 | - 0.2 |
| Service | 13.6 | 13.0 | 6.1 |
| Domestic | 0.9 | 0.6 | -25.2 |
| Other[1] | 12.7 | 12.4 | 8.1 |
| Total[2] | 99.1 | 97.9 | 8.3 |

[1] Excluding protective services.
[2] Mining and protective services excluded from total.
Sources: See Table 2.1.

All of this adds up to a major shift in the composition of the female labor force in Japan, and a major shift in a Japanese woman's "life chances" for taking up paid employment. Compared to her grandmother, a Japanese woman today is much more likely to take a paid job and to remain in it for some time, although women still are moving in and out of the labor force at much higher rates than men are. Whether Japanese women today are more likely to hold lifelong careers is something we cannot determine from the census data. What our information does indicate is that although the so-called revolving-door pattern of labor force participation still prevails for some women, women at every age are more likely to work. Some women continue to enter the labor force for a time after leaving school, withdraw during their childbearing years, then later return to paid work until retirement. Declining rates of withdrawal for each younger cohort suggest that it is increasingly common for women to have continuous labor market careers or to experience only short interruptions in their work, if they do withdraw at all.

Women, particularly older women, are coming to make up a larger and more stable component of the Japanese labor supply. What this trend implies for such matters as the industrial wage structure, employment and retirement policies, rates of college attendance, women's career expectations, and family incomes is unclear. It is a new source of career uncertainty for Japanese women as individuals, and a significant source of uncertainty for the Japanese economy as a whole.

## Notes

I have focused my analysis here on changes in paid employment. A similar kind of analysis also needs to be done on women who are self-employed or who are unpaid family workers. If the numbers of women in these categories are on the downtrend (e.g. equalling 25.6% of women working outside the agricultural sector in 1975, in contrast to 28.0% in 1960), they still account for a substantial number of Japanese women of working age. Occupational development analysis has given a good deal of attention to what industrialization and economic growth do to agricultural employment. We still know rather little about what industrialization does to job opportunities for the self-employed and for unpaid family workers *outside* of agriculture.

1. Cohort-specific changes by occupation will be furnished by the author on request.

## References

Cain, Glen G.
   1966   Married Women in the Labor Force: an Economic Analysis.
          Chicago: University of Chicago Press.
Evans, Robert, Jr.
   1971   The Labor Economies of Japan and the United States. New
          York: Praeger.
Fuchs, Victor R.
   1968   The Service Economy. New York: National Bureau of Economic
          Research.
Holden, Karen C.
   1973   A Comparative Study of Labor Force change: Japan, 1920-69,
          and the United States, 1890-1955. Ph.D. dissertation, University
          of Pennsylvania.
Japan Bureau of Statistics, Office of the Prime Minister. Polulation Cen-
       sus of 1950, III, Part I. Tokyo, n.d.
   1960   Population of Japan, 1955 II, Tokyo.
   1962   Population of Japan, 1960 II, Part 1. Tokyo.
   1967   Population of Japan, 1965 II, Part 1. Tokyo.
   1973   1970 Population Census of Japan 5, Part 1, Div. 1. Tokyo.
   1978   1975 Population Census of Japan 5, Part 1, Div. 1. Tokyo.
Oppenheimer, Valerie K.
   1970   The Female Labor Force in the United States. Berkeley and Los
          Angeles: University of California Press.
Singelmann, Joachim
   1978   The Sectoral Tranformation of the Labor Force in Seven In-
          dustrialized Countries, 1920-1970. American Journal of Sociol-
          ogy 83 (5): 1224-1234.
Sorrentino, C.
   1971   Comparing Employment Shifts in 10 Industrialized Countries.
          Monthly Labor Review 94, (10): 3-9.
Sweet, James A.
   1973   Women in the Labor Force. New York: Seminar Press.

# Part Two

# BUT AM I GETTING
# ANYWHERE?

I suppose that every normal adult thinks, now and then, about the broad currents of employment that flow around him. Thinks, too, about how history and demography channel those currents and about his own location within them. But more often he will gauge his progress, or lack of it, directly against the career phases that are standard in his own line of work, and against the career fates of co-workers around him. In the next two chapers, Kenneth A. Skinner and Paul H. Noguchi guide us from the wider scene into the micro-climates of an executive office and a blue-collar work site in Japan. They show us how tenured employees at different levels in large organizations answer for themselves the constant career question: "Am I movin' on or only standing still?"

Read in tandem, these two reports complement one another and add up to a worker's-eye view of life in that crystal palace of modern employment, the large-scale corporation with its well-marked routes for personnel passage and with what sometimes is too-generously referred to as an escalator system of promotions.

To be more precise, I should say that these reports provide a *male* worker's perspective on lifetime employment. If you want a more complete view of the corporation as a career setting, I suggest that along with these two chapters you read Chapter Eight. There you will find the much more truncated career perspectives of young "of-fice ladies," who are put under pressure to resign within a few years and give their energies instead to homemaking.

As Skinner and Noguchi portray him, the Japanese Organization Man is no sociological fool. He knows that few job histories will ever replicate the perfect careers outlined in the personnel handbook. Perhaps he was idealistic during his first days on the job; if so, he soon learned that one should not expect more than a loose correlation between effort and reward within the organization. Factors beyond a man's control may twist or halt the "escalator". Skinner's executives in Chapter Three find that the top-level positions in their organization are reserved for outsiders; Noguchi's railway men of Chapter Four are in an industry that is debt-ridden and being forced to retrench. One simply has to accept such limitations. But within these limits a man can hope — cannot avoid trying — to influence the direction and speed of his advancement.

So the worker confronts a never-ending task: of assessing where he is and of taking action on the basis of that assessment. Executive or ticket-taker, both scrutinize the lists of promotions and reassignments, evaluate the performance-and-reward patterns of co-workers, note the whims of supervisors — in short, conduct a daily intelligence operation on the job and after hours in the bar. They formulate strategies, adjust work course and life course. For example, says Skinner, if a man moves out of the company apartment project and buys a house of his own, he probably believes that he is in line for eventual promotion to middle management. Only middle-rank managers earn enough to pay off a mortgage.

Each of the two promotion schemes — blue collar and white collar — elicits a different style of career development action, whatever the level of one's aspirations. The National Railways' scheme for its operating employees is explicit, abstract, built around formal written examinations; but in the office where Skinner worked the scheme is tacit and obscure. The railwayman has to be a lifetime student, always preparing for yet another round of promotion tests. The executive is not troubled with examinations; by contrast he has to be a lifetime gossip — always asking about the job histories of his colleagues so that he may infer, from a snarl of arbitrary job-reassignments, just where his own trajectory may be carrying him.

These chapters are not offered in a spirit of sour grapes, although they tend to talk more about the losers and the less successful. These men value their job security. And if the promotion outlook is less than glorious for most of them, they have pride and self-respect enough not to use the situation as an excuse for mere time-serving. The important point, conceptually, is this: If these men are working to achieve the organization's purposes, at the same time they are playing with the system in order to achieve their own goals. The dramas of this corporate underlife, brought alive by two talented ethnographers, are one of the most humanly fascinating features of life in the Japanese corporate palace today.

KENNETH A. SKINNER is Assistant Professor of Anthropology at Widener University. PAUL H. NOGUCHI is Associate Professor in the Department of Sociology, Bucknell University.

# CHAPTER 3

# Aborted Careers in
# a Public Corporation

KENNETH A. SKINNER

Large Japanese organizations are said to favor permanent or lifetime employment: hiring people with the expectation that they will remain in the organization until they are retired. Thanks to annual salary increases and to promotions based largely on seniority, recruits into such organizations are thought to be able to look forward to thirty years of career predictability. Such employees can predicate decisions and plans for their lives outside the organization by projecting the foreseeable course of their work careers. Ishida Takeshi (1971:47) has even suggested, perhaps ingenuously, that an employee's future is so clearly calculable in terms of income and promotions that his dreams and hopes seem futile.

Reviewing the evidence, Levine in Chapter One finds that only a fraction of the Japanese labor force actually is in any form of permanent employment. But even among these employees we cannnot assume the career predictability which current notions of permanent employment imply. In this chapter I take you to a public corporation in Tokyo where employees expect to remain until retirement, but where they have difficulty prediciting what course their work careers will take.

During their initial years in the organization, employees usually follow a "normal" course of work assignments, moving horizontally within and across sections of the organization. This is similar to what happens to young white-collar employees in most large work organizations in Japan or elsewhere (see Rohlen 1974, Yoshino 1968, Dore 1973). However, in JKII (my acronym for this particular organization), as employees approach the conclusion of this "learning stage" (Schein 1971), they find limited possibilities for advancement. Their "apprenticeship" is not necessarily followed by assignments to positions of middle rank. JKII's formal structure of jobs holds out the promise of promotion, but in practice this promise tends not to be fulfilled. For this reason I think it appropriate to characterize these careers as "aborted."

A person's entire work career in JKII is likely to be a succession of movements from one unrelated assignment to another, making futures difficult to foretell. Confronted with this uncertainty, employees must devise personal plans of action, or strategies, which they hope will bring about an acceptable or desired sequence of assignments. "Negotiating the structure" is part of life in any organization. But in JKII structural factors heighten career unpredictability and accentuate the need for carefully formulating personal strategies. Examination of these strategies reveals how employees perceive their relationship to the organization. By recognizing how people use strategies within a context of career course uncertainty we also gain a new purchase upon social relationships among personnel.

## Public Corporations

The Japanese government has established public corporations to perform a variety of social and economic functions. Generally government-owned and -financed, these organizations provide public services, implement economic and social policy programs, and administer capital for economic projects. Some of the better-known public corporations are the Japanese National Railways (see Chapter Four), Japan Housing Corporation, Small Business Promotion Corporation, Japan Broadcasting Corporation (NHK), and Japan External Trade Organization. A public corporation has the legal status of *tokushu hōjin*, "special juridical person," meaning that it was established by a Diet-enacted law which sets forth its functions, governance, structure, and financing. There are other *tokushu hōjin*, but only those organizations subject to scrutiny by the Central Administrative Management Agency (Gyōsei Kanri Chō) are properly termed public corporations. In 1976 when I studied JKII, it was one of 113 such public corporations in Japan.

There are distinctions among public corporations according to functions, finanaces, and laws governing labor relations. The Administrative Management Agency divides public corporation into eight categories, as shown in Table 3.1, although differences are often not as clear as the terminological distinctions imply. The law establishing a public corporation generally specifies which national ministry or agency will supervise its operations, budget, and appointment of officers (see Table 3.2). Some public corporations are attached to two or more supervising bodies.

Though a few public enterprises were established prior to 1945, public corporations are primarily a postwar phenomenon. Only four of the 113 existed before 1945. The growth in the number of public corporations has paralleled Japan's economic resurgence. The Japanese government chose the corporate device for a number of reasons, the major one being that it allows the government to accomplish certain tasks without expanding the size of ministries and agencies. As shown by the variety of functions and structures of this device (Table 3.1), the government has been imaginative in its use. Once the Occupation authorities had removed the national railways, tobacco monopoly, and telephone service from the ministries and converted them into *kōsha*, "public companies," the number of public corporations began to grow steadily. Many of those established in the early 1950's were mandated to provide financing for private industry or to aid low productivity sectors such as agriculture and small business. Those established during the late 1950's and early 1960's reflect more diverse functions, a response to needs created by Japan's rapid economic growth, technological advancement, urbanization, emerging international position, and expanding communications networks. Between 1958 and 1966, the number of public corporations increased from 53 to 108. All public corporations in the *jigyōdan* category and three-fourths of those in the "other" category were formed after 1958 (see Yoshitake 1973, Johnson 1978).

As of the end of 1975, public corporations employed 932,738 people. When employees of the three *kōsha* (Japanese National Railways, Japan Monopoly Corporation, and Japan Telegraph and Telephone Corporation) are removed, this figure falls to 142,354. Among the remaining 110 corporations, the largest has over 21,000 employees (Japan Air Lines) and the smallest has five (Fisheries Mutual Aid Fund), the average being around thirteen hundred employees (Gyōsei Kanri Chō 1976a). Workers in public corporations are nominally government employees. They are not considered *kokka kōmuin*, "national civil servants," however, and so do not share the legal status of people in the ministries and national agencies. Labor relations in a public corporation are not governed by the

Table 3.1. Types of Japanese Public Corporations

| Category | Characteristics | Number | Examples |
|---|---|---|---|
| Kōsha | Provide major public services. Fully government-owned and financed. | 3 | Japanese National Railways<br>Japan Monopoly Corporation<br>Japan Telegraph and Telephone Corporation |
| Kōdan | Carry out large-scale public works projects. Whole or partial national government ownership, capital fully financed by national government or by national and local governments. | 16 | Japan Housing Corporation<br>Japan Highway Corporation<br>Honshu-Shikoku Authority |
| Jigyōdan | Implement economic and social policy programs. Smaller in scale than kōdan, with less commercial character. Generally government-owned and financed. | 20 | Small Business Promotion Corporation<br>Japan International Cooperation Agency<br>Public Nuisances Prevention Corporation |
| Kōko | Finance corporations for specific areas. Fully financed by national government. | 10 | Housing Loan Corporation<br>People's Finance Corporation |
| Kinko and Ginkō | Banks and depositories having similar functions as kōko, but with some entrepreneurial autonomy. Fully financed by national government. | 4 | Export-Import Bank of Japan |
| Eidan | Essentially the same as kōdan. From the Pacific War period. | 1 | Teito Rapid Transit Authority |
| Tokushu gaisha | Provide public services. Joint-stock corporations with relative autonomy as special companies with capital financed both by the national government and the private sector. | 12 | International Telegraph and Telephone Company<br>Japan Air Lines<br>Electric Power Development Company |
| Others | Various types — foundations, research institutes, promotional organizations, mutual benefit associations for certain occupations, etc. Largely government financed. | 47 | Japan National Tourist Organization<br>Japan External Trade Organization<br>Japan Broadcasting Corporation |

Sources: Gyōsei Kanri Chō (1976a, 1976b).

53

Table 3.2. Distribution of Japanese Public Corporations Among Supervising
Ministries and Agencies

| Ministry or Agency | Number of Public Corporations Supervised |
|---|---|
| Prime Minister's Office | 1 |
| Hokkaido Development Agency | 1 |
| Economic Planning Agency | 2 |
| Science and Technology Agency | 7 |
| Environment Agency | 2 |
| Okinawa Development Agency | 1 |
| National Land Agency | 5 |
| Ministry of Foreign Affairs | 2 |
| Ministry of Finance | 16 |
| Ministry of Education | 10 |
| Ministry of Health and Welfare | 10 |
| Ministry of Agriculture and Forestry | 19 |
| Ministry of International Trade and Industry | 27 |
| Ministry of Transportation | 15 |
| Ministry of Posts and Telecommunications | 5 |
| Ministry of Labor | 6 |
| Ministry of Construction | 11 |
| Ministry of Home Affairs | 4 |

Source: Gyōsei Kanri Chō (1976a, 1976b).

National Public Service Law. Except in three *kōsha,* employees
come under the Trade Union Law, the same law that applies to
private enterprises. The Trade Union Law permits workers to
organize, bargain collectively, and strike. The three *kōsha* are under
the Public Corporations and National Enterprises Labor Relations
Law, which, like the National Public Service Law, denies the right
to strike.

In order to protect my informants, I choose not to identify the
public corporation I studied. JKII is an acronym for neither its actual name nor a fictitious one. Like other *jigyōdan,* JKII exists
because the Diet has set a specific socioeconomic policy goal.
Specifically, JKII provides financing, planning, technology, and expertise for public works projects. Requests for JKII's involvement
come primarily from public agencies, and JKII staff members work
closely with these governmental groups in developing and carrying
out a variety of locally designed projects. Together these projects
contribute to the achievement of JKII's legislated goal. Unlike some
public corporations, JKII enjoys the support of both politicians and
the public. In fact, its activities are generally considered vital to the
nation's future.

JKII employs over one thousand people, about 90 percent of

whom are men. It is organized into twenty divisions, each containing two to eight sections. I interviewed employees in all divisions, but most of my participant observation efforts took place in the largest division, which has over one hundred staff members. I had two periods of contact with the organization: first, during the two years when I was a full-time employee of the organization; and second, three and one-half years later when I returned for ten months of intensive field research.

## Reward Structures in the Organization

Most regular staff members have entered JKII directly from universities. But in the early years of the organization, some positions (especially for section and division chiefs) were filled by people hired away from other public corporations or ministries. For most new recruits, JKII is their second or third choice; first choice is usually one of the ministries, especially the ministry which supervises JKII. The similarity of JKII's activities with those of its supervising ministry attracts these individuals, and their failure to become national civil servants does not diminish their commitment to JKII's goals. Moreover, the fact that employment in JKII is second choice to a ministerial career reveals that most recruits desire the long-term careers which government service offers.

JKII's salary schedule reflects an assumption that employees will remain until retired. Salary increases are given to all employees each year. With some exceptions, employees interpret the steady rise in salaries as a system which pays them in later years for working hard in early years (see Tsuda 1974). While it is possible to transfer to other public corporations, employees recognize that leaving JKII for private enterprise would mean forfeiting one's accumulated seniority. Salaries in public corporations are generally lower than those in large companies, but they are sufficiently high to discourage temptations to leave.

The major component of an employee's monthly pay is called *kihon kyū*, "base salary," comprising 70 to 80 percent of the total. The remainder is composed of various *teate*, "allowances," such as housing, commuting, family support, lunch, and overtime. The system operates according to a set scale of levels of base pay, with employees automatically moving from one level to another at least every twelve months. The schedule has six grades, each of which contains ascending levels of base salary according to years of service.

Table 3.3 is an abbreviated reproduction of the base level schedule in use in 1975.

A middle school or high school graduate begins in Grade 6, but since almost all recruits are university graduates Grade 6 is rarely used. A recruit with a university degree begins at the first-year level in Grade 5 at a base salary of 89,600 yen per month. In principle, a person advances to the next level in each grade each year in the month of his entry. After four years in Grade 5 he reaches a salary level which is equivalent to or higher than the first-year level in Grade 4. Then, theoretically, management decides whether to advance him to Grade 4 or to continue him in Grade 5. In fact, advancement has become practically automatic, largely as a result of labor union insistence. Moving to Grade 4 is desirable because the yearly increments are greater. A similar automatic advancement from Grade 4 to Grade 3 occurs when a person's monthly base equals the first-year level for Grade 3, although it takes eight years to reach this level.

Grade 2, however, is only for section chiefs and persons appointed as advisers after having been section chiefs. People who are not appointed section chief continue in Grade 3, following a base-level salary sequence beyond the amount equivalent to the first-year level of Grade 2. Grade 3 includes base-level salaries for up to 26 years of service in that grade. A university graduate who was in Grade 5 for four years and Grade 4 for eight years could remain in Grade 3 through his thirty-eighth year of employment. He would reach his fifty-seventh birthday, the mandatory retirement age, a few years before arriving at the final base-level salary of Grade 3.

Base salary at each Grade 3 level is over 99 percent of what a person would receive as base salary were he a section chief and in Grade 2 with the same number of years of service. However, section chiefs receive higher salaries than other staff members. Seventeen percent is added to a section chief's base salary. This is done as a supplemental percentage increment rather than as a raise in base pay in order to maintain a base-level schedule that can be applied to persons who become section chiefs but subsequently are not advanced to Grade 1. Only division chiefs are in Grade 1, and they too receive a 17 percent supplemental increment. The top executives (president, two vice-presidents, 12 governing board members, and two auditors) have salaries set by the supervising ministry.

The salary schedule illustrates two things. First, rising to a middle management position involves significant monetary gain. Second, provision is made for people who will advance in salary but not be

*Table 3.3.* Base-Level Monthly Salary Schedule of JKII, a Japanese Public Corporation, 1975

| | Grade | | | | | Years of Service |
|---|---|---|---|---|---|---|
| 1 | 2 | 3 | 4 | 5 | 6 | |
| Y246,300 | Y198,800 | Y160,800 | Y115,300 | Y 89,600 | Y 64,500 | 1 |
| 251,800 | 204,300 | 166,400 | 120,900 | 97,100 | 67,300 | 2 |
| 257,300 | 209,800 | 172,000 | 126,500 | 104,500 | 70,200 | 3 |
| 262,700 | 215,200 | 177,600 | 132,200 | 111,900 | 73,200 | 4 |
| 268,000 | 220,500 | 183,200 | 138,000 | 115,500 | 76,500 | 5 |
| 273,300 | 225,800 | 188,800 | 143,800 | 119,000 | 79,800 | 6 |
| 278,600 | 231,000 | 193,700 | 149,600 | 122,500 | 83,100 | 7 |
| 283,800 | 236,200 | 198,800 | 155,300 | 126,000 | 86,400 | 8 |
| 289,000 | 241,300 | 204,000 | 160,800 | 129,500 | 89,600 | 9 |
| 294,000 | 246,300 | 209,100 | 165,000 | 133,000 | 92,800 | 10 |
| 299,000 | 251,100 | 214,300 | 169,100 | 136,400 | 96,100 | 11 |
| 303,900 | 255,900 | 219,300 | 173,200 | 139,700 | 99,600 | 12 |
| 308,800 | 260,700 | 224,400 | 177,300 | 143,000 | 103,100 | 13 |
| 313,700 | 265,500 | 229,400 | 181,400 | 146,300 | 106,600 | 14 |
| 318,600 | 270,300 | 234,400 | 185,500 | 149,600 | 110,100 | 15 |
| | | | | | | |
| | 299,100 | 287,000 | 235,600 | 194,600 | 155,200 | 21 → / 26 → |
| | | | | | | 26 |
| | | | | | | 27 |
| | | | | | | 28 |
| | | | | | | 29 |

In 1975, 300 yen equalled approximately one dollar.
Arrows indicate continuing yearly salary increments.
Source: From author's field notes, based on JKII unpublished internal memorandum.

promoted to positions of authority. The schedule makes clear to staff members that there is no "escalator" of automatic promotion to middle-management positions simple because of seniority.

## Organizational Dependency and Aborted Careers

In an organization having 20 divisions and 58 sections, one would expect that most of the regular staff could anticipate promotion to section chief at some point, and that a sizable number would eventually attain division chief positions. In 1976 approximately 250 regular staff members were between the ages of 35 and 45, the age level when appointment as section chief is most likely. Therefore, a person had about one chance in four of being a section chief. If these positions are rotated at three- or four-year intervals, with no one given a second term, the majority would receive appointments. In fact, very few do, making the careers of most JKII staff "aborted." To understand how this has come about, we must examine JKII's relationship to its supervising ministry.

Because public corporations are supervised by one or more ministries, they can be considered "dependent organizations." There are four facets to ministry control. First, the ministries stand as the source of a public corporation's legitimacy. Second, the budgets, salaries, and financial dealings of most corporations must be approved by its supervising ministry in consultation with the Ministry of Finance. Third, if the ministries wish, they can have final voice in the selection and promotion of personnel. And fourth, the ministries oversee policies and performance.

This situation benefits the ministries by allowing them to regularize their own flow of personnel. Japan's civil service policies emphasize permanent employment and seniority, making them similar in principle to those of most countries. The route and timing of a minsitry official's promotions are highly predictable. The general pattern is that most of those hired in the same year achieve the section chief level after the same length of service. People are conscious of belonging to an entrance-year cohort, and when preference in promotion is given to some members of a cohort it is often resented by other members.

Above the section chief level the pyramid narrows, and not all individuals in a cohort can expect to be elevated at the same time. The norm is that no person is demoted, nor is one member of a cohort allowed to become the direct supervisor to others. It is thought to be awkward and therefore inefficient for a person to exercise authority over his peers. Those in a cohort who are not appointed to division or bureau chief positions are sent to temporary posts of equivalent rank either inside or outside the ministry. They may be assigned to bodies which the ministry can influence: field offices, agencies, auxiliary organizations — or public corporations.

The custom has developed that when one member of a cohort is promoted to an administrative vice-ministership, all others in the cohort resign to allow him absolute seniority in the ministry. Such "voluntary retirement" is called *yūtai* and occurs not only when an administrative vice-minister is appointed but also when an individual recognizes that his best option is to retire early. The average age of departing ministry personnel is 51. Retiring officials usually find high-level positions in private enterprises or in public corporations. Either way, they can expect high salaries, and many are able to serve in a succession of positions until they are into their 60's (see Johnson 1974, Watanabe 1976, Okabe 1970).

The ministries, then, place two types of personnel into positions in public corporations: retired officials (pejoratively called *amakudari* because they "descend from heaven") and personnel in active service who are transferred temporarily. JKII's law of establishment gives to the supervising ministry the authority to appoint the president and auditors. The law does not specify that these and other executive positions be filled only, or even predominantly, by men with backgrounds in the ministries. But all of JKII's executives are *amakudari*. A 1975 survey of 72 public corporations found that 81 percent (N = 350) of the executives were *amakudari* (Seirōkyō 1975). Regular JKII staff refer to executive positions, especially on the governing board, as *zabuton:* "cushions" on which retired ministry officials can sit and collect high salaries. Officials of the Administrative Management Agency admit that one of the motives for ministries' encouraging establishment of public corporations is that they open up positions for retiring bureaucrats.

The careers of regular staff members in JKII are not directly affected by *amakudari*, since the staff members do not consider executive positions to be open to them. The practice contributes, however, to a general feeling that JKII is being "used" by the ministries, with little concern for the integrity of the organization or welfare of its personnel. Employees of large organizations in Japan have often been described as identifying closely with their place of work (see Nakane 1970, Rohlen 1974, Ballon 1969, Vogel 1979), but staff members of JKII complain that their desire to identify with it is undercut by their ill-feeling toward *amakudari* executives. Some staff members compare JKII to a colony, saying that the supervising ministry treats JKII's staff members with the same disdain a colonial power shows to subjugated people. As evidence for this, they point to the temporary transfer of outsiders into middle-level positions, often described in labor union literature as *shinnyūsha,* "invaders." JKII's laws of establishment make no provision for ministries to assign their own personnel to middle-level positions on a regular basis. The prerogative to do so rests not on legal statutes but on the structural dependency of the corporation.

Ministry officials claim that people temporarily posted to JKII bring it needed expertise. To JKII's labor union that is a rationalization which reflects ministry officials' belief that public corporation personnel are inherently inferior. The labor union has urged that training programs be offered to better prepare regular JKII staff to assume middle-level positions. But JKII's executives have refused, thus contributing to the ministry's ability to justify appointing their own personnel. Executives thus tacitly recognize that even with training programs JKII few regular staff will be appointed to middle-level positions in their own agency.

According to employment data gathered in 1975 by labor union members in 37 public corporations, 46 percent (N = 204) of the division chief and assistant division chief positions were filled by temporarily assigned ministry officials. In 20 of the 37 public corporations, half or more of these postions were filled by ministry personnel. Nineteen percent (N = 190) of section chief positions also were occupied by people from the ministries (Seirōkyō 1975).

In 1976, 16 of JKII's 24 division and assistant division chief positions were filled by ministry personnel, as well as 26 of its 58 section chief postions. Over the years the proportion has varied only slightly. A small number of regular staff have been section chiefs at some time and are now advisers or are in other auxiliary positions. The vast majority of the 900 regulars, however, have never held middle-level positions. Rather, each has moved through a unique sequence of assignments, none of which is designated as a promotion in rank or responsibility.

Figure 3.1 shows the limited number of middle-level positions that regular staff are allowed to fill. But the opportunities are restricted even more by the fact that the few regular staff members who *are* promoted to middle-level positions usually occupy a series of such positions. In other words, middle-level positions are not distributed among a wide range of staff members. In the division for which I obtained the most complete employment records, only 13 of the 103 staff members working in 1976 had ever held one of the eight section chief positions. Only two had held section chief positions in other divisions. Some staff members complain that a person becomes a repeater in middle-level positions less for ability than for proven support for executives' policies.

*Figure 3.1.* Number and Level of Positions in JKII, 1976.

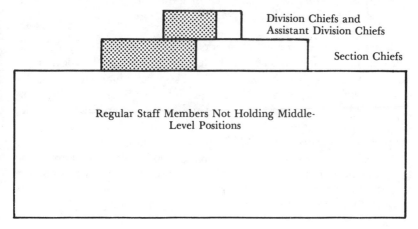

Division Chiefs and
Assistant Division Chiefs

Section Chiefs

Regular Staff Members Not Holding Middle-
Level Positions

Shaded areas represent positions occupied by personnel of supervising ministry.
Source: From author's field notes.

## Career Course Orientations

Harold Wilensky (1964:314) defines a work career as a succession of related jobs through which an individual moves in an orderly and predictable sequence. This or similar definitions have shaped most discussions of careers in large organizations. But the situation in JKII does not allow an employee to subscribe to such a definition. In terms of predictability and orderliness, a JKII staffer finds his work career consisting of two dissimilar parts. On the one hand, he has a channel of secure employment and predictable increases in salary. On the other hand, his movement through jobs is far from orderly or predictable, and the contents of the jobs themselves are not necessarily related.

JKII staff members view their career movement in one of three distinct and alternative ways, which can be called their career course orientation. These are subjective notions about the kinds of work a person would like to be doing or expects to be doing. In discussing

what they believe will be their futures in JKII, a significant number of staff members express views which reveal one of these orientations. For others I have made inferences from actions, statements, and employment histories. Briefly stated, the three orientations are:
  (1) to expect and/or seek advancement to middle-level postions
  (2) to be satisfied with the status quo, or
  (3) to think only about short-term gains, with no clear sense of of where one might go over a long range.

A small number of staff members, in holding to the first orientation, have not abandoned hopes for promotion to a middle-level position. In most cases these are men whom superiors have singled out as having mangerial potential. Consequently they have been given important jobs during most of their time in the organization. Expecting promotion, they devote themselves to performing well and express their commitment to JKII's goals. An indication of the expectation of advancement is that in comparison to fellow workers of the same age more of these men have brought homes, rather than live in apartments heavily subsidized by JKII. The debt incurred places these individuals in the position of needing the additional salary attainable only through promotion.

The second career course orientation is also found among relatively few staff. In essence, these people are comfortable in the jobs they are doing, show few signs of wanting to do any other job, and have routinized their work as much as possible. Promotion is unlikely, as they see it, since they have been given little indication by superiors that they are considered skilled. Staff members with this orientation realize that they are subject to assignment changes, but they do not appear to be acting to influence decisions about the assignments they will be given.

It is the third orientation which is not only the most interesting but also the most widespread. Most staff members see their work careers as being at best a succession of unrelated reassignments. Resigned to the unlikelihood of promotion, they are primarily concerned about movement from one section to another, from one assignment to another. Finding little order in their personal involvement in JKII's activities, many of these people have become disillusioned and have difficulty sustaining devotion to the organization's goals.

Assignment changes are relatively frequent, with 23 months being the average length of service in one post. I base this figure on the complete employment histories of 87 staff members hired in 1971 or earlier. Rarely is an individual in the same assignment for as long as three years; some assignments last only one month. Although a person may be reassigned at any time during the year, most changes take place at the beginning of the fiscal year in April or six months later in October when budget allocations for projects begin or are adjusted. Also, field assignments generally begin and end at these times.

An assignment change may trigger a chain of personnel movements. The original vacancy created by moving one individual is almost always filled. Because division chiefs make reassignments primarily at two points during the year, a number of vacancies appear simultaneously. This results in long chains of personnel movements, of which some are complete loops and others terminate in newly created posts. In many Japanese organizations, work roles are non-specific within a team or section (see Nakane 1970, Vogel 1979, Rohlen 1974, Noda 1975), but in JKII's sections an individual's responsibilities are clearly delineated. Each section has its function, and each position within the section has its task. Ideally, individual talents are matched with role tasks. But as a consequence of the chains of personnel movements, individuals are placed in assignments which they neither like nor feel prepared for.

Harrison White (1970:18) states that intraorganization mobility characterized by long chains of movement suggests that there is a central authority with the power of coordinate such movements. Division chiefs in JKII have this authority. In contrast to what has been reported for many other Japanese organizations (see DeVos 1975, Nakane 1970, Yoshino 1968), leaders in JKII, especially division chiefs, do not act primarily as group facilitators or coaches, nor do they encourage staff participation in their decisions. Rather, division chiefs tend to be authoritarian and to keep decision-making power in their own hands. There is little to constrain a division chief when reassigning staff. He need not, for example, be concerned about maintaining a person's hierarchical status according to some objective assessment of a previous assigment's status. People are often moved from a post which they and others view as important to one that is clearly unimportant. Staff members believe that superiors, who if ministry personnel are often more interested in their home ministry than in JKII, are either not concerned about staff career development or feel that their own short tour of duty in JKII makes such concern impractical.

People find themselves being moved for a variety of reasons, and usually the reasons are not clear. Is a person being reassigned because a chief values his skill? Or because his performance is less than adequate? Is he being moved simply to make room for someone else, even though his performance has been satisfactory? Is he being put into a less desirable assignment because he is too active in the labor union? Is the move designed simply to give a younger person experience in the section? On most occasions a division or section chief will indicate the rationale for a move. But staff mebers generally treat these explanations as *tatemae*, "statements for public consumption," not as *honne* or "real reasons" (see Nieda 1973).

Staff members do not believe they can refuse reassignment. Those who have tried to do so have found division chiefs unsympathetic. In most instances, a refusal would disrupt the chains of reassignments which division chiefs have devised. Only if a person hears rumors about an impending reassignment far in advance of the implementation date does he have any chance of persuading chiefs not to make the change.

## Career Strategies

Assignment changes are highly visible events. A staff member uses them to assess his situation in the organization and also the situations of others. The limited possibilities for altering one's formal status make assignment changes one of the few, and certainly the most tangible, indicators of where one stands. They are also material for introspection about the unfolding of one's career. Consequently, personnel shifts are of great interest to JKII staff, probably more so than among people in organizations in which promotion possiblities are not as narrow (see Cole 1979:114-115). Predicted and announced assignment changes are major topics of conversation, with people trying to discover the motives behind the division chiefs' directives. Such probing brings into general discourse notions about the personal qualities, work performance, and reputations of any individual slated for reassignment. Staff members are not reticent in discussing how division or section chiefs, as well as other staff, are thought to evaluate fellow workers. Because they know that reassignment will touch everyone at some point, understanding the bases for decisions is essential for formulating strategies. Keeping abreast of gossip about fellow employees is helpful in thinking about one's own future, and this seems to dissolve whatever reluctance people might have about discussing fellow employees in frank terms.

No formal procedures for evaluating staff members have been instituted. Division and section chiefs acquire much of their information about a person in casual conversations with his fellow workers, such as during drinking sessions in local bars. Since the brief tenure of ministry personnel does not allow them to develop extensive knowledge about individuals, they must rely heavily upon information derived from a person's peers. Knowing this, staff members conclude that the type of reassignments they can expect depends largely on the reputation they have among their associates.

In an organization with a fairly stable work force, reputations become widely known. A person's movement to a new section is generally preceded by the surfacing of his reputation. People in the section he is leaving speculate about the reasons for his departure, and his new section mates are interested to learn why he is coming and, if they do not already know him, what his background is. Much of a person's behavior can be attributed to attempts to shape how others view him. Many staff members want their self-perception of being hardworking and skilled to be confirmed by others and to be translated into personally challenging assignments which they consider important to the organization. Both actual hard work and carefully constructed presentments of hard work are expressions of this strategy. It assumes that division chiefs put hardworking and skilled people into such assignments, an assumption not always confirmed by events. By contrast, people who hope to have relatively easy assignments tend to present themselves as being competent while doing their work without enthusiasm. Avoiding assignments requiring hard work results in no financial loss since there is no merit pay in JKII.

Staff members' thoughts about future assignments include a variety of other considerations. Some of the more common ones are listed below. Depending on the individual and the situation, these may be viewed as desirable or undesirable in an assignment:

- performing work which requires extensive contact with superiors,
- being assigned to a field office,
- having experience in a variety of jobs,
- being assigned to sections having certain people in them,
- returning to a section in which one had already worked,

65

- participating in new projects whose success is uncertain, and
- being given a job in which nothing novel occurs.

## Some Examples of Strategies

One staff member, whom I shall call Mr. Tamura, was told by his division chief that he would be sent to a new post. Mr. Tamura did not want this assignment and argued that he had a medical problem which prevented him from undertaking more strenuous work. The chief encouraged him to undergo treatment, and so every day for a year Mr. Tamura left the office at 3 p.m. to see a doctor. Other staff told me that Mr. Tamura's medical condition was not at all serious, but by making regular trips to the doctor for as long as possible Mr. Tamura hoped to postpone reassignment, perhaps eventually resulting in the chief reconsidering his decision.

Another man, Mr. Wada, said that he was trying to establish himself as an expert in work he found enjoyable. His hope was that the division chief would consider him indispensable in that assignment. His "passion" for doing good work, therfore, was in fact an indication of his fear of reassignment. Other staff members expressed skepticism about the likelihood that such strategies would succeed, arguing that superiors were inconsistent in recognizing and rewarding expertise. Some of these staff members stated that strategies aimed at currying favor among superiors have more chance of success. Even while disapproving of ministry officials in middle-level positions, a number of staff members have adopted this strategy.

Though some observers report a cooperative relationship between union and management in Japan (see Shirai 1973, Kawada 1973, Clark 1975, Hanami 1969), between JKII's union and the organization's executives there is unremitting hostility. The union's opposition to *amakudari* and to "invaders" nurtures a basic disinclination to support executives' policies or seek even temporary accommodations. Another issue is the fact that the governing board makes its salary decisions on the basis of the National Personnel Authority's (Jinji-In) annual salary recommendations for civil servants. This is seen as a denial of the union's right, under the Trade Union Law, to negotiate pay and working conditions.

The labor union receives support from staff members who see it as the only means for obtaining higher salaries. It owes much of its strength to the fact that members are denied careers with some form of "normal" advancement. The union is a vehicle both for expressing anger at this situation and for moderating the consequences by securing higher salaries and greater benefits. In these efforts, the union has been fairly successful. Union negotiators argue that staff should be compensated for the restricted possibilities for promotion, but are careful not to give the impression that they are abandoning opposition to temporary transfers from the ministries. Despite the union's stance, some members try to influence decisions about their reassignments by impressing upon chiefs that they are willing to be cooperative and provide information. But if they do this too openly they risk being ostracized by fellow union members for revealing union plans to management.

The presence of "traitors" in the union reveals that temporary posting of ministry personnel as chiefs offer opportunities to regular staff. It gives one a chance to execute new strategies and to have a brief respite from the influence of one's reputation. A person can present himself in a manner that counteracts the unflattering aspects of one's reputation, although these actions have less impact once the new supervisor has been around long enough to plug into the gossip network. The rapid turnover among superiors means that changes in strategies, and even in career course orientations, are not uncommon. My two periods of contact with the organization allowed me to see shifts in people's approaches. For example, a number of staff members who had once tried to demonstrate their qualifications for positions of responsibility were later found to have resigned themselves to routine tasks.

Strategies can backfire. For example, Mr. Tanaka had worked hard in an assignment he did not like in order to show the division chief that he could handle a job he preferred. After being given the desired job, however, he was allowed to remain in it for only two months. The person who replaced him in his earlier assignment did not perform to the division chief's satisfaction, and so the chief elected to move Mr. Tanaka back. In another instance a man followed his division chief's dictum that staff members should improve skills in their spare time. He enrolled in evening classes in subjects he thought would enhance his qualifications for a desired assignment. After a year, however, it became apparent that the division chief planned to keep him where he was for a long time; so he dropped the classes. Despite such unpredictability, staff members with the third career course orientation believe it would be foolish to abandon the struggle, and as proof they point to uninteresting and meaningless jobs of people holding the second orientation.

Understanding career course orientations provides insight into office and after-hours relationships among JKII personnel. People who share career expectations tend to associate with one another. Beyond this, few generalizations can be made about staff members' lives outside the organization. Predictably, a person with the second or third career course orientation is unwilling to make major financial commitments. Rarely does he own a home or foresee buying one. Nearly half of JKII staff live in apartments owned by the organization, for which they pay modest rent. About 20 percent live in public housing or parents' homes. The high cost of private housing itself might account for the small number of homeowners, but one's calculation of future salary (barring promotion) effectively eliminates any hopes of home ownership. For married men, employment security removes worries about meeting basic needs of a family. My observations in staff members' homes, however, do not permit generalizations about how career course uncertainty affects family life, although interesting questions can be put forward. For example, to what extent has career uncertainty in JKII resulted in a compensatory clarity in the defintion of role expectations among family members as they move through stages of family life? Or has the flexibility required for negotiating career courses in the work organization also been adopted in family relations?

## Discussion

In large organizations a career is often thought of as the succession of formal positions which an individual holds, each position being logically precedent to the next. This case study of a public corporation demonstrates that the concept of career must be separated into two parts. On the one hand, an individual in JKII can expect security in that his employment is virtually guaranteed until he is retired. On the other hand, there is no certainty about the course his career will take. With middle-level positions limited, a person's career course is likely to be a series of jobs, none of which represent advancement. These job assignments are not differentiated in a manner which signifies that movement from one to another represents advancement or "normal" progress. In the literature on organizations in Japan there is a recurring tendency to assume that the security offered by "permanent employment" also means a career of increasing responsiblity and authority as employees move through their years of association with an organization. Case studies which examine participation in organizations in terms of indivudual careers, as opposed to an emphasis on formal structures, allow reappraisal of this assumption.

The case study of JKII reveals that in the absence of career predictability an employee is forced to make his own assessment of what constitutes a satisfying career. This assessment is the outcome of an individual's reflections on his level of skill, commitment to the organization, willingness to perform certain tasks, and desired self-image. Strategies are devised in hopes of influencing the course of one's career. While a few staff members strive for promotion, most seek only short-term successes in maintaining an acceptable career course. A person's experiences in the organization and his observations of the experiences of others contribute to the formulation of this strategy.

The tying together of strategies and career lines can be significant for a focus on careers in any social or institutional setting. While a person's career can be plotted along some line or through stages, the process by which movement takes place is often masked. A myriad of factors may affect career movement. Our ability to assess the impact of these factors is aided by identifying what factors the actors themselves feel they have to take into account in devising career strategies. In JKII, however, I found a number of strategies being employed, an indication of staff members' uncertainty about what will affect their careers.

Studies which have reported on "typical" career paths in Japanese organizations usually present seniority and work performance as the major factors in determining career progress. Because of this emphasis, an employee's relationships with others in the organization are either neglected or presented as having comparatively little influence on his career course. But we have been made aware of patron/client relationships between superiors and subordinates that may facilitate successful performance as one moves through a career, although these relationships do not necessarily affect a person's changes for promotion. The situation in JKII draws our attention to the significance of a person's many relationships with co-workers in the unfolding of a career. The kind of relationship a person has with any of his co-workers can become the content of gossip which directly affects superiors' decisions about reassignments. Any act or statement may become part of the body of information making up a person's reputation. Employees' behavior reflects an awareness of this fact. From my experience in JKII, I am convinced that such a perspective provides a better way of getting at the motivations for employees' actions than does an approach which emphasizes the influence of culturally defined role expectations or behavioral norms.

By any standard, JKII is a successful government bureaucracy. Its activities are applauded by the public; its budgets increase by 10 to 20 percent each year. Staff members take pride in the organization's success, but this does not alleviate the anxiety and frustration experienced in negotiating one's involvement in the organization. While JKII's goals are supported by most staff, the organization's goals do not take precedence over individual career goals. At best, the desire to participate more fully in JKII's activities shapes personal strategies and heightens frustration over limited access to middle-level postions. Observers of Japanese organizations have often appeared to be so impressed by employees' ritualistic expressions of support for an organization's goals that they fail to get below the surface and identify more significant personal goals.

The case study demonstrates that careers cannot be adequately understood if the organization in which they unfold is treated as an isolated social unit, which has often been the case of studies of Japanese companies. Outside forces can extend their influence deep into an organization, affecting its actions and its employees' careers. One significant factor may be differentials in power among interacting organizations, as shown in this case study by the supervising ministry's ability to regularize careers for its officials at the expense of career predictability for JKII employees. A consequence of the ministry's power is an employment structure in which an individual's unquestioning obedience, surrender of self-interest to group interests, and reliance on superiors' beneficence are rarely conducive to the achievement of a satisfying career.

Employees in JKII do not fit the mold of the supposedly passive Japanese worker who can direct his attention to productivity without being overly concerned about promotions. Most employees of JKII are actively involved in efforts to shape their own work careers. In presenting themselves to fellow employees and in performing work, they are intensely conscious that they must rely on themselves far more than on formal provisions of the organization in order to achieve satisfying careers. The consequence of aborted careers has been the creation of a highly fluid situation in which the advantage goes to those who have the ability to deal with uncertainty.

*Data for this chapter are drawn from research funded by a Japanese Foundation Fellowship, a Putnam D. McMillan Fellowship, and a University of Minnesota Foundation Special Grant.*

## References

Ballon, Robert J.
  1969  Participative Employment. *In* The Japanese Employee, Robert J. Ballon, ed., pp. 63-76. Tokyo: Sophia University Press.
Clark, R. C.
  1975  Union-Management Conflict in a Japanese Company. *In* Modern Japan: Aspects of History, Literature, and Society, W.G. Beasley, ed., pp. 209-226. London: George Allen and Unwin.
Cole, Robert E.
  1979  Work, Mobility, and Participation. Berkeley and Los Angeles: University of California Press.
DeVos, George A.
  1975  Apprenticeship and Paternalism. *In* Modern Japanese Organization and Decision-Making, Ezra F. Vogel, ed., pp. 210-227. Berkeley and Los Angeles: University of California Press.
Dore, Ronald P.
  1973  British Factory — Japanese Factory: the Origins of National Diversity in Industrial Relations. Berkeley and Los Angeles: University of California Press.
Gyōsei Kanri Chō [Administrative Management Agency]
  1976a Tokushu hōjin sō ran [A Register of Public Corpora — tions. Tokyo.
  1976b Public Corporations in Japan. Tokyo.
Hanami Tadashi
  1969  Labor Disputes and Their Settlement. *In* the Japanese Employee, Robert J. Ballon, ed., pp. 241-248. Tokyo: Sophia University Press.
Ishida Takeshi
  1971  Japanese Society. New York: Random House.
Johnson, Chalmers
  1974  The Re-Employment of Retired Government Bureaucrats in Big Business. Asian Survey 14(11):953-965.
  1978  Japan's Public Policy Companies. Washington, D.C.: American Enterprise Institute for Public Policy Research.
Kawada Hisashi
  1973  Workers and Their Organizations. *In* Workers and Employers in Japan: the Japanese Employment Relations System, Ōkochi Kazuo, Bernard Karsh, and Solomon B. Levine, eds., pp 217-268. Tokyo: University of Tokyo Press; and Princeton: Princeton University Press.
Nakane Chie
  1970  Japanese Society. Berkeley and Los Angeles: University of California Press.

71

Nieda Rokusaburō
1973　Tatemae to honne. [Official Explanations and Real Intentions] Tokyo: Daiyamondo Sha.

Noda Kazuō
1975　Big Business Organization. *In* Modern Japanese Organization and Decision-Making, Ezra F. Vogel, ed, pp. 115-145. Berkeley and Los Angeles: University of California Press.

Okabe Shirō
1970　Kōdan kōsha, jigyōdan [Public Corporations] Tokyo: Kōkigyō Kenkyū Chōsa Kai.

Rohlen, Thomas P.
1974　For Harmony and Strength: Japanese White-Collar Organization in Anthropological Perspective. Berkeley and Los Angeles: University of California Press.

Schein, Edgar H.
1971　The Individual, the Organization, and the Career: A Conceptual Scheme. The Journal of Applied Behavioral Science 7(4): 401-426.

Seirōkyō [Public Corporation Labor Unions Council]
1975　Amakudari Hakushō [White Paper on "Those Descending from Heaven"]. Tokyo: Seifu Kankei Tokushu Hōjin Rōdō Kumiai Kyōgi-kai.

Shirai Taishirō
1973　Collective Bargaining. *In* Workers and Employers in Japan: the Japanese Employment Relations System, Ōkochi Kazuo; Bernard Karsh, and Solomon B. Levine, eds. Tokyo: University of Tokyo Press; and Princeton: Princeton University Press.

Tsuda Masumi
1974　Lifetime Employment and Seniority-Based Wage System. Hitotsubashi Journal of Social Studies 7(1):1-16.

Vogel, Ezra F.
1979　Japan as Number One: Lessons for America. Cambridge, Mass.: Harvard University Press.

Watanabe Yasuo
1976　Kōmuin no kyaria [Careers of Public Officials]. *In* Gyōseigaku kōza [Lectures on the Science of Public Administration], Tsuji Kiyoaki ed., pp. 169-207. Tokyo: Tokyo Daigaku Shuppankai.

White, Harrison
1970　Chains of Opportunity: Systems Models of Mobility in Organizations. Cambridge, Mass.: Harvard University Press.

Wilensky, Harold
1964　Work Careers and Social Integration. *In* Comparative Social Problems, S. N. Eisenstadt, ed., pp 306-319. New York: Free Press.

Yoshino M. Y.
1968    Japan's Managerial System: Tradition and Innovation.
Cambridge, Mass.: MIT Press.
Yoshitake Kiyohiko
1973    An Introduction to Public Enterprise in Japan. Tokyo:
Nippon Hyōron Sha.

# CHAPTER 4

# Shiranai Station: Not a Destination But a Journey

PAUL H. NOGUCHI

## Introduction

One occupational culture that demands a keenly mechanical, segmented time orientation is the railroad industry. With Cottrell (1939) I find that railroad workers have an unique linkage with the passage of time. In this chapter I look at how workers on the Japanese National Railways (JNR or Kokutetsu) cope with the timing of their career options. Wilensky's definition is useful here: "A career is a succession of related jobs, arranged in a hierarchy of prestige, through which persons move in an ordered (more-or-less predictable) sequence" (1968:323). I approach this with what Klerman and Levinson label the "career perspective" — the subject's "evolving occupational role, goals, and identity" (1969:412). This perspective examines changes in the individual's career direction, including discontinuities as well as continuities. In order to understand promotions, the major punctuation points, one must place them in the context of an evolving career. Promotion represents both an opportunity for growth and a threat to early aspirations and identity elements that must be limited or abandoned because of the requirements of a new position.

Many workers employed by the Japanese National Railways claim that trains symbolize life's journey and the transiency of human existence. This prompts the investigator to hypothesize that there is a close relationship between life line and career line for JNR employees. To explore this relationship, I ask how a worker deals with certainty and uncertainty as he moves up the occupational ladder. Are there serious disparities between career expectations and achievements in the case histories of train station personnel (from platform workers to station masters)? What are the adaptive strategies of these workers? When do they consider themselves to be "on time" or "running late" in reaching their career goals? This awareness of timing in careers heightens the individual's awareness of age (Neugarten 1968a:96) and provides the investigator with a cultural time clock that is superimposed over the biological clock (Neugarten 1968b: 146).

The first part of the chapter discusses the macro-structural processes which delineate the career options of a modern-day railroad worker in Japan. These factors are mainly historical, demographic, economic, and political in nature. The second part offers case studies of individual career patterns, and looks at how individuals negotiate the promotion system in JNR. The process of "becoming a railroad man" not only involves the obvious early, middle, and late stages of career development; more important, a constant reassessment of self becomes a prevailing theme. As a railroad worker matures, he encounters a period of greater introspection and increased sensitivity to his position within a complex social environment. His lesson is one of greater self-tolerance.

Roth (1963:107) makes the important point that the analysis of any career timetable must include study of the manner in which failure is handled. Surely a typical career is not only a series of successes; in the JNR there are "sidetracks" that impede one's progress. Success and failure must also be considered within the framework of other careers, occupational and nonoccupational, which surround them. It is within this complex maze that JNR employees seek the signposts and reference points by which they define themselves, and that helps them to answer when asked, "Where are you now?" The answer "I don't know" (*shiranai*) would be a melancholy one.

## JNR Careers and the Macro-Society

### Historical Factors

In the early days of Japan's modernization, the railroad worker commanded respect from all quarters because the industry was so instrumental in the economic, political, and social development of the nation. Closely linked with his occupation was the idea of unending self-sacrifice in the line of duty and a deep sense of national purpose. People often spoke of a *tetsudōin katagi* ("pride of a railroader") which was symbolized in *abura* ("grease") and *ase* ("sweat"). At the forefront of the idea of industrial familism was the example of the railroad industry, as echoed in the phrase *kokutetsu ikka* ("One National Railways Family") (Nakane 1970:7).

For young people of that early modern era, the engineer and the passenger conductor became role models. It was a common sight to see children playing near local stations to watch the steam locomotives pass by. Mothers encouraged their daughters to marry railroad men. Today, some older workers claim that when a station master entered an eating establishment, the proprietor would get on his knees to clean the man's shoes. Often the station master was not charged for his meals. Even today in some country towns the station master is given the seat of honor at athletic contests. The railroad worker, in short, was a special kind of human being. In his study of a Tokyo neighborhood, Dore (1958:233) alludes to the episode of the ten-year-old boy who interviewed Tokyo's Central Station master, and of the honor which surrounded the occasion. In the late 1960's an NHK television drama serialized a best-selling novel that spanned the career of a railroad worker from 1925 to 1955.

But for all the nostalgia about what railroading once may have meant, the status of the JNR worker has fallen markedly. The glamour now goes instead to the television or movie celebrity, the baseball player, or the astronaut. Today the railroad worker is associated with the staging of illegal strikes and slowdowns which greatly inconvenience the public. In surveys conducted in 1955 and 1964, male residents of Tokyo ranked the railroad worker thirteenth among occupations. In the 1964 survey the railroad worker shared a similar occupational status with the barber, carpenter, or garage mechanic (Befu 1971:128). Many of the young JNR workers I interviewed in 1971 claimed that they themselves did not think their occupation carried much prestige. In fact, many of their peers in high school had not been interested in the railroad because of low pay and harsh working conditions. Many young males confessed that they saw no future (*saki ga nai*) in the railroad.

But recruitment problems in the JNR seem to be confined to lower levels of the organization. At management levels, young college graduates find JNR attractive. They seek out the *hanagata* ("star") and *ninki* ("popular") employers. And the JNR is among the most popular of the public corporations, along with the public radio and TV network (NHK) and the public telephone and telegraph service. Figure 4.1 summarizes JNR's ranking by college students as a place of employment over a recent eleven-year period. While college graduates regard the management level as lucrative, middle and high school graduates relate to the organization in a less enthusiastic way. JNR management now has two- and even three-generation families well represented within its ranks — according to the *Japan Times Weekly* for October 22, 1977, page 6 — but lower level workers discourage their sons from joining and their daughters from marrying railroad workers. The overall decline of the industry to one of low standing (workers doing monotonous tasks and working for a declining, deficit-ridden organization) serves as a backdrop for viewing careers in the JNR today.

*Figure 4.1.* College Graduates' Ranking of Japanese National Railways as a Place of Employment, 1969-1979

Year

| 1969 | 1970 | 1971 | 1972 | 1973 | 1974 | 1975 | 1976 | 1977 | 1978 | 1979 |
|------|------|------|------|------|------|------|------|------|------|------|

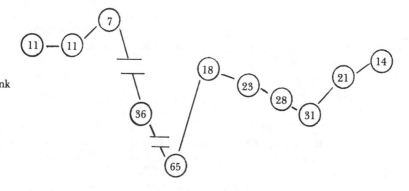

Rank

Source: *Shūkan Asahi*: (1978:20).

*Demographic, Political and Economic Factors*

The current employee age structure and promotion schedules of the JNR were influenced by several other elements. First was the ending of World War II. The dilemmas that JNR management faces today can be traced back to the practices of an earlier administration. The peculiar age pyramid derives directly from these practices. And the budget deficit problem which has plagued the organization for many years not only touches upon the realm of national economic issues but also the political arena as well.

During the war, females took over many posts that normally had been filled by men. Hence a female conductor or ticket taker was a common sight, especially during the later years of the conflict. With the termination of the war came a surge of ex-soldiers and repatriated civilians in need of employment. The railways, then government-owned, tried to find jobs within its ranks for the newly returned soldiers. This policy was primarily responsible for the current shape of the organization's age pyramid. Figure 4.2 shows an overabundance of workers in the 40 to 50 year age bracket. These are the workers who returned home from the war. This unusual bulge creates problems. From the point of view of management, the large number of workers causes strains on the reward system since wages are based on seniority, and even the years in military service count as time spent on the job. From the vantage point of the employees, the increased numbers generate keen competition for promotion, especially in the higher supervisory positions.

JNR workers have evolved two models for the age structure. In the first, they compare it to a Japanese lantern; i.e., the age pyramid is *chōchin-katachi* ("lantern-shaped"). The *chōchin* is fairly narrow at the top and bottom but bulges in the middle. Then in the early 1970's workers noticed that management was attempting to entice younger recruits. Because of the future possibilities of an extremely narrow base to the age pyramid, the workers began to speak of it as *rakkyō-katachi* ("scallion-shaped").

Another major factor which influences the options of JNR workers is that the entire corporation has long been running a deficit. In 1977, as the nation's top red-ink enterprise, JNR tallied a deficit of about 800 billion yen.

One of the main sources of strain on JNR's income is that only a handful of its lines operate in the black. Scattered throughout the country are many local lines which carry few passengers but which Diet members refuse to close for fear of losing popularity with their respective constituencies.

JNR is unable to operate and expand like a private business. Over the years it has been authorized to invest only in industries closely related to transporation, such as managing bus terminals or station buildings, or the running of retail shops within the stations. The problem was somewhat lightened by a revision of the Japanese National Railways Law in 1977 which allows the organization to engage

*Figure 4.2.* Age Distribution of Japanese National Railways Employees, 1970

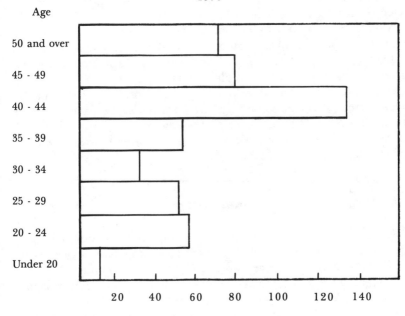

Number of Employees (in thousands)

Source: Japanese National Railways (1970).

in a greater variety of business activities. Real estate holdings in particular promise to be a good source of new income.

Furthermore, the JNR cannot automatically raise fares when operating costs increase. This task is left to the Diet, but it is the JNR organization which becomes the culprit in the eyes of the public. Public outcry is a predictable outcome of fare increases, and a shift to other modes of transporation. In 1976, a 50 percent fare hike prompted many commuters and travelers to switch to airlines and other means of transportation. In some areas of Japan, it is now less expensive to fly than to take a train.

Indeed, a major external factor leading to the financial ills of JNR has been the increased competition from land, air, and sea transportation. At one time the railways enjoyed a virtual monopoly on land transportation. But over the years, according to JNR officials, the financial crisis of the railways has been brought about because the government has emphasized investment in the auto industry and has not implemented rehabilitation measures for JNR. The high-speed railroad network currently under construction is an attempt to remedy the situation.

Nevertheless, mounting personnel costs and interest payments on loans keep the JNR in a financial bind. If the JNR were a private company it would have to declare itself bankrupt under current laws. A 10 year reconstruction plan which began in 1972 calls for the elimination of unprofitable local lines, for limitations on annual wage increases, for periodic fare hikes, for personnel cutbacks, and for raising productivity. These points have met resistance and will no doubt continue to be sensitive issues for both employees and the general public.

## The Promotion Examination System

Kokutetsu has long held the reputation for providing lifetime employment. In a questionnaire which I gave to a sample of seventy-six lower ranking employees, almost 65 percent responded that their main reason for joining the railroad was that it was indeed "a secure place to work" *(antei shita shokuba)*. But while employment may be "secure," in reality a career in JNR, especially at the lower levels of the organization, is filled with obstacles that cause anxiety and concern. One such cause for bitterness among the lower ranking workers is the promotion system for managers.

In contrast with JNR managers, the station-level employees' struggle with formal written examinations does not end once they have been hired. Lower-ranking station employees are quite vocal about the contrasts between the two promotion systems. They complain that incompetent managers can reach high positions merely by convincing the right people that they did not cause any ripples along the way *(taika naku)*. This "escalator system," they say, applies only to the elite.

Atsukawa (1968:40) draws an analogy between trains and promotion speed. College graduates who are at JNR Central Headquarters in Tokyo are riding the *tokkyū* ("special express") while employees at the branch divisions are riding the *junkyū* ("limited express."). All other employees who are not college graduates are riding the *donkō* ("ordinary train").

Riders of the special express are at the top of the organization. They can be divided into office workers and technicians. These employees have passed a highly competitive entrance exam. When talented recruits join the main office and work there for ten years, they can hope to become *kachō* ("section chief"). This level can be reached when the employees are in their 30's. Recruits who begin their careers in the branch offices, however, will reach this level only in their 40's.

Riders of the "limited" career train also are sometimes referred to as the *otsukan,* or "second trunk," group. This is a carry-over from the wartime era when a similar distinction was made between those with primary potential for becoming a military officer and those with only secondary potential. *Otsukan* are college graduates who did not attend universities of the highest prestige. Because they were hired through the examination for the branch offices, not for Central Headquarters, they cannot hope to match the promotion speed of the "special express" riders. Of the more than five hundred posts above *kachō,* more than half are filled by graduates of the Faculty of Law at Tokyo University.

The "ordinary" train riders are the field unit employees *(genba shokuin).* The highest-ranking position they can hope to attain is that of station master. The key to a successful career in JNR for the *genba* worker is to maintain steady performance on the promotion exams (see Figure 4.3).

The new employee begins in a probationary status. Once his supervisor recommends him for full employee status he is ready to begin his long journey. His level of education will determine how long he must wait at successive intervals before taking exams. This is first noticeable in the qualifying examination for apprentice conductor and later for the test to become assistant station master. Thus, even beginning the journey, the middle school graduate must wait two years longer than the high school graduate before taking his first exam.

An extremely talented worker can join the railroad at 18, become a conductor at 22, reach the level of assistant station master at 29, and then become a station master at 35. Of course, this kind of rapid promotion rarely happens. Passing these exams is crucial to rapid mobility in JNR but success on the exams does not always ensure promotion: personal ties and recommendations come into play after the exams. When I asked workers about this promotion system, their attitudes varied, although in general about one-third favored it and two-thirds wanted it to be revised. Younger workers especially complained about the volume of information for which they were responsible. For example, the examination for passenger clerk might include questions on railway mottoes, the reading of difficult

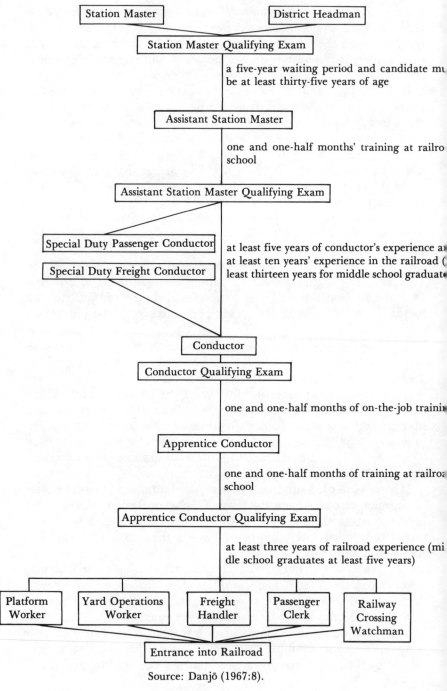

*Figure 4.3.* "Ordinary" Employee Promotion Schedule, Japanese National Railways

Station Master        District Headman

Station Master Qualifying Exam

a five-year waiting period and candidate mu
be at least thirty-five years of age

Assistant Station Master

one and one-half months' training at railro
school

Assistant Station Master Qualifying Exam

Special Duty Passenger Conductor        at least five years of conductor's experience al
                                        at least ten years' experience in the railroad (
Special Duty Freight Conductor          least thirteen years for middle school graduat

Conductor

Conductor Qualifying Exam

one and one-half months of on-the-job trainii

Apprentice Conductor

one and one-half months of training at railroa
school

Apprentice Conductor Qualifying Exam

at least three years of railroad experience (mi
dle school graduates at least five years)

Platform     Yard Operations     Freight     Passenger     Railway
Worker       Worker              Handler     Clerk         Crossing
                                                           Watchman

Entrance into Railroad

Source: Danjō (1967:8).

Chinese characters used in station names, complicated calculation of fares using the abacus, and essays about how employees should respon to a particular situation. While some feel it is the best way to reward talent, others find it too limited and narrow in the abilities it taps. Some men insist that the success rates are dismal and sap employee morale. Test results for the Tokyo Western Division for a typical year are summarized in Table 4.1.

Table 4.1. Promotion Examination Results for Tokyo Western Division, Japanese National Railways, 1971

| Examination Category | Number Taking Exam | Number Passing Exam | Percentage Passing Exam |
|---|---|---|---|
| Station Master | 174 | 16 | 9.2 |
| Assistant Station Master | 321 | 40 | 12.5 |
| Conductor | 226 | 37 | 16.4 |
| Business Clerk | 213 | 57 | 26.8 |
| Supervisor of Security | 12 | 11 | 91.7 |
| Supervisor of Electrical Operations | 157 | 30 | 19.1 |
| Office Worker | 101 | 4 | 4.0 |
| All Categories (N = 14) | 1849 | 471 | 25.5 |

Source: From a Japanese National Railways unpublished internal report, 1971, as abstracted and given to the author.

## Some Career Patterns: Journeys with Many Stops

In order to highlight the general set of problems faced by workers and the strategies they employ to solve these problems, I now turn to some examples of career scenarios. I will isolate stages along the ideal career line given in Figure 4.3, and show how examination barriers prevent rapid mobility. The contrasts between bright and dim career lines will serve to illustrate how the uncertanties that surround the promotion system lead to a reassessment of self as the worker marks time in his career.

### Employee Adachi: A False Start

All the men in my sample entered the industry as "platform workers" (ekimu gakari). Employee Adachi was one such. He and other platform workers confess that their tasks are not very exciting, since most of their day is spent flagging down trains, announcing arrivals and departures, ensuring passenger safety by making certain the doors are clear for closing, sweeping the litter from the platforms and rail beds, scrubbing the bathrooms, recording lost and found

83

items, answering the telephone and telegraph, and giving directions to passengers.

Worker Adachi was adopted by a former JNR worker who wanted a son to follow in his footsteps. After graduating from high school in Hachiōji, he entered Kokutetsu with the hope of rapidly moving up the promotion ladder. In his three years at Shiranai Station he had become well-liked by his co-workers and supervisors. During this time, he gained valuable work experience and knowledge of railroad culture, which would help him in his first attempt at promotion. He chose to try the exam for "passenger clerk" *(ryōkaku gakari)*. Although he and other young employees studied diligently, all of them failed the test. After they drowned their dismay at a local beer garden, they proceeded to discuss their futures. Employees Adachi, Yoshida, and Ishida decided to retake the exam the next year while worker Nakamura chose an alternate route.

Employee Adachi must wait for the next round of exams. Although he is bored with his daily job tasks, he does plan to remain with the railroad. He claims that through hard work and perservance he will be able to attain the level of assistant station master before he retires. As a young worker, he has not yet become active in union affairs and takes a moderate stance towards station labor issues. His major complaint is the schedule of his workday. He feels that 24 hours on duty alternating with 24 hours off is exhausting. During the duty day the employee is allowed only four hours of sleep. This rigorous schedule, he feels, interfers with his social life; some days of the week he finds himself extremely tired, sleeping most of the day.

We find two ways of coping with failure at this level. While Adachi will retake the exam, employee Nakamura will instead take the test for entrance into the railroad police. Another option would be to withdraw from the competition and be trapped as a platform worker for the remainder of one's career. I noted such a case at Station Tonari. A very career-conscious assistant station master claimed that this employee, who was in his late 40's, should have been embarrassed at working on the platform next to teenagers. Age and career status were out of joint.

At this level of the organization another cause for concern is on short notice being reassigned due to rationalization programs. Two of Adachi's co-workers on the platform were suddenly reassigned to a maintenance crew. One was happy with the transfer because his work schedule was confined only to the day shift; the other was unhappy because he was small in stature and his new job required that he move heavy materials. Many Shiranai Station workers were concerned that the latter's new assignment had been given without due consideration for the man's abilities.

*Employee Tanaka: The First Bright Signpost*

Twenty-four-year-old Tanaka was the son of a railroad worker in Kyushu. Oddly enough, he claims that it was through the influence of a school friend and not his father that he decided to join the railroad. After he graduated from a special railroad school near his home town, he spent a year at Tokyo Central Station as a freight handler and then was transferred to Yokohama where he was an assistant to the railroad police. Then came a year at Ueno Station, after which he took the examination for passenger clerk. He passed, and was reassigned to Shiranai Station. His career plans are optimistic and he hopes to be transferred from Shiranai to a larger station such as Shinjuku where a more challenging work experience will help him prepare for the conductor's exam. Reaching conductor status is the best indicator of progress towards becoming a supervisor. If one becomes a conductor early in one's career, his chances for further promotion are enhanced. The exam for conductor is difficult, and very few pass it. A talented conductor will be assigned a post on the high-speed "bullet trains." These men wear a special tan uniform which contrasts with the usual blue uniform of JNR workers.

Tanaka sees himself "on schedule." Aligned with his occupational career are his plans for marriage. He and his fiance are optimistic about his promotion chances. By contrast, another co-worker, Nakamura (also 24 years old), failed his first exam for passenger clerk. This came shortly before he proposed to his girl friend. She rejected his proposal because she and her parents felt that a platform worker in JNR can offer little financial security. Workers in JNR become more marketable in the marriage scene if they have passed their first promotion exam.

The rank of passenger clerk may become a side track. This is Honda's situation. Honda became satisfied very early in his career with this position. Although he passed the exam fairly early in his career, he waited more than twenty years before he attempted his next exam. Both Honda and Tanaka hold the same job classification; both work at adjacent ticket windows in the same office. The difference is that Honda is eighteen years older. Honda claims that he is completely satisfied with his position at Shiranai Station. He only has a 10-minute walk to and from his job. His work day begins

85

at ten o'clock in the morning and ends at 6:45 in the evening. He has become accustomed to this routine, having been at the same desk for 23 years.

For Tanaka, Shiranai Station is merely a stopover; he hopes that his personal ties will be increased at a larger station. For Honda, Shiranai is a haven from the pressures of promotion schedules.

## Employee Murakami: The Last Hurdle

Assistant Station Master Murakami was born the first son of a farmer in Gumma Prefecture. He was the oldest of seven children and aspired to attend college and become a lawyer. Even today he reads books about Japanese law in his spare time. During his long career with the JNR he has served as freight handler, truck driver, ticket office worker, and operations clerk. He passed and failed various examinations along the way. He successfully completed the exam for assistant station master in his eighteenth year (the average number of years is 15). Of all the men at Shiranai Station, Murakami was perhaps the most eager about promotions. He was the most ambitious of the assistant station masters in trying to become a station master. When the productivity movement was in full swing, no one cooperated more than Murakami. When the monthly sales records for soliciting group travel tickets were posted, his name would be at the top of the list. His enthusiasm was directed toward convincing his supervisors at the main office that he deserved the promotion.

When another assistant station master arrived at Shiranai to fill a post vacated by promotion, competition arose between this newcomer and worker Murakami. The new man had been transferred from another station and should have received the higher ranking. Although the two rivals had entered the railroad in the same year, the new worker was older than Murakami. However, Murakami had a better sales record for group travel tickets, and he won the promotion. The younger platform workers were upset because the new assistant master was a more effective leader and was better liked. Murakami, on the other hand, was overbearing and complained too often. He became overly enthusiastic about encouraging young workers to sell group tickets and to study for their exams.

It is at this stage, the level of assistant station master, that one faces several sidetracks and intense career competition. A hitherto successful employee may be slowed down. When this occurs, chances are greater for him to lose interest in his work and for serious morale problems to ensue. In a national sample of assistant station masters (and equivalent supervisory positions) taken by the Japanese National Railways Labor Science Research Institute (1970: 65-66), almost 30 percent of the 2600 workers who were questioned felt that promotions were "fairly slow." Approximately 10 percent of the sample felt that promotions were "fairly fast." It is most likely that the former group of respondents contains those whose morale is sagging and those who, according to the younger workers, are merely "waiting for retirement."

The difficulties of this period are illustrated by the situations of Murakami and another assistant master, Hatta, who also worked at Shiranai Station. Hatta had passed the exam for station master. Yet he was in poor health and had to take a hospital leave. When he returned to the station, he found that he had been demoted to the position of reserve assistant station master, the lowest rank among the four assistant masters. Murakami, although he enjoyed excellent health, did not pass the station master's exam. For different reasons, both men are stuck on the promotion ladder. They face a series of transfers every two years to stations of similar size. One worker suggested a model for this system of lateral transfers: the coiled, serpentine device the Japanese burn to ward off mosquitoes (*katori senkō*). Murakami will try the promotion exam again. If he fails, he will try to become headmaster at a JNR bachelor employees' dormitory. He feels tht he can reach that goal before he retires. Hatta can only hope that his health improves. One man has test-taking ability; the other has good health. Both qualities are necessary to become a station master.

Management offers a consolation prize to workers who have failed promotion exams by making certain that they are shifted to a new social environment through lateral mobility. The system of transfers is management's way of softening the harshness of failure — helping the worker adjust by "cooling the mark out" (Goffman 1952: 451-463).

## Employees Inoue and Ushiba: The Final Reward

Like most Japanese workers, railroad men face compulsory retirement at age 55. Up until this time they diligently save part of their earnings with the hope of someday building a home. The careers of Station Masters Inoue and Ushiba show alternative ways of adapting to the uncertainties of retirement.

87

Station Master Inoue was born in Tokyo but spent his early years in Taiwan. When he was eight years old, his family returned to Kanagawa Prefecture, where he attended local schools. He showed much promise as a student, but the economic pressures of the Great Depression forced him to join Kokutetsu for immediate employment. His work history (Figure 4.4) shows a considerable disparity with the ideal JNR promotion schedule given in Figure 4.3. Worker Inoue's promotion history covers a longer time span, with more hurdles and sidetracks along the way. He feels that nowadays one can become an assistant station master much more quickly than in earlier years, but that becoming a full station master takes a longer time.

In part Inoue was hampered by the war and the destruction and rebuilding of the railroad. After 35 years of service he had reached the pinnacle in his career. Before arriving at Shiranai Station, he served as chief assistant station master at another small station. He, too, was momentarily caught in the age bulge of JNR's overabundance of middle age and older workers. Management has attempted to appease these personnel by staffing large stations with one station master and a host of assistant station masters who are carefully ranked. Sometimes it is possible for a station master who has passed his promotion exam to find himself posted to a large urban station but with the rank of assistant master. As assistant station master there he will have more status than he would as master at a smaller urban station such as Shiranai. At a large station such as Tokyo Central, Shinjuku, or Ueno, he commands more respect. In any case, the Shiranai workers admired Inoue because they judged him to be a fair, hardworking man who had made it to the top of the ladder without leaning upon a strong network of connections (kone).

Retirement became a concern during his last year in office. Everyone remarked about his sharp mind and quick gait. However, he had reached the age of compulsory severance. The majority of station personnel who retire from the JNR find jobs with the Railroad Mutual Aid Association. A lower-ranking employee will enter a post-retirement position such as salesman (tachiuri), or temporary worker at a hand baggage counter (te nimotsu azukarijo), or clerk at a station box lunch stand (bentōya). A higher-ranking employee, such as a former master of Ueno Station, may become regional section chief of the catering service. Worker Inoue's anxiety was heightened by his lack of a network of contacts who could ensure that he would be well-placed. Higher-ranking officials find less difficulty in securing second-career jobs with transportation-related

*Figure 4.4.* Promotion History of Station Master Inoue, Japanese National Railways, 1935-1972

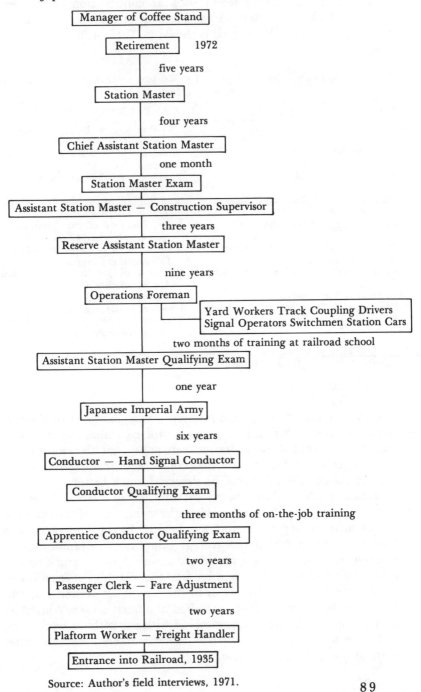

Source: Author's field interviews, 1971.

industries in the private sector such as construction companies, tourist agencies, or hotels. A sample of post-retirement positions taken by ranking JNR officials is shown in Table 4.2.

*Table 4.2.* Retirement Jobs of Former Top-Ranking Japanese National Railways Managers, 1968

| Last JNR Position Held | Post-Retirement Position |
| --- | --- |
| President of JNR | Vice-President of the Japan Railroad Construction Corporation |
| Vice-President of JNR | President of the Japan Tourist Association |
| Vice-President of JNR | President of the Corporation for Trucking |
| Vice-Minister of Railway Transportation | Vice-Minister of the Municipal Rapid Transit Corporation |
| Director of JNR Public Relations | Board Member of the Japan Railroad Construction Corporation |
| Director of the JNR Labor Science Research Institute | Vice-President of the Japan Railroad Construction Corporation |
| Director of the Tokyo Division of JNR | President of the Railroad Mutual Aid Association |
| Director of Transportation | President of Japan Express |
| Director of Railway Security | President of the Agency for Traffic |
| Station Master of Ueno Station | Regional Section Chief of the Directors of the Japan Catering Association |

Source: Adapted from Atsukawa (1968:51-53).

Station Master Inoue's new position was as manager of a coffee stand in a station building. He was complacent about his new job, but the workers at Shiranai Station were angry that his reward for 35 years of service was a new job that consisted of making and selling cups of coffee. They felt that he deserved much better.

Station Master Ushiba joined the railroad in 1936 and spent a total of 33 years in JNR before his retirement. One of Ushiba's anxieties surrounding retirement was health. In my interviews with him, he mentioned that the average salary man in Japan lives 19 more years after retiring from his company. He was quick to add that a friend of his in JNR had ignored the warnings of friends and family and had worked hard until the day of his retirement. Immediately after, he collapsed and died of a heart attack. Almost all assistant station masters must contend with the 24 hour work shift, and have their own stories of how fellow workers became ill after years of the grueling schedule.

At Ushiba's station a sign on his office door welcomes the general public to enter, but on his last day of work he locked that door and wrote a final entry into his journal. He reflected on his long career as railroad worker, husband, and father. He drew an analogy between his family and his line of work. While the husband is the driver of the train, the wife is the coal tender. The cars that they together must pull are their children. The proverbial road of life is the track, which is in constant need of repair and always seems to go uphill. The track must also cross mountains, valleys, and rivers. He laments that he wants to give his coal tender a rest, but he knows that he cannot since he must make another transfer to still another line. He has no choice but to close his entry with the thought that his destination remains unknown.

Some men see the act of retirement as the same as getting fired or being served with divorce papers. Many JNR workers spoke to me in these idioms. For workers Inoue and Ushiba, retirement meant a cut in pay plus citations for good service and a parting gift of a necktie. According to Ushiba, the size of the JNR's severance pay is like a sparrow's tear (suzume no namida). Both workers think ahead of a household without children. Ushiba's wife wants to travel overseas; Inoue wants his daughter to study in the United States. Inoue expects his wife to supplement their income by continuing her part-time job while he makes and sells cups of coffee. Since Ushiba and his wife do not have enough in their savings account to build their own home, they plan to use his retirement pay as a down payment for starting a Western-style sewing shop.

When JNR workers retire they are forced out of JNR housing. Employee Inoue was fortunate enough to have saved enough money to build a home; Ushiba had not. In Ushiba's case, it becomes clear how his occupational career line and its timing influence the other careers which intersect with his, since he openly states that not building a home will hurt his sons' chances of finding good brides. Inoue can use part of his retirement allowance for his daughter's education to brighten her chances on the marriage market.

Even if a worker reaches the level of station master before he retires, with the rising cost of living, the retirement allotment is not sufficient to provide security. This is a problem that railroad workers face in the latter part of their careers. At this stage paradox and irony prevail. Many assistant station masters know that they will not reach the level of station masters, and so simply give up hope (akirameru); they lose morale and wait out retirement. When retirement does arrive, it brings still another series of problems.

## Summary and Conclusions

Japanese National Railways workers face a most unusual paradox in their careers. While they are participants in a service industry that demands a conscious, accurately segmented concept of time (every railroad worker owns a watch which must be in good working order), the time junctures in their careers are not as evenly or clearly punctuated. Furthermore, while their jobs require that they keep the trains moving on time, the majority of the workers themselves are "running late" in their career schedules. They gradually must learn to think in terms of longer time perspectives.

Most railroad workers would concur that the ideal career pattern is seldom actualized. They think it naive to believe they will pass all of the promotion exams according to management's schedule. Most have resigned themselves to the fact that their performance on these exams is limited, and they alter their expectations of themselves accordingly. They would argue that there is no *one* way of "becoming a railroad man." These reformulations of self-definition and self-awareness are ways of viewing themselves within readily available strategies and options. After confronting the promotion exams, a worker increases his self-knowledge and has a more realistic appraisal of his strengths and weaknesses.

Like any other organization, the JNR rewards and punishes. Few railroad workers are complete winners and few are absolute losers. Most must rationalize their disappointments in light of limited satisfactions, and content themselves with some middle ground. The current promotion system does not offer a single plan that will guarantee an equal reward for all. Because of the limited successes and many failures in the sphere of promotion, a career in the national railroad by necessity becomes a process of constant reinterpretation.

Career unfoldings in JNR mean job changes not only temporally but spatially. It is a rare employee who spends his career in one geographic locale. Many young workers who begin their careers in small country stations and then decide to migrate to Tokyo have no idea of their next assignment. In some cases the transfer of an older worker means a long commuting distance from his family. These transfers may even entail renting an apartment away from family and home. Commuting long distances is less anxiety-causing for a young bachelor than for a worker in the later stages of his career. However, even if an older worker is transferred to a new station for only two years, he must establish a new network of social capital. Being transferred to a distant or small, isolated station remains a constant concern for workers at all stages of their careers.

A source of anxiety, and one of the most commonly-heard complaints of railroad workers, is that they work unconventional hours. If a worker is assigned the 24-hour *tetsuya* shift, his schedule does not match that of his family or nonrailroad friends. His off-duty hours are spent catching up on lost sleep, watching television, or doing postponed errands. Because of the pulse of this work schedule, work shifts and days off must be scheduled far in advance. More than one worker insisted that year after year of this work tempo takes a toll on one's health. One station master commented that attaining the rank of master carried with it the secondary reward of not working this shift, of having instead a work day that ended in the early evening.

Another source of career insecurity in the JNR is the rationalization program that could reduce the labor force in future years. If stations are closed down, the number of higher supervisory positions would be decreased and lessen a worker's chances for upward mobility. It remains an issue for management and the unions to decide whether streamlining the financial state of the railways should include a plan for the reduction of the work force.

The retirement system has also been viewed as a source of uncertainty. Workers can start their careers very early in the railroad, move up the ladder of promotions, and be rewarded with post-retirement jobs that do not match their expectations. In fact, if the worker is late in reaching the post of station master, he could conceivably work at the position for only a few years and then be retired by the JNR. The status reward could be short-lived. Furthermore, retirees complain increasingly that the retirement sum is inadequate to meet the soaring cost of living.

In many ways a career in the railroad is a journey, not a destination. A destination carries the connotation of an ultimate design with a predetermined end. A journey, on the other hand, involves a context of the unknown, the mastery of which will lead to growth in self-knowledge. An organization of JNR's size is normally associated with providing the employee with "lifetime" employment security. This stereotype of lifetime employment masks many of the sources of insecurity that are interwoven into any occupational career. This veil of security does not do justice to the anxieties and uncertainties that arise from the existing structures themselves.

The study of careers in organizations such as JNR becomes especially important in the analysis of failure timetables. Martin and

PAUL H. NOGUCHI

Strauss (1956: 110) note that the fateful periods in a person's life are frequently associated with personal and public recognition of failure. One certain sign of such a career pattern is continual and rapid transfers in which horizontal movement is the rule for sidetracked employees. For the further study of the life cycle an important issue is: What does it mean to the individual when he is given a cue to assess his performance and position in life later than expected?

## Notes

Fieldwork for this paper was conducted in Japan in 1971 under a Fulbright-Hays grant for dissertation research. I wish to thank Bucknell University for a grant which helped prepare these materials. The train station where the fieldwork was conducted bears the fictitious name of Shiranai Station. The field site was a small, urban station and was the workplace for platform employees, ticket sellers and takers, and supervisory personnel. The data in the paper include interview and questionnaire material from 76 Japanese National Railways employees.

## References

Atsukawa Masao
   1968   Kokutetsu no kutō [JNR's struggles]. Tokyo: Tokuma Shoten.
Befu Harumi
   1971   Japan: An Anthropological Introduction. San Francisco: Chandler.
Cottrell, W. F.
   1939   Of Time and the Railroader. American Sociological Review 4: 190-198.
Danjō Kanji
   1967   Akai wanshō [The Red Armband]. Tokyo: Tetsudō Tosho Kankōkai.
Dore, Ronald P.
   1958   City Life in Japan. Berkeley and Los Angeles: University of California Press.
Goffman, Erving
   1952   On Cooling the Mark Out: Some Aspects of Adaptation to Failure. Psychiatry 15: 451-463.
Japan Times Weekly
   1977   October 22: 6.
Japanese National Railways
   1970   Facts and Figures. Tokyo.

Japanese National Railways Labor Science Research Institute
  1970   Joyakusō no ishiki chōsa [A Study of the Consciousness of the
         Assistant Station Master Grade]. Tokyo: Japanese National
         Railways.
Klerman, Gerald L., and Daniel J. Levinson
  1969   Becoming the Director: Promotion as a Phase in Personal-
         Professional Development. Psychiatry 32: 411-427.
Levinson, Daniel J., et al.
  1978   The Seasons of a Man's Life. New York: Knopf.
Martin, N. H., and Anselm L. Strauss
  1956   Patterns of Mobility Within Industrial Organizations. Journal of
         Business 29: 101-110.
Nakane Chie
  1970   Japanese Society. Berkeley and Los Angeles: University of
         California Press.
Neugarten, Bernice L.
  1968a  The Awareness of Middle Age. In Middle Age and Aging, Ber-
         nice L. Neugarten, ed., pp. 93-98. Chicago: University of
         Chicago Press.
  1968b  Adult Personality: Toward A Psychology of the Life Cycle.
         In Middle Age and Aging, Bernice L. Neugarten, ed., pp. 137-
         147. Chicago: University of Chicago Press.
Plath, David W. (ed.)
  1975   Adult Episodes in Japan. Leiden: Brill.
Roth, Julius
  1963   Timetables: Structuring the Passage of Time in Hospital Treat-
         ment and Other Careers. Indianapolis: Bobbs-Merrill.
Shūkan Asahi
  1978   September 9: 20.
Ueda Yoshiyuki
  1970   Ekichōsan shūten desu [Last Stop, Mr. Station Master]. Tokyo:
         Asahi Shimbunsha.
Wilensky, Harold L.
  1968   Orderly Careers and Social Participation: The Impact of Work
         History on Social Integration in the Middle Mass. In Middle
         Age and Aging, Bernice L. Neugarten, ed., pp. 321-340.
         Chicago: University of Chicago Press.

# Part Three

# PATHS AND PRIORITIES

Career development issues look pretty straightforward for the typical Organization Man. If the ladder of positions is simple, and alternative routes are few — as we saw at Shiranai Station — about all that a worker can influence is his speed of promotion. But the issues quickly become complicated the moment we turn from the fixed channels of one organization and look at the wavering currents of a whole occupational flow. Continuity across the years of labor no longer is anchored in a particular institution; it resides instead in the worker's ability to find and fill an array of different positions. He may be simultaneously pursuing part-time career lines in two or more institutions. With each line he adds, his problems of managing the direction and speed of his working life will multiply. In the next three chapters we explore three facets of this many-faceted process.

In place of lifetime employment we might call this "lifetime involvement". A person's own life goals, his sense of mission, come to the foreground; the organization and its purposes recede. Institutions are seen more as present vehicles in which to realize his more distant mission — whether as healer or leader or defender of the motherland. "Professionalism" is the buzz word now for this sense of moral purpose, as "calling" was in an earlier era. And the three reports in this section all happen to deal with professionals in the everyday meaning of the word. But if the mission is more evident, better articulated, in some lines of work, I assume it will be present, if shadowy, in all.

As in other parts of the book, so in this one I have grouped these three chapters because of what they add to one another. Each by itself brings out elements in the tapestry of an occupational pathway; together they suggest the full configuration that only could be documented, even for a single occupation, by massive research. Exploring the postwar fates of Imperial Army officers in Chapter Seven, Theordore F. Cook, Jr., alerts us to the importance of mission. Even when in uniform, the officers tell him they were not mere "careerists" grubbing for promotion. And their mission continues in civilian life. By contrast, Susan O. Long and Jack G. Lewis take professional commitment for granted among the physicians and local politicans they studied. Instead they illuminate issues of career path management. In Chapter Five, Long reports on the optional "styles" of medical practice open to a doctor, each with its entailed package of involvements in other sectors of the lifecourse. Lewis in Chapter Six analyzes the election records for the city assembly in a small town, and shows how a man's success in maintaining a seat in the assembly hinges in large part upon his success in sustaining some other line of income-producing work.

There is a bothersome issue of terminology in Parts Three and Four. The social science vocabulary offers us no standard set of terms to use in verbally separating the multiple long-run lines of conduct that a normal adult will pursue across the decades. The result is that different tags may be attached to the same phenomenon by different writers.

In its wider sense, "career" could be used to mean any course or path of action that has a recognized direction, speed, and sequence. One can speak of the career of a mental patient or the career of a dry-fly trout fisherman. The sociologist can be found using career to indicate almost any norm-hedged succession of roles within an institution. But in popular idiom "career" usually means a course of paid employment. To some people the idea of "family careers" for example is a contradiction in terms. (However, there are rather ponderous coinages and euphemisms such as "career homemaker" and its Japanese counterpart, *okusan sen'gyō*).

Typologies get invented when needed, and the present lack of a timeline typology in the social sciences probably reflects the long-standing mood of indifference to lifecourse issues. We did not appoint ourselves as conceptual law-givers in preparing these chapters. Nor did I, as editor, insist that contributors hew to my whims of vocabulary choice, although I have tried to insure that each author's use of terms is clear and consistent. There is a challenge here to anyone who holds conceptual orderliness to be part of his scholarly mission.

98

SUSAN O. LONG, is Instructor in Anthropology at Western Illinois University. JACK G. LEWIS is Program Associate in the Executive Development Center, University of Illinois at Urbana-Champaign. THEORDORE F. COOK, JR. is Assistant Professor of History, University of Maryland — Far Eastern Division.

# CHAPTER 5

# Intertwined Careers in Medical Practice

SUSAN O. LONG

Research on Japanese salarymen has stressed the strong interrelationship of the work career with other aspects of the individual's life and self-definition. As he progresses through each level of company organization, his work colleagues and responsibilities greatly influence his family and social life (Vogel 1971; Rohlen 1974). But how, if at all, does this conception of careers in Japan apply to professionals? A lawyer or an architect may or may not work in the type of institutional setting that produces a highly structured progression of work responsibilities. A Japanese physician has several practice-style alternatives, ranging from the hierarchically organized university department to private practice. Studies of physicians in Western societies have found that whether the doctor works independently or in an institutional setting will make important differences in how he organizes his professional and personal life (Elliott 1972; Friedson 1960). Other research has suggested that aspects of his nonmedical life, such as family background, influence the decision as to which practice-style a physician will choose (Hall 1948; Johnson 1971; Marshall, et al. 1978).

The notion of "lifetime commitment" that has dominated recent thinking about careers in Japan has been based on the assumption that workers remain in one institutional setting for all of their working lives. A physician may have a kind of lifetime commitment to his profession, but his career is not the orderly progression of the organizational model. To understand how he makes his work career decisions and the effects of these decisions on his personal life, a broader definition of "career," incorporating ideas of Roth (1963) and Goffman (1974), is useful. A career in this broader sense is any connected sequence of social positions. The work career is thus only one of a number of careers an adult may be engaged in at any particular time. He may also have family, consumer, hobby, and other careers.

In this chapter, I examine the relationships of these other careers to the Japanese physician's professional practice changes, focusing on his decision to leave the university and on his decision to enter private practice. After briefly describing the practice-style alternatives which are objectively available to the physician, I will ask if the decision to choose a particular option can be attributed to changes in one or another of his other careers. Then I will suggest some of the ways in which, in turn, the choice of a new direction influences changes in the doctor's nonmedical careers.

This chapter is based on interviews done in 1977-1978 with more than fifty physicians in a major Japanese metropolitan center, in a regional city, and in a small town. I gained additional understanding of Japanese physicians' lives through participant-observation in five university hospitals, nine public or private nonuniversity hospitals, 13 clinics, and through visits to numerous physicians' homes. To obtain supplementary information I also administered a questionnaire to all staff physicians in several hospitals and university medical departments, and to all members of a community Medical Association.

## Careers and Goals

I begin with the assumption that career movement is not so much a result of the structure of the work setting as it is the result of individual decisions made in a variety of social contexts. A university or hospital setting imposes constraints on the physician's decisions, but each physician responds with his own strategies. A strategy is a plan of action directed toward a particular goal. As LeVine (1978:2) points out, "it is goals rather than roles that organize career activity." An individual usually holds several goals simultaneously, and these change over time as he encounters new situations and experiences.

I have defined a career as a connected sequence of social positions. In daily behavior, this translates into a series of interpersonal relationships in specific social contexts. Career movement must be seen in shifts in the composition and patterning of these relationships. A shift in one career affects the individual's network of social ties, creating movement in other careers. Johnson (1976:158) adds that the conflicting or intersecting of several career lines may effect major transitions in the life course. Thus it is individual decisions, based on consideration of structural restrictions *and* of other careers, that help to determine the direction and timing of career movement.

I use the terms "linked careers" and "intertwined careers" as reminders of the importance of goals and interpersonal relationships in a person's career strategies. In each of his careers, some people in his social network provide feedback regarding his goals and decisions, and offer their own definitions of his situation. A medical student, for example, decides which specialty to enter based on a number of factors, such as interest and the lifestyle of its practitioners. But more important considerations often include expectations held by a physician-parent, relationships with professors, or encouragement from young doctors already working in a department. In this way, as he enters a speciality, his career becomes linked to these people, for the medical careers of his seniors will affect his own, as his will have an impact on theirs. The doctor will make his own decisions based on his perceptions of his relation to events in the careers of the others (cf. Neugarten 1968), such as the promotion or retirement of a colleague. Linked careers thus refer to the careers of two or more individuals in the same sphere of activity.

Intertwined careers, on the other hand, refer to the careers of a single individual in his various endeavors. A person's work career will likely be intertwined with his career as a family member. Economic needs of aging parents may be a significant factor in a physician's decision to open his own practice. Once he has done so, he may be better able to pursue a career as a community leader.

Viewed subjectively, then, a career stage in one realm can be seen as a period of *relative* stability in the individual's relations to others in linked careers. A career transition, on the other hand, is dynamic, the shifts over time in the constellation of the individual's intertwined careers. It involves changes in his relationships to others (as when a younger colleague is promoted over him to become professor) and in the makeup of the network of people to whom he is linked (as when most of one's age-mates have left the university and most links in that stage of one's work career are now to younger colleagues).

We can distinguish, at least crudely, between major and minor transitions by the extent to which change in one career sets in motion changes in others. In a minor shift, there is less drastic change in one's social network, or in the "significant others" portion of it. A major change may affect nearly all of an individual's careers. A physician's decision to enter private practice may mean a change from salaried hospital worker who spends free time reading and relaxing at home to an independent businessman who becomes active in the Medical Association and gains satisfaction through community service. However, I am not merely describing a switch in roles. A physician does not simply become a private practitioner, shedding his past identity like a butterfly emerging from a cocoon. He maintains relationships with his university, though these may be severely altered; he continues his contacts with former colleagues at the hospital; he still enjoys quiet times at home with his family, although these may decrease in frequency.

Thus in investigating work career decisions, we must look for changes in interpersonal relations. We need to examine the effects of work career movement on these intertwined careers. In the following sections I discuss the intertwining of the physician's work career with his collegial, family, and civic careers. While one can find that physicians pursue many other careers, these three seem to be the most closely tied to professional career movement.

The collegial career refers to relations with other doctors both in and out of the workplace. It includes, but is not limited to, *sempai* (elder colleague), *kōhai* (younger colleague), and *dōkyūsei* (age-mate) relationships. Some writers have failed to recognize a distinction between collegial and work careers, as when Becker and Strauss (1968:319) write, "the significant others shift and vary by the phases of a career . . ." While I agree that these shifts occur, changes in interpersonal relations are not automatic results of movement in the work career. The individual retains a large element of choice in the determination of collegial ties. For doctors, merely leaving the university physically does not mean severance of ties, although their nature may change over time. Likewise, the setting up of a private practice does not result in instantaneous identification with the Medical Association. To be sure, dependency on the Association's services creates a shift, but in most cases it is gradual and incomplete.

There is a further reason for recognizing a separation of work and collegial careers. A doctor's "significant others", even in the work-related portions of his social network, may be other physicians. But they may also be nurses, laboratory technicians, or patients. A doctor's relations with his patients, for example, may change little with

103

a promotion that has a large impact on his relations with his colleagues, or vice versa. It is therefore analytically useful to view the collegial career as distinct from the work career.

Family is often recognized as intertwined with work career, but little scholarly attention in this area has been devoted to physicians, probably because sociological studies have concentrated on defining the professions and the process of professionalization. But even without detailed background, we can see that family cooperation and support are crucial elements in medical school admission in Japan. Other factors, such as marriage, a child's entry into college, or the death of a physician relative, can also have a strong impact on work career movement. The choice of a particular practice-style severely influences the lifestyle and interpersonal relations of family members, especially the wife's.

Finally, I look at the civic careers of physicians. This involves the development of adult values regarding, and participation in, political and social affairs of the nation and community. It may be possible to refine this category into several separate career strands, but for the purpose of this chapter, a broad conceptualization will be sufficient.

## Work Career Options

Medical school in Japan is a six-year program entered after high school. Admission is highly competitive, based on examination scores and, at the private schools, on personal and family factors as well. In the early years after World War II, a rotating one-year internship followed graduation, but this American importation was abolished in 1968 due to pressure from young doctors and medical students. However, graduate education has, since the introduction of Western medical schools a century ago, centered around university hospitals. Generally each young doctor selects a specialty department where he does research (eventually receiving the *hakase* degree) and receives clinical training for an indeterminate number of years. During some of that time, the young doctor is "banished" from his university hospital to improve his clinical skills by working in affiliated public and private hospitals. Those who were required to do an internship followed the same pattern upon completing the mandatory year of interning.

In contrast to the formal entry into a university department which is marked by a welcome ceremony or party, there are few fixed times or ritual markers for departure. But like companies and government bureaus, university departments are pyramidally structured, so opportunities for advancement become increasingly limited as the doctor moves up the hierarchy. Few can make it to the top to become full professor. Unlike the company or bureau, the university department has few sideline jobs into which to shuffle the less successful. (In practice, this function has been partially served by affiliated hospitals.) The vast majority, somewhere along the way, choose alternatives to university employment. Table 5.1 indicates the most common options and the frequency with which they have been chosen. The following section suggests how these may become subjectively real options through the impact of intertwined careers.

*Table 5.1.* Proportion of Physicians in Types of Practice, Japan, 1975

| Personnel of Medical Facilities | % |
|---|---|
| hospital owner-administrators[1] | 2.5 |
| clinic owner-administrators[1] | 45.2 |
| hospital (nonuniversity) employees | 28.7 |
| clinic employees | 6.5 |
| university hospital employees[2] | 12.2 |
| Others | |
| nonclinical employees of educational or research facilities | 2.2 |
| public health physicians | 1.6 |
| others | 1.1 |
| Total | 100.0 |

[1] referred to in this chapter as "private practitioners."
[2] includes all clinical doctors, from residents to full professors.
Source: Nihon Ishikai (1977:396).

## Influences on Work Career Movement

Many Japanese physicians choose to remain at the university until they recognize clearly that the direction of "up" has been closed to them. This may be evident in a number of ways. Most directly of all, a doctor will be considered but not chosen for a higher position. In an extreme situation, the Assistant Professor does not receive his Professor's endorsement for promotion; or, even having received it, is not elected to the faculty. For a fictional account of political intrigue in a unversity hospital and medical school faculty, see Yamazaki's best-selling novel *The Great White Tower* (1965) and Befu's interpretation of it (1977). For reasons of self-esteem and interpersonal effectiveness, at that point the Assistant Professor will find his position untenable. He must activate his networks of colleagues to find him another job. Colleagues may locate an acceptable position for him at another university or at a hospital. Former classmates and medical friends may advise and assist him in setting up his own practice. Or he may be able to enter a practice already operated by a family member.

More likely, however, a doctor will realize earlier in his work career that he will not make it to the top. One signal which makes this real is the failure of his mentor or a close *sempai* in the department to get an expected promotion. One of my informants described his own reason for leaving the university in such terms:

> The assistant professor who directed my research was a good friend. He lost out in the professorial selection though . . . . Fortunately, his father owns a private hospital that he was able to go back to.

In such cases, the older colleague may provide a job for the younger man who follows him to a new place of employment. The doctor quoted above was offered a position in the family hospital; but recognizing that his chances of advancement were as limited there as at the university, he chose instead to open his own practice. To do so, he relied on introductions and advice from other colleagues who already were in private practice.

The doctor may also turn away from the university because of family obligations. Inheriting the practice of a father, father-in-law, or occasionally another relative, is common. The occupational successsion rate is about 33 percent for Japanese physicians, but 60 percent of medical student sons of private practitioners questioned by Tanaka (1974) expected to enter private practice. Many doctor' sons go through medical school intending eventually to take over the family clinic or hospital; for others it is a decision that comes later. Usually, however, it is not until the death or retirement of the relative that private practice becomes a reality for the doctor. In some cases, he may have been working part-time at the relative's clinic or hospital, and the discontinuity is less sharp. In other situations there is an element of surprise. I was told of one young doctor whose father died shortly after the son graduated from medical school. The son needed to complete several more years of training before he was fully competent to operate the private rural clinic, yet he had the immediate responsibility for keeping the clinic open and providing care for its patients.

Similarly, the birth of children or their nearing college age has been a significant factor in changing career directions. Marriage, but even more, arrival of children in the family, means increasing financial responsibility. Particularly when parents and in-laws are neither physicians nor wealthy, young doctors have been forced to leave low-paying university work (and in the past, hospital work as well) to provide the family with financial support. Usually, by the time children reach college age, aging parents need support as well.

The third career has to do with a doctor's civic orientation. Before or during his years at the university, the doctor may develop political or social values which lessen his commitment to the department. A number of doctors profess a goal of community service in their work, a goal best accomplished away from the research-oriented university. Some explicitly derive their values from a formal religious tradition such as Christianity or Buddhism. Others are products of wartime education and postwar experience. After service in the military, some doctors of that generation accepted placements in doctorless villages or in infectious disease hospitals, in hopes of making life better for their countrymen in a difficult period. Some retained ties to the university and completed their advanced degrees; others claim that they could not do so for financial reasons.

Some doctors educated in the 1960's have refrained from continuing at the university because of involvement in the left-wing student movement. These doctors viewed (and many continue to see) the university department as a feudalistic institution over which the professor has absolute and arbitrary control. As part of their protest, many vowed that they would not do research toward an advanced degree. To accept the degree was to perpetuate the hated feudal order. Private practice was not regarded as a viable alternative due to the capitalist orientation in running a clinic as a business. Others have maintained university ties but (realistically, since they will not take the *hakase* degree) do not envision their future there. They will leave when a better opportunity appears. Reading and involvement in a leftist political movement have led some to positively value community service and the solution of social problems (cf. Krauss 1974).

## Career Movement and the Reordering of Goals

Once the physician has left the university setting, he faces a new set of structural constraints, to which he must adjust his behavior. While at the university, regardless of his personal feelings, a doctor

107

engages in research activities and participates in departmental affairs. In his behavior he should exhibit a loyalty to his department that assures him a reputation in the medical world and in the public eye.

However, when a doctor moves to hospital employment, he has a choice of several strategies. If his goal is to remain in academic medicine, he continues to participate in the activities of his university department, including its research, conferences, and social functions. Since he may not advance in his domain, he may redefine his own role in relation to it. One man, for example, had been sent by his professor to begin a new orthopedics department at a nearby public hospital. It seemed unlikely to him that he would ever return to the university, yet he remained committed to the values of university style medicine. He gradually came to see his role at the public hospital as a necessary support of the university: a teacher of clinical skills to young doctors rotated to his hospital. This is a function, he claims, not adequately performed by the university, but critical to its reputation.

Other hospital doctors have chosen different strategies. Some have left the university because of dissatisfaction with personal relations or with the type of medicine practiced there. Many profess a goal of community service. This demands greater attention to the needs and expectations of patients, with decreased emphasis on academic medicine and university ties. A hospital doctor may occasionally meet former university friends for a night on the town, but he is also likely to spend time performing administrative duties, serving on civic committees, or working at the public health clinic.

Still other physicians working at hospitals see their careers as continuing within that institution, and they work toward advancement there. They turn their professional loyalties to the hospital administration, and their social ties toward hospital colleagues. Their work is clinical and administrative, with little concern for research. They define their place in the wider society through their association with the hospital.

Physicians who leave salaried employment for private practice do so for a wide variety of reasons, from a desire for greater professional independence to a goal of greater income. Some switch allegiance to a new professional organization, substituting the Medical Association for the university department. These doctors comprise a visible minority of private practitioners who reject the values of university-style medicine and devote themselves to political activity to improve the status of private practitioners in society. Although as an independent professional his livelihood depends on reliable service to his clients, such a physician spends much professional and social time with other Medical Association activists.

The majority of private practitioners, however, choose not to ally closely with any group. They may maintain ties of friendship or expedience with their university department and their local Medical Association. Yet they choose a strategy of community orientation to achieve their career goals. They are dependent on patients rather than on colleagues for their livelihood and their reputation (cf. Friedson 1960). This shifts their focus from the medical community toward greater contact with patients, neighbors, and other business men and professionals. In this way, they attempt to build their practices, provide public service, or achieve goals in other careers.

## The Impact of Work Career Choices on Intertwined Careers

### Choosing the Hospital Option

When the young doctor is first sent out to an affiliated hospital for a period of clinical work and training, he expects to return to his university department for additional training and research. Even if the hospital is physically distant from the university, he retains professional and social ties with department members there. His primary loyalty remains with the doctors of his university department.

When, however, watching colleagues' careers suggests the possibility of not being called back to the university, these ties weaken or change. Many former classmates and *sempai* will have already left the university. The doctor is forced to consider that future professional growth (promotion in the hospital or opening a practice) lies with other collegial groups.

The move to hospital employment may also have an impact on family careers. The point where one becomes financially independent from parents will vary greatly with the family's circumstances. But in recent years it has become comfortably viable by the time the doctor leaves the university for better-paying hospital work. Until then, even if a man has well-paying part-time jobs offered through the university department, it is difficult for him to support a family; many continue to rely on supplementary aid from parents or in-laws. It is rare, especially in cases of arranged marriages, for a young doctor to marry before some period of hospital experience. In some

109

cases marriage, or even the search for a spouse, may be postponed, occasionally until completion of the advanced degree. The average age of marriage among the male physicians I surveyed was 29, while the national average for Japanese males is 27. In talking with wives and children of private practitioners or hospital doctors, one is told that the period of hospital employment represents a settling down into family life and routine. Many compare the life-style of a hospital physician to that of a salaryman.

The impact on civic careers is less evident. Hospital doctors have more contact with patients, or at least contact with greater numbers of patients than they did at the university. However, this numerical increase alone seems to have little influence on the doctor's world view. If, however, he has already acquired a community outlook, then hospital employment, with its regular hours and lack of emphasis on research offers more opportunity to pursue relationships with patients and to participate in service activities. Most doctors working in hospitals, however, prefer to spend their time with medical friends and family. Hospital administrator-physicians, of course, often participate in service clubs and serve on local and regional committees. These activities are considered a natural result of having achieved a high position in the hospital hierarcy.

### Changes upon Entering Private Practice

Taking up private practice means an even sharper work career discontinuity than moving to a hospital, not only because of differing work activities and opportunities, but because of its greater impact on other careers.

Unless the doctor makes an effort to maintain university ties, his collegial career shifts toward greater contact with other private practitioners. *Sempai-kōhai* ties remain, but strong social ties among "equals" increase in importance. This does not happen at once. Many doctors just entering practice adhere to the values of scientific medicine taught in the university, despite difficulties in applying these in a clinic setting with its simpler equipment and small staff. Suddenly they are making medical decisions without the support of other physicians, so they call their former teachers for advice and refer patients to the university hospital. The Medical Association is often viewed as a necessary evil and as one doctor in his early 40's explained,

Most of the members (of my local medical association) are a lot older

110

than I — a different generation, really. They're not the ones I see as friends. My friends are mostly doctors, that is true, but they are classmates and friends from my university days.

But private practice necessitates at least a mimimum of contact with other practitioners through the Medical Association, whose approval is virtually required to open a new clinic. Very likely, a new private practitioner already has ties to the area — as the son of a doctor, as a long-time resident, or as a university classmate of someone in practice in the area. These people will have already been called upon for introductions and for advice in opening a clinic. To show cooperation and gratitude, the new doctor is expected to participate in such Medical Association events as the formal New Year's party and the annual golf tournament. As more of his age-mates participate in these activities, he gradually shifts his social ties away from the university and spends more time with local colleagues, often in local Medical Association interest clubs. University ties are rarely completely dropped, especially if the doctor remains in the same part of the country. It is also unusual for a doctor in private practice to identify himself with the Medical Association to the extent he formerly did with his university department.

Private practice means a drastic and sudden change in family life. When he was at the university or hospital, the doctor's life was similar to that of a salaryman; now suddenly his entire business seems to be moved right into the home. Rented or purchased clinic space away from the home does seem to be becoming more common, but nearly three out of four clinics adjoin the home (*Nikkei Medical* 1977-78.) Most clinics are open from 9 to 12 in the morning and another two to three hours in the late afternoon and/or evening; doctors make house calls and/or attend meetings during the midday break. Not only is Papa home for a long lunch but a wife's freedom to pursue her own interest is curtailed by the responsibilities of patient and staff contact, and of helping to run the family business. Even when the wife does not actually work in the clinic, she assists at least with the insurance forms. This results in a lesser separation of activity spheres of husband and wife than has been noted for white collar families (cf. Vogel 1971). There may also be a change in the doctor's relation to his children. He may see them more, and may take a greater interest in their scholastic success, particularly when it relates to a child's ability to inherit the clinic.

A doctor's relations with local and national society also change with the move to private practice. The new clinic owner, previously politically neutral or apathetic, may suddenly be mobilized by his encounters with insurance forms and government regulations. I asked a doctor whose clinic had only been open a year and a half what the most significant change in his life had been. "The biggest surprise was all the paperwork," he said. "At first, my wife and I spent every night working on insurance forms. Even now that we are more familiar with them, it still takes way too much time. The system [of multiple private and public programs for medical insurance] has just got to change."

Some men become active in the local Medical Association, and a few run for public office with Association backing. This type of participation, though, takes time, which cannot be spared until after the clinic is well-established. Thus, most of those who are politically active are in their 50's and 60's. This also suggests that for an individual with such interests, it is best to inherit an established practice.

Even those not politically inclined find their social horizons broadened and their civic responsibilities heightened. When they were at the university or hospital, their standing in the community was often visualized by association with that institution. Once out on their own, they become, in a sense, community property. For business and personal reasons, they are compelled to define a place for themselves in this new arena. They may be asked to serve as school doctors, to sit on local government committees, or to join the Lions Club. For some, this is an additional chore; a few find great personal fulfillment in active participation. For most, it is simple an expected part of adult community life.

## Physicians and the Stereotype of Lifetime Commitment

Much research on Japanese society has focused on defining a culturally unique work organization, suggesting that Japan's "groupism" has been a key factor in the nation's "rapid modernization" and high levels of industrial productivity. In this approach, organizational form has been viewed as serving broader societal goals, and individuals in turn serving organizational ends.

I start from individuals and their personal goals, and ask instead how one uses the institutional forms of the workplace to organize his own careers in numerous realms of activity. In doing so, many a physician develops a kind of "lifetime commitment," but it is a commitment to his occupation, as is characteristic of the professional in

112

any society. He may at times have a deep attachment to his university department or to his hospital, but these are loyalties which serve his own careers. It is not some culturally absolute group affiliation. For a physician to identify with a hospital or university department need not mean that he loses his identity in it.

The notions of linked careers and intertwined careers may help bring together the concepts of constraint and strategy as a way to better explain career choices. The larger social environment limits available options; individuals draw on their own goals and perceptions of the situation in deciding how to deal with the options. Options may exist objectively without having meaning for an individual. They become real when recognized subjectively, as for example when a doctor decides to leave the university because his physician-father is retiring. Until that time, private practice had existed for others, including his father in his own linked career, but with little subjective relevance for the young physician in his own life.

Intertwining of careers implies intertwining of goals. A person is likely to rank success as more important in some of his careers than in others. One physician puts his effort into publishing research results, another perhaps into bettering his golf score. The stereotype of "lifetime commitment" has distorted this picture by implying that success in the work setting take priority over all other goals. The rank-ordering of goals may change as the pattern of intertwined careers changes across career transitions. The order may also change historically, as different age cohorts experience diverse sequences of events (Elder 1977).

The cohort of Japanese physicians educated during World War II had virtually no options upon graduation: They became military doctors. Their postwar career choices, based partly on consideration of family careers and economic conditions, helped strengthen the power of the university departments, a system which incited rebellion in the next cohort. Those who participated in the medical-student and young-doctor movement of the 1960's had new work career options available. Changes in society and in medicine had also led to new definitions of old options. Elder asks, how much variation can be explained by the historically unique circumstances a cohort experiences at a given stage of life, and how much can be attributed to maturation and aging? Will the former student activists settle down to private practice when they get into their 40's and 50's?

My guess is that they will remain in salaried practice in greater numbers than their predecessors. But only one of the causes is

113

motivational. (The most recent cohort of graduates did not directly experience the comradeship of the student movement, so the parameters will again be different for them.) All physicians face common constraints such as universal health insurance, disease prevalence patterns, and public attitudes toward doctors that are different from those of a generation ago. Moreover, the postwar cohorts of doctors are part of a society that has undergone great economic and ideological changes; it is no surprise that not only their options but their priorities might be different from those of their predecessors. They have had different experiences in their intertwined careers, new kinds of transitions which influence their career decisions. And if I am correct in predicting that there will be substantial shifts in the distribution of doctors by type of practice, we can reasonably anticipate continuing shifts as well in the patterning of linked and intertwined careers.

## Notes

The research on which this chaper is based was supported by a Fulbright-Hays Doctoral Dissertation Fellowship and a National Science Foundation dissertation grant.

## References

Becker, Howard S., and Anselm L. Strauss
    1968   Careers, Personality and Adult Socialization. *In* Middle Age and Aging, Bernice L. Neugarten, ed., pp. 311-320. Chicago: University of Chicago Press.
Befu Harumi
    1977   Power in *The Great White Tower:* Contribution to Social Exchange Theory. *In* the Anthropology of Power, Raymond D. Fogelson and Richard N. Adams, eds. New York: Academic Press.
Elder, Glen H., Jr.
    1977   Family History and the Life Course. Journal of Family History 2(4):279-304.
Elliott, Philip
    1972   The Sociology of the Professions. New York: Herder and Herder.
Friedson, Eliot
    1960   Client Control and Medical Practice. American Journal of Sociology 65:374-382.

Goffman, Erving
1974   Frame analysis. Cambridge, Mass.: Harvard University Press.
Hall, Oswald
1948   The Stages of a Medical Career. American Journal of Sociology 53:327-336.
Johnson, Malcolm L.
1971   Non-Academic Factors in Medical School Selection: A Report on Rejected Applicants. British Journal of Medical Education 5:264-268.
1976   That Was Your Life: A Biographical Approach to Later Life. *In* Dependency in Old Age, Joep M. A. Munnichs and Wim J. A. van den Heuval, eds. The Hague: Martinus Nijhoff.
Krauss, Ellis S.
1974   Japanese Radicals Revisited. Berkeley and Los Angeles: University of California Press.
LeVine, Robert A.
1978   Adulthood and Aging in Cross-Cultural Perspective. Social Science Research Council Items 31/32 (4/1, March): 1-5.
Marshall, Robert J., Jr., John P. Fulton, and Albert F. Wessen
1978   Physician Career Outcomes and the Process of Medical Education. Journal of Health and Social Behavior 19:124-138.
Neugarten, Bernice L.
1968   The Awareness of Middle Age. *In* Middle Age an Aging, Bernice L. Neugarten, ed., pp 93-98. Chicago: University of Chicago Press.
Nihon Ishikai [Japan Medical Association]
1977   Kokumin iryō nenkan [People's Health Yearbook]. Tokyo: Shinshūsha.
Nikkei Medical.
1977   October 25.
Rohlen, Thomas P.
1974   For Harmony and Strength. Berkeley and Los Angeles: University of California Press.
Roth, Julius A.
1963   Timetables. Indianapolis: Bobbs-Merril.
Tanaka Tsuneo
1974   Ishi shi shikōsha no kaikei to seikatsu jōken. [Budgets and Living Conditions of Prospective Heirs to Private Practices]. Igaku Kyōiku 5. Cited in Nikkei Medical, October 25, 1977, 50.
Vogel, Ezra F.
1971   Japan's New Middle Class. 2nd ed. Berkeley and Los Angeles: University of California Press.
Yamazaki Toyoko
1965   Shiroi kyotō [The Great White Tower]. Tokyo: Shinchō Sha.

# CHAPTER 6

# Where Security Begets Security: Concurrent Careers of Local Politicians

JACK G. LEWIS

A considerable number of individuals in Japan pursue multiple careers, even if "career" is narrowly defined as applying to income-producing or working roles. For example, many rural Japanese engage in farm work throughout their lives, while also maintaining careers in the secondary or tertiary economy. Many Buddhist clergy continue to offer their priestly services while pursuing careers in the business world. Professional athletes often maintain both athletic and business careers. Many urban Japanese housewives combine their homemaking careers with careers as teachers of an art or skill (tea ceremony, *ikebana*, calligraphy, cooking, etc.), as door-to-door saleswomen (Yakult, cosmetics) or in other door-to-door work (newspaper fee collectors, gas meter readers), or as part-time workers in small enterprises.

Yet another example is that of the local politican. There are 74,940 elected officials in Japan, only 763 of whom serve at the national level (Jichishō 1978:552). The remainder serve as chief executives or members of the assembly in Japan's prefectural, city, town, and village governments. In some cases, elected politicans' political careers are so time-consuming or located so far away from home that they are forced, once elected, to concentrate on political activities. In Japan, national-level politicians, prefectural governors, and city mayors have a difficult time sustaining an active vocational role concurrent with their political duties. Most other politicians, however, carry on dual work careers while serving in public office.

In this chapter I look at the concurrent careers of members of the assembly in a single Japanese city from the earliest postwar election in 1947 to the most recent election in 1979. Mishima, a city of approximately 90,000 residents, is in eastern Shizuoka Prefecture, an hour by high-speed train southwest from Tokyo. It is the 198th largest of Japan's 645 cities (Nihon Shichōkai 1978: 102). Approximately one-half of the city's residents live in its densely populated central sector, while the remainder live in outlying agricultural and "suburbanizing" districts. Over half of the residents work in the tertiary "service" sector of the economy, while somewhat less than 40 percent are engaged in manufacturing and about 10 percent primarily in agriculture (Lewis 1975:45).

Images of continuity and security, derived for the most part from research on salaried workers in large-scale private enterprises, permeate our understanding of Japanese work careers. Yet a large portion of the Japanese population is not engaged in salaried work or in large private enterprises. How much security and continuity do they have in their careers? This is the question that I apply to the lives of Mishima's city assembly members. How orderly are their political and occupational careers? When do they enter into political careers, how long do they remain active in elective politics, and what do they do after their political careers end? How are their political and occupational careers related?

To set the scene, I first discuss the nature of city assembly work. Thereafter, I look for patterns in assembly careers and discuss whether these patterns have changed since 1947. I am particularly concerned with how secure local political careers are. Then, looking first at all members of the assembly since 1947 and second at those who have experienced long, "successful" careers, I describe their backgrounds and how their work and political careers are related. In closing, I write in more general terms of the context of local political careers and the lifecourse implications of what I have found.

## The Job of Members of the City Assembly

There are 20,331 assembly members in Japan's 645 cities (Jichishō 1978: 552). City assemblies range in size from 20 to 100 seats, with a national average size of 31.5 seats. The Mishima assembly has had 30 seats since Mishima first became a city in 1941. Since the first postwar election in 1947, there have been nine assembly elections. Thus, 270 individuals could have served as assemblymen since 1947 had no one ever been reelected. In fact, as indicated below, considerably fewer have served assembly terms.

City assembly elections occur every four years. As there are no electoral districts in medium and small Japanese cities, candidates can campaign throughout all of Mishima in hopes of securing enough votes to win. As Mishima has grown in population, the minimum number of votes necessary to secure an assembly seat has increased from 298 in 1947 to 1,132 in 1979, making campaigning increasingly expensive and time-consuming, and less and less a personal, "friends and neighbors" type of experience.

The assembly member's job has also become increasingly time-consuming. Mishima's assembly normally meets for four regular sessions each year in March, June, September, and December. Each session lasts from two to three weeks; extraordinary sessions are occasionally required. The assembly day begins at 10:00 a.m. and lasts into the late afternoon. Half of all members must be present for a quorum to be met, and my personal observation of the Mishima assembly indicates that more than two-thirds of them attend regularly. The assembly may meet in plenary session or in committees; Isomura and Hoshino (1969:79) indicate that more time is spent in committees than on the assembly floor.

The job is time-consuming not only because of its formal duties, but also because of its informal requirements. Members of the assembly spend hours performing such service tasks as attending weddings and funerals, helping constituents deal with city government officials, and attending meetings of local organizations such as the PTA and neighborhood associations. In addition, they are usually members of assembly political party caucuses. The caucuses have their own meeting rooms in City Hall, and members spend hours there together. In 1971, for example, the Mishima assembly was split into six different caucuses, four conservative ones of from four to eight members, a Socialist group, and one other caucus consisting of representatives of the remaining centrist and progressive parties.

There are careers to be made within the city assembly. An ambitious or goal-oriented person will be looking for assignment to particular assembly committees and eventually to selection as a committee chair. After a few terms in office, he or she may hope to be selected as a city auditor (kansa-iin) or be elected by the assembly as its vice-chair or even chair, positions which receive more remuneration.

If increasingly time-consuming, the job is also increasingly remunerative. Perhaps reflecting this, two candidates seeking reelection have listed their occupations officially as "city assemblyman." In 1977, Mishima assembly members were paid 150,000 yen per month in salary, an amount supplemented by various additional allowances (Nihon Shichōkai 1978: 143, 174). By comparison, Mishima city employees received an average salary of 138,000 yen per month, and administrative employees (*ippan gyōsei shokuin*) received 144,200 yen per month. The national average for city assembly members in 1977 was 192,400 yen (these in larger cities tend to recieve more compensation). Nationally, city assembly vice-chairpersons receive 210,700 yen per month, while chairpersons receive 239,800 yen.

## Political Careers in the Mishima Assembly, 1947-1979

Consider the following contrast in careers. Wada Shōgorō — reporter, publisher, and owner of a small local newspaper. Some attribute his political career to ambition, others to an interest in politics or a commitment to an ideal. Some candidates in American elections, often lawyers or real estate salemen, are said to repeatedly run for election as "advertising", regardless of the result. Whatever the reason for his efforts, Wada had a difficult time in Mishima as a would-be public servant. For twenty years, from 1947 through the election of 1967, he entered the city assembly race unsuccessfully six times, never coming close to victory, never substantially expanding his support base. Perhaps as relief from the monotony of defeat, in 1952 he also sought election to the local school board, finishing fifth among five candidates. Beginning his postwar political career at age 60, he retired from the local political wars after his last assembly defeat at age 80.

Consider on the other hand the case of Takatō Tadao, a farmer in Mishima's Kitaue district and 47 years old when he first became an assembly candidate in 1947. Takatō succeeded comfortably in that effort, placing fourteenth among the 30 successful contestants, and thereafter easily won five more times until his retirement after 24 years of assembly service. Takatō was able to cap his assembly career with selection as assembly chairman, his political party career as leader of the assembly faction of the Liberal Democratic Party, and one of his occupational careers (he was, of course, also a farmer) as Managing Director of the Kitaue Agricultural Cooperative.

Between these two extremes lies tremendous variety in the political career patterns of assembly candidates and members. At first glance, it appears that residents who embark on an electoral career in Mishima face a hazardous venture. Throughout the postwar period, individuals have registered 386 times to compete for 270 assembly positions (i.e., 30 seats in nine elections). This represents an overall competition ratio of 1.43 contestants per seat. Yet this figure masks significant change in the level of competition over time, hiding an almost continuous decrease in the number of competitors for assembly seats since 1947.[1] As was the case throughout Japan at that time, in the initial flush of democratic spirit after the war's end, many Mishima citizens rushed to participate in the first assembly elections. Sixty-nine candidates competed in the 1947 election (a ratio of 2.30), 45 candidates entered in 1951 (a ratio of 1.50), while 1979 found only 33 candidates for the 30 assembly seats (a ratio of 1.10). Only a temporary surge of discontent with plans to construct a huge petrochemical complex in the city of 1963, when 54 candidates entered the election fray, broke the decline in postwar assembly competition.

In fact, because voters have chosen to reelect their representatives often, only 142 individuals have been assembly members in postwar Mishima. As a result, over the nine elections an average of 15 of the 30 assembly seats have been filled by freshmen members. Yet, while 24 of the 30 members were freshmen in 1947, the number of freshmen has steadily declined since that time. Table 6.1 evidences this progressive decline from 24 freshmen in 1947 to nine in 1979. It also indicates that the average number of terms and years served by newly elected assembly members has steadily increased from 0.2 to 1.63 terms and from 0.8 to 7.32 years. Clearly, members of the local assembly have been blessed with increasingly lengthy elective careers. Yet, these figures provide an inadequate indication of career security, as they fail to indicate whether assembly members have suffered electoral defeat at some time during their career.

Table 6.2 provides a comprehensive picture of the character of assembly careers. In this table, the "year elected" columns indicate the lifetime career patterns of the 30 persons elected in the year noted. The final column summarizes the lifetime career patterns of all 142 individuals elected at least once. Table 6.2 indicates that approximately three-fourths (108) of the assembly members have experienced careers unblemished by electoral defeat. However, over one-half of these served only one term and did not run for office again. Four years in office seems to be sufficient to convince a large number of local political hopefuls that an extended political career is not attractive.

In the case of a limited number of those elected from Mishima's agricultural districts, a brief term of service reflects social dynamics

Table 6.1. Terms and Years in Office of Mishima City Assembly Members, 1947-1949

| Term | Year Elected | | | | | | | | | Average 1947-1979 |
|---|---|---|---|---|---|---|---|---|---|---|
| | 1947 | 1951 | 1955 | 1959 | 1963 | 1967 | 1971 | 1975 | 1979 | |
| First | 24 | 18 | 17 | 15 | 16 | 14 | 12 | 10 | 9 | 15.0 |
| Second | 6 | 8 | 7 | 9 | 7 | 11 | 8 | 7 | 8 | 7.9 |
| Third | – | 4 | 3 | 3 | 4 | 2 | 7 | 5 | 6 | 3.6 |
| Fourth | – | – | 3 | 2 | – | 2 | 1 | 5 | 2 | 1.7 |
| Fifth | – | – | – | 1 | 2 | – | 2 | 1 | 3 | 1.0 |
| Sixth | – | – | – | – | 1 | 1 | – | 2 | 1 | 0.6 |
| Seventh | – | – | – | – | – | – | – | – | 1 | 0.1 |
| Average Prior Service: | | | | | | | | | | |
| Terms | 0.20 | 0.53 | 0.73 | 0.83 | 0.93 | 0.86 | 1.10 | 1.53 | 1.63 | |
| Years | 0.80 | 2.12 | 2.92 | 3.32 | 3.72 | 3.44 | 4.40 | 6.12 | 6.52 | |

Source: Mishima-shi Senkyō Kanri Iinkai (1958, 1961, 1966, 1967, 1971, 1976); *Mishima Nyūsu* (1979).

Table 6.2. Political Career Patterns of Mishima City Assembly Members, 1947–1979

| Pattern | Year Elected | | | | | | | | | Number of Members 1947–1979 |
|---|---|---|---|---|---|---|---|---|---|---|
| | 1947 | 1951 | 1955 | 1959 | 1963 | 1967 | 1971 | 1975 | 1979 | |
| **Assemblymen Never Defeated:** | | | | | | | | | | |
| Win once then retire or still incumbent | 14 | 6 | 7 | 3 | 7 | 3 | 5 | 2 | 9 | 57 |
| Win twice and retire/incumbent | 2 | 4 | 3 | 5 | 7 | 5 | 3 | 8 | 7 | 21 |
| Win three times and retire/inc. | 3 | 3 | 4 | 2 | 3 | 3 | 5 | 4 | 2 | 10 |
| Win four times and retire/inc. | 1 | 1 | 1 | — | 1 | 3 | 3 | 3 | 2 | 4 |
| Win five times and retire/inc. | 2 | 1 | 1 | 1 | 4 | 3 | 4 | 3 | 3 | 4 |
| Win six times and retire/inc. | 1 | 2 | 2 | 3 | 3 | 2 | — | 1 | — | 3 |
| Win twice, then higher office | 2 | 1 | 2 | 1 | 1 | 1 | — | — | 1 | 5 |
| Win three times, higher office | 1 | 2 | 1 | 1 | — | — | — | — | — | 2 |
| Win, not run (nr), win | 1 | — | 2 | — | 1 | — | — | — | — | 2 |
| Total Never Defeated | 27 | 20 | 23 | 16 | 27 | 20 | 20 | 21 | 24 | 108 |
| **Assemblymen Experiencing Defeat:** | | | | | | | | | | |
| *Win initially, then defeated, end career winning:* | | | | | | | | | | |
| Win, lose, win | — | — | 1 | — | — | 1 | — | 1 | — | 3 |
| Win, lose, win twice | — | 1 | — | 1 | — | — | 1 | 1 | — | 3 |
| Win, lose, win three times | — | — | — | 1 | — | 1 | 1 | 1 | 1 | 1 |
| Win twice, lose, win | — | — | 1 | 1 | — | 1 | 1 | 1 | 1 | 1 |
| Win twice, lose, win five times | — | — | 1 | 1 | 1 | 1 | 1 | 1 | — | 1 |
| Win, nr, lose, nr, win | — | — | — | — | — | — | 1 | — | — | 1 |
| *Win initially, end career losing:* | | | | | | | | | | |
| Win, lose | 2 | 2 | — | 2 | — | — | — | — | 1 | 7 |
| Win, lose, nr, win, lose | 1 | — | 1 | 1 | — | 1 | — | 1 | — | 1 |
| Win, lose, win twice, lose | — | — | — | 1 | — | — | 1 | 1 | — | 1 |
| Win, nr, win, lose | — | — | — | — | — | 1 | 1 | — | — | 1 |
| Win twice, lose | — | 2 | 2 | — | — | — | — | — | — | 2 |
| Win three times, lose | — | — | — | 1 | 1 | 1 | — | — | — | 1 |
| *Lose initially, end winning:* | | | | | | | | | | |
| Lose, win | — | — | — | 2 | — | 1 | — | — | 1 | 3 |
| Lose once, win three times | — | 2 | 1 | 1 | — | 1 | 1 | 1 | 1 | 2 |
| Lose twice, win three times | — | — | — | 1 | 1 | 1 | 1 | 1 | 1 | 1 |
| Lose twice, win six times, higher office | — | — | — | 1 | — | — | — | — | — | 1 |
| Lose, nr, win | — | — | — | — | — | — | 1 | — | — | 1 |
| *Lose initially, end losing:* | | | | | | | | | | |
| Lose, win, lose | — | 2 | — | — | — | 1 | — | — | — | 2 |
| Lose, nr, lose, win, lose | — | 1 | — | — | — | — | — | — | — | 1 |
| Total Defeated at least once in Career | 3 | 10 | 7 | 14 | 3 | 10 | 10 | 9 | 6 | 34 |

Note: Data for 1979 is for then-incumbent

more than individual choice. In these cases, two or three villages have historically cooperated to elect a single representative. To maintain the relationship, assembly candidacy is rotated each term to a resident in a different hamlet. Solidarity and social pressure remain strong enough within these villages to ensure that the joint effort will succeed. Yet a representative from such an area cannot plan an extended political career.

Other assembly members who have never suffered defeat (36%, as indicated in Table 6.3) have served from two to six terms in office. Only 13 of the 142 persons, including two who suffered defeats early in their careers, have served 16 or more years in the assembly.

Table 6.3. Electoral Success According to Terms Served by
Mishima City Assembly Members, 1947–1979

| Terms Served | Never Defeated | | Defeated | | Total | |
|---|---|---|---|---|---|---|
| | % | (N) | % | (N) | % | (N) |
| One Term | 40 | (57) | 10 | (14) | 50 | (71) |
| Two or More Terms | 36 | (51) | 14 | (20) | 50 | (71) |
| Total | 76 | (108) | 24 | (34) | 100 | (142) |

Note: Percentages based on total n of 142.
Sources: See Table 6.1.

Eight persons moved on to higher office after two or more terms of service. In Mishima's case, members of the city assembly have contended for only two types of higher office, the mayoralty and the perfectural assembly. These two types of elections are similar to city assembly elections in that the voting district is citywide. National office appears unattainable, in part because the city's population constitutes only a fraction of any larger electoral district. All but one of the eight who moved on had consistently placed high in assembly elections and had never tasted defeat. In general, one can conclude that strong city assembly personalities have dominated the three mayoral and prefectural assembly positions throughout the postwar period. It was not until 1977 that someone of a different background was elected to one of these positions.

As indicated in Tables 6.2 and 6.3, 34 of the 142 postwar representatives have had their assembly careers disrupted by defeat at least once. Nearly half of these served only a single term. There are a wide variety of career patterns among these individuals. Few members end their careers on a losing note. Only 16 of 142 (11%) fall into this category. Almost 90 percent of the members retire or

123

move on to contend for higher office after a final victory at the assembly level. Furthermore, few of them lose more than once during their careers (5 of 142).

Finally, it is clear that incumbents, as in other democratic systems, suffer defeat rather infrequently. Fifteen of the 34 assembly members who were defeated at some time suffered defeat as an incumbent seeking reelection. Clearly, candidates most likely to be defeated are those seeking a seat for the first time, or are past members not seated in the previous assembly. Incumbency is a resource for reelection.

## Personal Backgrounds and Local Political Careers

Democratic political processes rarely produce leaders whose backgrounds proportionately reflect their constituencies (Putnam 1976:21-44). A large number of studies have shown that political elites are drawn disproportionately from among males, upper-status occupations, higher income groups, and higher educational levels. Such characteristics serve as resources for election to public office. On the other hand, it has also been shown that this advantage tends to decrease as one moves from higher political offices to local level ones. Thus, while the backgrounds of city assembly members or mayors cannot be expected to reflect the backgrounds of local residents, they may approximate local society more than, for example, national Diet members.

What are the social and political backgrounds of the 142 individuals who have had terms on the Mishima city assembly since 1947? In Table 6.4, the first column presents a composite picture. The second column indicates the percentage of candidates in each category who have been elected. For example, while 70.3 percent of all male candiates have been elected, only 40 percent of the women have succeeded. Approximately 70 percent of all candidates (270 of 386) have been elected. Thus, if a particular category significantly exceeds this level, there is presumably something about candidates who share this characteristic that promotes their chances of election.

As Table 6.4 indicates, women have rarely been candidates. Only three women have sought assembly seats in the postwar period, suffering three defeats and two victories. The first woman assembly member, an officer of the city's federation of women's associations, was not elected until Mishimas's eighth assembly election in 1975. She was reelected in 1979. Assembly careers are almost exclusively for men.

*Table 6.4.* Social Backgrounds of Mishima City Assembly Members and
Their Electoral Success, 1947–1949

| Characteristics Category | Assembly Members, (N = 270) | Candidates Within Category Elected | Winners/ All Candidates |
|---|---|---|---|
| | % | % | N |
| Sex: | | | |
| Male | 99.3 | 70.3 | 268/381 |
| Female | 0.7 | 40.0 | 2/5 |
| | 100.0 | | |
| Age: | | | |
| | winners: | losers: | |
| Average age at election | 51.6 | 53.2 | |
| 25–34 | 4.8 | 68.4 | 13/19 |
| 35–44 | 13.3 | 70.6 | 36/51 |
| 45 + | 81.9 | 69.9 | 221/316 |
| | 100.0 | | |
| Area: | | | |
| Inner-city | 51.5 | 63.5 | 139/219 |
| Outlying agricultural and suburbanizing districts | 49.5 | 78.4 | 131/167 |
| | 101.0 | | |
| Occupation: | | | |
| Small business owner or company manager | 50.2 | 69.0 | 136/197 |
| Farmer | 26.3 | 74.0 | 71/96 |
| Company employee or worker | 9.6 | 68.4 | 26/38 |
| Agricultural cooperative or labor union leader | 6.6 | 85.7 | 18/21 |
| Professional (doctor, dentist, writer, priest, etc.) | 4.8 | 65.0 | 13/20 |
| Unemployed/retired | 2.2 | 42.9 | 6/14 |
| Political party official | 1.9 | 83.3 | 5/6 |
| | 101.6 | | |
| Political Party Affiliation: | | | |
| No affiliation registered (*mushozoku*) | 76.3 | 69.6 | 206/296 |
| Liberal Democratic Party or predecessor conservative party | 5.6 | 60.0 | 15/25 |
| Socialist Party | 7.8 | 63.6 | 21/33 |
| Clean Government Party | 4.8 | 100.0 | 13/13 |
| Communist Party | 3.0 | 66.7 | 8/12 |
| Democratic Socialist Party | 2.6 | 100.0 | 7/7 |
| | 100.1 | | |

Note: totals do not always equal 100% due to rounding.
Sources: See Table 6.1.

The pool of potential assembly members seems further limited by age. The average representative is over 50 years old. Less than 20 percent are elected at an age under 45. However, since all age groups appear to succeed to the same degree (see column 2), it is not so much that voters look unfavorably on young candidates as that young residents do not run for office. The cost of election campaigns, negative feelings about political involvement, lack of community or social status, and the demands of family and occupational life may all contribute to the fact that more than 80 percent of those in the assembly are over 45 years old.

While the number of "young" candidates has not increased substantially during the postwar period, their degree of success has. Before 1959, more than half of all young candidates were defeated; since then almost 85 percent have been successful. This can be attributed to the fact that candidates of Japan's centrist and leftist political parties — the Socialists, the Clean Government Party, the Democratic Socialists, and the Communists — have been increasingly successful in Mishima. These parties tend to select young candidates. With strong organizational backing, young candiates can succeed and then be reelected repeatedly.

There is no significant distortion by place of residence. Candidates from Mishima's outlying agricultural districts have historically had a higher rate of success in assembly elections than those from the central area, however, and this has become increasingly so, even though these outlying areas are becoming more populated and heterogeneous. Fewer candidates from these areas contend for election and, since 1959, over 90 percent of them have been elected. Presumably, the social homogeneity of farm communities and the power of their agricultural cooperatives continue to be effecitve even in the face of an inflow of new residents. The number of farmers or officers of agricultural cooperatives in the assembly has not fluctuated, even though the number of people who regularly engage in farming has dropped substantially.

Most of the members of Mishima's assembly have been small businessmen or farmers (see Table 6.4). This has not changed significantly since 1947, with each election producing an assembly with 22 to 24 such members. Other occupational groups are, therefore, found in only small numbers. White-collar workers, blue-collar workers, and professionals usually contribute less than five members. Lawyers play an insignificant role in Japanese politics; this group has never been represented in the assembly. Small businessmen and farmers have advantages for political participation;

for example community status, wealth, freedom from rigid time constraints which would interfere with assembly attendance, support from their employees or from related business or agricultural interest groups. The importance of organizational support is attested to by the high level of success (see column 2) of those who list their occupations as officers of agricultural cooperatives, labor unions, or local political party branches.

The political backgrounds of assembly members have changed to some degree over the postwar period. In the early years, almost all those elected ran as "independents" *(mushozoku)*, fearing that identification with a party would lose them votes. Most conservatives, in particular, ran as independents even if they were active in one of the local conservative parties up to 1955, or in the Liberal Democratic Party (LDP) branch after 1955. Until the early 1960's, leftist party candidates ran as party-affiliated candidates and were as often defeated as elected. So until 1967 independent conservatives and a handful of brave LDP candidates always captured 26 or more of the assembly's 30 seats.

After 1967, a significant shift can be noted. Conservatives, even more than before, have run as independents. And conservatives gradually have begun to lose assembly strength, dropping most recently to 19 of 30 members. Furthermore, all major centrist and leftist parties have come to be represented in the assembly by two or more members, and candidates of these parties are almost never defeated. In the four elections since 1967, only three out of 37 of their candidates have been defeated. These parties carefully calculate their prospects and fully utilize their organizational resources to ensure success.

## Political Veterans

Which individuals have had the most lengthy and successful local political careers? As political careers increase in length or as the individuals reach higher office, do occupational careers change? Do local politicans exit from politics in the same vocational roles in which they first entered politics? Does a lengthy political career disrupt one's work career? Tables 6.5 and 6.6 address these questions. "Successful" assembly members are defined as (1) those with assembly careers of 16 or more years unblemished by defeat, or (2) those who served in the assembly for two terms or more and proceeded to higher elective office.

*Table 6.5.* Social Backgrounds of "Successful" Mishima City Assembly Members, Other Assembly Members, and Losing Candidates, 1947-1979

| Characteristics Category | "Successful" Assembly Members | Other Assembly Members | Losing Candidates |
|---|---|---|---|
| | % | % | % |
| Sex: Male | 100.0 | 99.0 | 97.5 |
| Female | – | 1.0 | 2.5 |
| | 100.0 | 100.0 | 100.0 |
| Age: Average age | 48.2 | 52.0 | 53.2 |
| at first election | 41.3 | | |
| Area: Inner-city | 54.0 | 50.5 | 69.0 |
| Outlying areas | 46.0 | 49.5 | 31.0 |
| | 100.0 | 100.0 | 100.0 |
| Occupation: | | | |
| Small business owner or company manager | 60.0 | 44.5 | 52.5 |
| Farmer | 15.7 | 30.0 | 22.4 |
| Company employee or worker | 2.9 | 12.0 | 10.3 |
| Agricultural cooperative or labor union official | 14.2 | 4.0 | 2.6 |
| Professional | 2.9 | 5.5 | 6.0 |
| Unemployed/retired | – | 3.0 | 6.8 |
| Political party official | 4.2 | 1.0 | – |
| | 99.9 | 100.0 | 100.6 |
| Political Party Affiliation: | | | |
| No affiliation registered | 64.3 | 80.5 | 77.6 |
| Liberal Democratic Party or predecessor conservative party | 8.6 | 4.5 | 8.6 |
| Socialist Party | 2.9 | 9.5 | 10.3 |
| Clean Government Party | 12.9 | 2.0 | – |
| Communist Party | 4.3 | 2.5 | 3.4 |
| Democratic Socialist Party | 7.1 | 1.0 | – |
| | 100.1 | 100.0 | 99.9 |

Notes: "Successful" candidates were those serving four terms or more without defeat in the city assembly, or two or more terms in the assembly without defeat and then becoming mayor or prefectural assembly member.

The N for "successful" assembly members is 70, for other assembly members is 200, and for losing assembly members is 116; N represents terms rather than individuals. (Thus, in the case of "successful" assembly members, 18 individuals served a total of 70 assembly terms.)

Occupation is that indicated by the candidate when registering his candidacy. In most cases, this represents the main source of income for the individual. Some candidates, however, have multiple sources of income (e.g., farmers who also serve as officials of agriculture cooperatives, or workers who are union officials). This is not reflected in the table.

Sources: See Table 6.1.

*Table 6.6.* Political and Occupational Careers of "Successful" Mishima City Politicians, 1942–1979

**City Assembly (A) and Mayoral (M) Career**

1. Conservative — 1942A, 1947A — owner, small oil refining company; 1947M — no occupation; post-incumbency — officer, shipping firm.

2. Conservative — 1942A, 1947A — company employee; 1951A, 1953M — president, Mishima branch of nationwide shipping firm; 1957M — mayor; post-incumbency — owner, local business.

3. Centrist — 1955A, 1959A, 1961M — owner, furniture manufacturing and sales firm; 1965M, 1969M, 1973M — mayor; post-incumbency — owner, furniture manufacturing and sales firm.

**City Assembly (A) and Prefectural Assembly (PA) Career**

4. Conservative — 1942A, 1947A, 1951PA, 1955PA, 1959PA — farmer; post-incumbency — head, agriculture cooperative.

5. Conservative — 1951A, 1955A, 1959A, 1963PA, 1967PA, 1971PA — owner, small retail firm; post-incumbency — same.

6. Socialist — 1951A, 1955A — writer; 1963PA, 1967PA — employee, accounting firm; 1971PA, 1975PA — managing director, accountancy firm; post-incumbency — same.

7. Conservative — 1963A, 1967A, 1975PA, 1979PA — owner, medium-size manufacturing firm; post-incumbency — same.

**City Assembly (A) Career**

8. Conservative — 1942A, 1947A, 1951A, 1955A — owner, printing firm; post-incumbency — same.

9. Conservative — 1942A, 1947A, 1951A, 1955A, 1959A, 1963A — owner, produce company; post-incumbency — same.

10. Conservative — 1947A — farmer; 1951A, 1955A, 1959A, 1963A, 1967A — head, agriculture cooperative; post-incumbency — same.

11. Conservative — 1947A, 1951A, 1955A, 1959A, 1963A — owner, restaurant; post-incumbency — same.

12. Communist, then independent leftist — 1959A — owner, small glass company; 1963A — Communist Party official; 1967A, 1971A — organization leader; 1975A, 1979A — publisher, local political newspaper; present incumbent.

13. Conservative — 1963A, 1967A, 1971A, 1975A, 1979A — owner, small business; present incumbent.

14. Democratic Socialist — 1963A, 1967A, 1971A, 1975A, 1979A — employee, large synthetic fiber manufacturing firm, and head, labor union; present incumbent.

15. Clean Government — 1963A, 1967A, 1971A, 1975A, 1979A — owner, polishing/grinding equipment wholesale firm; present incumbent.

16. Conservative — 1963A, 1967A — farmer; 1971A, 1975A — farmer and auditor, agriculture cooperative; post-incumbency — same.

17. Clean Government — 1967a, 1971A, 1975A, 1979A — owner, foodstuff manufacturing and sales firm; present incumbent.

18. Conservative — 1967A, 1971A, 1975A, 1979A — farmer; present incumbent.

Sources: See Table 6.1.

Table 6.6 indicates that political veterans are males who build their political careers on the owning of property or of leading an important local economic organization. These individuals have been able to enter politics at a younger age than other electees. Over one-half of all those first elected at an age of less than 45 are included among the "successful" eighteen.

Three-fourths of them own small businesses or farms. Almost all of the remaining persons have been supported by labor unions or political parties. Some, e.g., the farmers who also serve as officers of agricultural cooperatives, or the Clean Government Party assembly members who are also small businessmen, can rely on dual bases of support. Small businessmen and farmers are even more heavily represented among veteran members of the assembly in general. And the tendency is even more pronounced among those who reach higher levels of elected office.

Veteran politicans seem to experience secure, stable occupational careers while serving in office. Most of them leave politics in the same vocational role as when they entered politics. This security might seem natural considering the circumstance. Most of these individuals were able to begin political careers partially *because* of the success, status, and stability of their vocations. Entry into a time-consuming political career is eased by the fact that such people, business owners or farmers, control decisions as to how their time is to be used more than can most people. In American politics, similarly, such occupations as real estate or insurance sales, law, or the ownership of a small business will facilitate the holding of public office (Eulau et al. 1960:230-231).

What little discontinuity in occupational careers there is that can be seen in Table 6.6 can be divided into three categories. First, an assembly member who becomes mayor devotes himself almost completely to public office. His business is not given up, but is attended to by sons, wife, or others; after a defeat sometime later, these men return to their business careers. A second minor change is found in the careers of three of the four farmers. After their election to the city assembly, they moved into top leadership positions in one of the agricultural cooperatives. Again, political careers and vocations reenforce each other. Assembly careers are helped by prominence in farm communities or by rising importance in an agricultural cooperative. After election, a long political career increases the prospect of one's rising to even higher ranks within the coop's leadership.

The third type of occupational discontinuity is displayed by the two politicians farthest on the left of the local political spectrum. Both of them experienced occupational insecurity as a result of their political beliefs. One, purged by the Japanese government on the orders of the Allied Occupation (because he led the local teacher's union) lost his teaching position in the early 1950's. He entered his first assembly election campaign as a free-lance writer, and later took a position in an accounting firm. The second man lost his position as head of the local Communist Party branch when, in the early 1960's, the Party purged itself of members who favored the Soviet Union too strongly. He remains in the assembly to this day, yet his work career has been varied and unstable since that time. Politics is now his vocation, and the assembly has become his primary means of support.

## Conclusions

More than 70,000 Japanese adults engage in dual occupational and public roles as representatives in local assemblies. If the case of postwar Mishima is of general relevance, we can conclude the following about such concurrent careers and the conditions which nurture their unfolding.

Elective careers are often brief. Half of Mishima's postwar assembly members served a single four year term, thereafter defeated or retiring. Many other candidates never are elected. It is perhaps more appropriate to speak of political *careers* in the case of those who served eight years (24%), 12 years (17%), or 16 years or more (9%). Lengthy careers, especially those unblemished by defeat, are relatively few in number. Yet they are increasing in number as the years pass. For example, in 1979, over two-thirds of the assembly members had served two or more terms as compared to the postwar average of 50 percent; and 23 percent of the incumbents have served four or more terms as compared to an overall average of nine percent since 1947. Mishima assembly politics are less and less competitive, and lengthy elective careers are ever more possible.

Those who are elected to assembly positions tend to move into this role from positions of substance in the local economic system. Electees tend to be owners of property — of small businesses or farms. Otherwise they work for or can rely on the support of a local economic interest group or political party. Veteran politicans fit this pattern even more strongly than in the assembly. Often, they rely on both bases of support — property and associational sponsorship.

131

Veteran local politicians continue to enjoy secure, stable occupational careers from their point of entry into public office and on into post-incumbency.

This analysis has been limited by its use of aggregate data rather than intensive personal interview. Interviews most likely would have revealed more of the perils of local political careers and a richer picture of the relationship among work roles, family life, and politics. As I do not have interview data, I want to present a few speculations on the local political lifecourse based on my personal experience in Mishima.

Although it is difficult to postulate a "typical" career pattern for those in the assembly, we can say that the local elective career normally begins in late mid-life, when work careers are financially rewarding and secure, the formative family years are past, and status in the community has been achieved. Almost all assembly members, regardless of partisan background, have given considerable time to neighborhood association (*jichikai*) or PTA activities. Leadership of one of these groups greatly improves a candidate's prospects for success. Reflecting continued respect for age, such positions of leadership are seldom achieved before the mid-40's.

For many assembly candidates, the urge to enter the first campaign seems as much a result of outside forces as personal ambition. Those who rise to positions of prominence in neighborhood associations are already known for their social and leadership skills. Two types of events often lead others to press them to enter the campaign fray. In the one case, an incumbent assemblyman from an area resigns or is defeated, and area residents feel a need for continued representation. The second case results from partisan conflict, when a local party branch or assembly faction tries to build its strength by pressing someone with status and neighborhood support to run. In either case, the decision to run for office is as much a result of social as individual dynamics.

The first election campaign is the most dangerous. Once an assembly career begins, it is only infrequently ended by electoral defeat. Incumbents seem either to serve relatively short terms or to continue in elective politics for periods as long as 16 or 20 years. This lends the impresssion that they can be divided into those who see politics as a *vocation* and those who see it as an *avocation*, supplementing rather than equaling or replacing their work roles in importance. Those who see the assembly as an avocation find their major base of elective strength in the area-limited "small world" of associational life (i.e., a single neighborhood association or a PTA group). They tend to be conservatives, but are not very active in the local Liberal Democratic Party branch. Many find that four or eight years in the assembly is enough and recommend a younger association leader for the next term.

A smaller group of conservatives, and most assembly members from the center and left political parties, approach local politics more as a vocation. Before entering their initial election contest, they have risen in the "big world" of local associational life and have become more explicitly involved in local party branch activities. By "big world" of local associational life, I mean the citywide interest groups which represent local economic interests — labor unions, the Chamber of Commerce or merchants' associations, and agricultural cooperatives. There is a close relationhship between positions of importance in such groups and lengthy, stable careers in the assembly.

These careerists tend to enter local politics earlier than others, serve longer terms, and invest greater time in the political vocation. They are secure in their work and group leadership positons. Local assembly members on the left in Mishima have served as full-time party functionaries or union leaders since the 1950's. For conservative careerists, the rise to prominence in business associations and local party activities reflects success in their business activities. Thus, success and security beget security in elective politics.

Assembly careers sometimes end in defeat, but more often end in voluntary retirement, attempts at higher office, or death. Voluntary retirement for the "avocationist" is legitimated because the end of one or two terms normally falls in the incumbent's mid to late 60's, a natural time to withdraw from public life. Vocationists continue longer. Their personal investment, programmatic sentiments, and political antagonisms are greater. The meaning of their lives is more tied to politics. In Mishima, retirement from politics has more often come with electoral defeat or pressure from younger men within their partisan group.

For all who are elected to the assembly, it may be that service there is more rewarding than in comparable local political roles elsewhere, for suveys of the Japanese public have repeatedly shown that politics is more interesting at local than at higher levels (see Richardson 1974: 29-64). Local politics is seen as relevant to people's daily lives. Thus, the members of a city assembly may leave their political careers secure in the belief that they have been involved in something of importance.

## Notes

1. The competition ratio for 1947 was 2.30, 1951 = 1.50, 1955 = 1.56, 1959 = 1.16, 1963 = 1.80, 1967 = 1.16, 1971 = 1.13, 1975 = 1.13, and 1979 = 1.10 (Mishima-shi Senkyō Kanri Iinkai 1958, 1961, 1966, 1967, and 1976; *Mishima News* 1979).

## References

Eulau, Heinz, W. Buchanan, L. Ferguson, and J. Wahlke
  1960    Career Perspectives of American State Legislators. *In* Political Decision-Makers, Dwaine Marvick, ed., pp. 218-263. Glencoe, Ill.: Free Press.
Isomura Ei'ichi and Hoshino Mitsuo
  1969    Chihō jichi tokuhon. [A Reader on Local Self-Government] Tōyō Keizai Shimbunsha.
Jichishō
  1978    Chihō jichi no dōkō.[Trends in Local Self-Government] Dai-ichi Hōki Shuppan Kabushiki Gaisha.
Lewis, Jack G.
  1975    *Hokaku Rengo:* The Politics of Conservative-Progressive Cooperation in a Japanese City. Ph.D. Dissertation, Stanford University.
Mishima Nyūsu
  1979    Shigikai Senkyō Kekka Repōto. [A Report on Results of City Assembly Elections]. April 26, p. 1.
Mishima-shi Senkyō Kanri Iinkai
  1958, 1961, 1966, 1967, 1971, 1976    Senkyō kekka shirabe. [Studies on Election Results]
Nihon Shichōkai
  1978    Nihon toshi nenkan. [Japanese Cities Yearbook]
Putnam, Robert D.
  1976    The Comparative Study of Political Elites. Englewood Cliffs, N.J.: Prentice-Hall.
Richardson, Bradley M.
  1974    The Political Culture of Japan.    Berkeley and Los Angeles University of California Press.

# CHAPTER 7

# Cataclysm and Career Rebirth: The Imperial Military Elite

THEODORE F. COOK, JR.

I did not consider this an occupation. Payment and the improving of my standard of living were not what I had in mind.
— Former Lt. Colonel Kanda Taizō, Imperial Japanese Army

The term "military career," like the term "professional soldier" is intensely disliked by most former officers of the Imperial Japanese Army. Not only did the Allied Occupation brand them as "professional soldiers" in its postwar purge orders, but they themselves did not view their military service in terms which might facilitate comparison with civilian employment, or even employment in other governmental institutions. "Armed bureaucrats" though they may have been in some of their institutional roles (Feit 1973: 1.21), they maintain that they were not oriented to the miltiary for self-advancement or for employment. Again and again they made this point to me as we talked of their reasons for following the military route. Often they prefaced their remarks with, "I think this is difficult for a foreigner to understand," indicating the depth to which they felt their attitude to be "Japanese." This reflects both a powerful ideological commitment and, to a surprising degree, the realities of the military's demands on its officer corps. Japan's defeat in 1945 shattered the institutional base for that commitment, and in a sense the former officers had to begin adult life all over again. In this chapter I explore what it was in their military experience that may explain their relative success in postwar civilian life.

The Army officer corps was one of prewar Japan's most important elites. The upper echelons of the Army exercised vast influence over the policies and programs of the entire nation. By the 1930s the men who directed the Army were chosen from among the graduates of the Military Academy. A young officer candidate standing at attention, waiting for his name to be called to step forward on graduation day, or receiving his diploma from a General in the presence of a member of the Imperial Family in full military uniform, might, in his dreams, hope to one day be the man wearing the three stars. Yet, in the atmosphere of the mid-1930s his thoughts were directed first of all toward performing his duties, and consequently toward his part in helping the Army to defend the country.

Long and arduous years preceded graduation. For many, their direct association with Army education began with one of the Army Cadet Schools (Rikugun Yōnen Gakkō), where a select few youths, about fourteen years of age, gained admission. This was understood to be the most likely starting point for a climb to the top of the Army hierarchy. In the early 1930s, only 150 boys each year were accepted from all Japan.

For those unable to gain direct admission to Yōnen Gakkō, there was a second, hardly less competitive route via examinations taken in the fourth or fifth year of Middle School. A successful candidate would be able to join the Army Cadet School students at the Preparatory Course of the Military Academy (Yōka Shikan Gakkō).Two years there and a period of six months attached directly to a regular Army regiment preceded his progression on to the Military Academy and its course of slightly less than two years. Only after graduation there did he embark on his real military life.

It was not a life — or an occupation — that ended with retirement. Army patterns of officer personnel use and the nature of Japan's military system, particularly the structure of her reserves, ensured that an officer's connection with the service would continue well beyond his active duty *(gen'eki)* years. This system and the ideology of military service precluded the officer from giving much, if any, attention to thoughts of "second" or "post-service" careers. Even in the case of the very highest echelons of the military, for whom "post-service" careers were usually conceived of in terms of helping the nation by participating in politics, the top generals were traditionally promoted to Gensui (Field Marshal), a rank that had no upper age limit (Cook 1978).

So the younger officer candidate of the 1930s, having completed his professional preparation, was likely to see himself less as entering another "stage" of life but rather more as finally having an opportunity to realize the very purpose of that life. A nearly "total" commitment to that purpose, to the exclusion if need be of the personal and family careers of the usual life cycle, was his ideal. This broad dedication to a calling is, of course, characteristic in some measure of many professions everywhere. What stands out about the Imperial Army officer is the extent to which his commitment, made not only to his profession but through the state to the Emperor, was rooted in the socialization patterns that affected the bulk of the prewar populace (Tsurumi 1970:80-137). He became a special cultural cynosure.

Robert LeVine's assumptions about personal continuities, monitoring of performance, goals, and self-evaluation (1978:2-3) are key concepts here for my examination of the effects of destroying the institutional structure and disorganizing the ideological and social environment which had nurtured the career of the Imperial Army officer. If a career is indeed "a patterned sequence of movements through social networks and settings." (Elder cited in LeVine 1978:2), then the "subjective career," defined as the "moving perspective in which the person sees his life as a whole and interprets the meanings of his various attributes, actions, and the things which happen to him" (Hughes cited in LeVine 1978:2), of a man who had been an Imperial Army officer must be seen in terms of the discontinuities between the value systems and the norms of socialization he experienced over his life cycle up to August 15, 1945, and those since then.

## Cataclysm

It is unusual for members of an entire profession to find themselves plummeted from a level of high status and higher power to being the objects of revulsion, all within a short span of time. It is even rarer for such a transformation to occur in just a few months. In the early days after Japan's surrender, this was the career cataclysm that overtook the Imperial officer corps.

A war had been lost: the ultimate sign of failure for a military elite. The Army and Navy which had played such a prominent part in "preparing" the nation for that war (particular the Army, whose leaders had been so politically important and who had exhorted the public to sacrifice for war) were held to be responsible. And this all the more so because of the constant assurances that had come from military headquarters and propaganda offices proclaiming that the

Army and Navy forces were ever-victorious and executing a master plan sure to bring disaster to the Enemy. The discovery that these claims were disingenuous, and a recognition of the futility of much of the sacrifice, rebounded to the discredit of those who lead Japan's military institutions.

There was another impetus for their fall into disrepute. This was the purge, conducted by the Allied Occupation authorities, with its attendant war crimes trials. It became a stated aim of the Occupation to excise the institutions and to exorcise the spirit deemed to have been responsible for Japan's "aggression." Japanese "militarism" was seen to be foremost among the evils, and the agents of that militarism were the members of the officer corps.

Initially, the purge was addressed to war crimes. The directive of the United States Joint Chiefs of Staff ordering certain categories of individuals to be arrested and held as war criminals included "all commissioned officers of the Gendarmerie (Kempei), and all officers of the Army and Navy who have been important exponents of militant nationalism and aggression." (Baerwald 1959:7) Efforts to limit the purge to career officers of the rank of major and above were abandoned, although it may seem to have been "patently absurd" to put all members of the officer corps in the same category as General Tōjō. If, as Baerwald states, "The all-inclusive category was based on the elimination of the influence of the Army and Navy," the small fish were sacrificed in order to beach the whales.

The Allies' reasons for barring all military leaders from public life were linked with a desire to remake Japanese society on the basis of ideals most commonly associated with liberal democracy. Quoting again from Baerwald (8-9).

> By removing [Japan's wartime leadership], another step would be taken toward Japan's pacification. A new dimension was thereby added to traditional theories analyzing the causes of war. Leadership is placed alongside economic, social, historical, and military pressures. In fact, what emerges is the belief that an elite imposes its will on objective forces as opposed to being guided by them. Man's fate is self-determined.... Whatever position we take on the validity of this analysis, one objective of the purge clearly emerges — namely, that it was to eliminate the leadership potential in Japan's capacity to wage war.

It was also vital to the effort to free the Japanese people from the intellectual, emotional, and social straight-jackets which, it was assumed, stood between the Japanese people and democracy.

So the former officers found themselves after 1945 excluded from any institutional role in the rebuilding of Japan. And they saw the values which had formed the basis of their self-indentity and their primary career singled out for repudiation, first by their former enemies and secondly by home-grown forces seeking fundamental social change. Another major fact of life in postwar Japan was the economic and social chaos of defeat. The economic losses of the war, the repatriation of millions of former soldiers and civilians to Japan from formerly occupied and colonial territories, and the tremendous readjustments needed to meet changed patterns in the world economy, all upset any orderly process of career readjustment which might otherwise have been possible.

It is against this background — the lost war, the purge, the economic ruin — that we must evaluate the careers of Japanese officers after 1945. The discontinuities in their careers, the disorientation of men accustomed to elite status but now members of a near-pariah class, and the tremendous difficulties all Japanese faced in redirecting their lives, all must be kept in mind in what follows.

## Data Sources

Primary data for this chapter are drawn from the research I have conducted on the social origins, education, and service career patterns of Japan's prewar military officers. As part of this research I sent a questionnaire to more than one thousand graduates of the Military Academy (Rikugun Shikan Gakkō). I mailed the form to all surviving members of a number of selected classes. The classes were chosen to identify cohort groups, and so facilitate comparison over time. Other individuals were also selected and a random sample was made of all prewar classes, including the large wartime classes of the 1940's. A similar questionnaire was prepared and sent to a thousand former naval officers who were graduates of the Naval Academy (Kaigun Hei Gakkō) at Etajima. I received replies from approximately six hundred former Army officers and nearly four hundred Navy officers.

The questionnaire, a fairly complicated one with some open-ended items, included a query concerning the man's postwar employment record, and a number of attitudinal questions about career choice and socialization. These are useful in understanding

*Table 7.1.* Percentages of Questionnaire Respondents from Selected
Japanese Military Academy Graduating Classes, 1911-1944,
and Their Average Ages in Various Postwar Years

| | Graduating Class and Year | | | | | | | |
| --- | --- | --- | --- | --- | --- | --- | --- | --- |
| | 23rd | 27th | 33rd | 36th | 40th | 44th | 48th | 56th[1] |
| Number and Age | 1911 | 1915 | 1921 | 1924 | 1928 | 1932 | 1936 | 1944 |
| Number in Class | 740 | 761 | 437 | 330 | 225 | 315 | 388 | 1672 |
| Number Responding | 23 | 50 | 62 | 67 | 52 | 90 | 104 | 27 |
| Percentage Responding | 3 | 7 | 14 | 20 | 23 | 29 | 27 | 2 |
| Median Birth Year | 1890 | 1894 | 1900 | 1903 | 1907 | 1911 | 1915 | 1923 |
| Age in 1945 | 55 | 51 | 45 | 42 | 38 | 34 | 30 | 22 |
| Age in 1952 | 62 | 58 | 52 | 49 | 45 | 41 | 37 | 29 |
| Age in 1975 | 85 | 81 | 75 | 72 | 68 | 64 | 60 | 52 |

[1] Excluding Air Officers School

Note: The figures for "Percentage Responding" refer to percentage of all men who had graduated with that class. The actual rate of response by those sent questionnaires was about 60% overall and virtually 100% for the 23rd and 27th classes. Questionnaires were sent to all surviving men from each class, except the 56th, for which a sample was drawn.

the officers' perspectives on their postwar experiences. I will give special attention here to seven graduating classes: those who left the Military Academy in the years 1911, 1915, 1921, 1924, 1928, 1932, and 1936, the 23rd, 27th, 33rd, 36th, 40th, 44th, and 48th classes to graduate, respectively. (See Table 7.2). Men in the classes from 1911 to 1937 formed the backbone of the field-grade officers of the Imperial Army during the Second World War, and had been a substantial proportion of the company-grade officers during the early stages of the China Incident. They were the heart of the General Staff officers in the Pacific campaigns.

My respondents from these classes include 49 general officers (26 Lieutenant Generals and 23 Major Generals) from the classes of 1911 and 1915 alone, including Lt. General Tatsumi Ei'ichi, prewar military attaché to Great Britian and postwar head of the Kaikōsha (Officers' Association) and an aide to Prime Minister Yoshida Shigeru in the formation of the Self-Defense Forces. (One of the greatest frustrations in this project was the impossibility of following these classes to the completion of what might have been their normal military careers. Who, among the promising stars of the class of 1936, would have become the Generals of the 1950's? If I had been able to answer that and similar questions from actual historical events, this chapter would be very different. Surrender in 1945 rendered that an impossibility.)

I have compared the results from these military academy classes with the results of a random sample drawn from the class of 1944. In addition, I have made use of a large number of interviews and of personal testaments (in the form of diaries, memoirs, and "reports") which were made available to me. The Goyūrenmei (Veterans' Association of the Army and Self-Defense Forces) and Suikōkai (Naval Association, a modern outgrowth of the Naval Officers' Association, the Suikōsha), as well as the Kaikōsha, where the bulk of my reserach was conducted, were very helpful in allowing me access to their document collections and their membership records and lists. The personal histories of some four hundred and fifty former Army officers, thus supplemented, allow me to present a picture of the postwar careers of former officers which is accurate in the specific cases and broadly applicable to the entire officer corps, or at least to the classes that graduated before 1937.

*Table 7.2.* Highest Military Rank Attained by Selected
Japanese Military Academy Graduates

| Rank | Graduating Class and Year | | | | | | | | |
|---|---|---|---|---|---|---|---|---|---|
| (U.S. Army Equivalent) | 23rd 1911 | 27th 1915 | 33rd 1921 | 36th 1924 | 40th 1928 | 44th 1932 | 48th 1936 | 56th 1944 | Total |
| *Chūjō* (Lt. Gen.) | 8 ( 53%) | 18 ( 36%) | – | – | – | – | – | – | 26 |
| *Shōshō* (Maj. Gen.) | 2 ( 13%) | 10 ( 20%) | 11 ( 18%) | – | – | – | – | – | 23 |
| *Taisa* (Colonel) | 3 ( 20%) | 17 ( 34%) | 40 ( 64%) | 34 ( 52%) | – | – | – | – | 94 |
| *Chūsa* (Lt. Colonel) | 1 ( 7%) | 2 ( 4%) | 11 ( 18%) | 30 ( 46%) | 51 ( 98%) | 31 ( 36%) | – | – | 126 |
| *Shōsa* (Major) | – | 3 ( 6%) | – | – | 1 ( 2%) | 54 ( 63%) | 100 ( 99%) | – | 158 |
| *Tai'i* (Captain) | 1 ( 7%) | – | – | 1 ( 2%) | – | 1 ( 1%) | 1 ( 1%) | 26 ( 96%) | 30 |
| *Chūi* (1st Lieut.) | – | – | – | – | – | – | – | 1 ( 4%) | 1 |
| Total | 15 (100%) | 50 (100%) | 62 (100%) | 65 (100%) | 52 (100%) | 86 (100%) | 101 (100%) | 27 (100%) | 448 |

Note: Figures in parentheses show the percentage of respondents in that class attaining that rank.

141

THEODORE F. COOK, JR.

## Career Rebirth

Describing his postwar employment experience, former Colonel Morimoto Higekazu, who graduated from the Military Academy in 1915 as a member of the 27th Class, said he saw the years after 1945 as his "second life." It was a different existence from the one that he had led and had expected to continue. It was, as for many Japanese, and not only military men, in the closing days of World War II, a life which they had not expected to lead. Over the course of his postwar years, during which he came to be president of his own small company, Morimoto decided that he had been "liberated from the military" and had been reborn. For he had rejected his military values, accepted postwar ones as they evolved, and had approached himself as a new individual almost separate from the officer he had been.

The path was not nearly as clear cut for most of Morimoto's classmates and seniors in the classes of 1915 and earlier. The men of these classes were, in 1945, in their sixth decade of life. Born in the early 1890's, they would have been, in times of peace, approaching the completion of their active service and would have had the prospect of becoming military senior citizens. I have emphasized that this would not have meant "retirement" from responsiblity, nor for most, any "second career." But it would have marked an institutional milestone on their life-course, a point where they could pause and measure their successes and failures in age-specific terms. Perhaps, too, it would have been a time for them to look to their sons to carry on the family military tradition, as so many Academy entrants themselves had done.

However, for nearly ten years, Japan had been at war, first with China and then with the Allies. Fine distinctions among age benchmarks seem to have been lost or sublimated. Age limits for active duty service set in 1935 had specified 55 for Colonel, 58 for Major General, 62 for Lieutenant General, and 65 for full General; but these had little meaning after 1937, when reserve officers with white-flecked hair, some of them veterans of the Siberian Intervention, had been recalled to service in full mobilization. Casualties and the rapid expansion of the forces to maximum size had often led to rapid promotions not necessarily signifying exemplary performance of duties. Although some severe criticisms were voiced to me by non-Academy graduates troubled by what they called "careerism" and "leading from the rear," it still seems that death in uniform, perhaps even on home soil against an invader, was what most officers had come to expect by the summer of 1945.

142

The break occasioned by the Emperor's surrender message of August 15th was, therefore, all the more complete. Officers who were in their early and middle 50's at that time suddenly were cut adrift, and in a few months were to witness the dismantling of institutions which had been their frame of personal reference for as long as 40 years.

Yet, while it struck all the individuals simultaneously, the cataclysm hit the age cohorts at different "stages" of these individual careers. We can thus see in the different experiences of the classes some of the broad range of experiences of all former officers. We can also glimpse different postwar redirection patterns which were age-specific, or at least identified with a particular point in the "career life."

Several respondents from the Class of 1911 had not been on active duty during the war. One described himself as having been a *rōnin* (samurai without a master) after 1941. These men and a few others "retired quietly," as did Lt. General Sakurai Seijō and had no employment career after 1945. In fact that was the case for a fourth of all respondents in this class. For others, status as a Lieutenant General of the Imperial Army was quickly replaced by, for example, three years of work as the "lowest ranking janitor in a small company," the experience of Nagatsu Sahijū. Some men who had initially tried retirement soon felt the need of supplementary income and took up active farming "at sixty years of age." One started a salt manufacturing company, failed, and eventually founded an association for former officers in his home prefecture. Work in business companies, part-time teaching of painting in junior and senior high schools, and imprisonment in Sugamo as a war criminal were among the postwar occupations reported by the 23rd Class.

Similar patterns, with an increasing diversity of jobs and increasing frequency of job changes, appear in the succeeding classes. A very large number of officers initially turned to types of work with which they were familiar. Those who served as members of demobilization or repatriation boards in 1945 and early 1946, in effect carried on the routines of the Army in a semi-civilian status. But this work came to a virtual end when the Supreme Commander for the Allied Powers sent down the purge order barring former military officers from government service. Although some did work on, unofficially, many more found themselves without employment.

The officers' primary skill, the ability to exercise military command, was unwanted; and their efforts to use their experience, their abilities to work in and though large-scale institutions and bureaucracies, were thwarted by the purge order. Unlike middle-

143

and lower-ranking civilian bureaucrats (men who shared many of their ideological assumptions), officers were left with no institutional attachment, and for a time at least, without any successor organizations.

*Table 7.3.* Number of Postwar Jobs Held by Respondents From Selected Japanese Military Academy Graduating Classes in Percentages

| Number of Jobs | Graduating Class and Year | | | | | | | |
|---|---|---|---|---|---|---|---|---|
| | 23rd 1911 (N=12 | 27th 1915 46 | 33rd 1921 64 | 36th 1924 64 | 40th 1928 48 | 44th 1932 86 | 48th 1936 92 | 56th 1944 27) |
| | % | % | % | % | % | % | % | % |
| None | 21 | 15 | 6 | 0 | 0 | 0 | 0 | 0 |
| 1 | 50 | 43 | 30 | 19 | 23 | 15 | 11 | 33 |
| 2 | 14 | 20 | 36 | 28 | 25 | 29 | 16 | 26 |
| 3 | 14 | 11 | 12 | 25 | 40 | 8 | 37 | 15 |
| 4 | 0 | 6 | 11 | 23 | 8 | 17 | 20 | 11 |
| 5 | 0 | 4 | 0 | 5 | 2 | 7 | 8 | 11 |
| More than 5 or "many" | 0 | 0 | 5 | 0 | 2 | 3 | 9 | 11 |
| Total | 99 | 99 | 100 | 100 | 100 | 79 | 101 | 107 |

Note: Percentages do not always total 100% because of multiple responses.

Commercial corporations did not want them. The major industiral combines, the *zaibatsu* (financial factions), were themselves subject to a purge and therefore were reticient about drawing attention by hiring former officers. The same may be said of schools and universities, particularly public ones, for "militarists" were not wanted in institutions seeking to cleanse themselves of the taint of "ultra-nationalism."

The professions also were closed to men of the earlier graduating classes, mainly because they were unable to acquire the educational prerequisites. This was not so, however, for the classes still in the military academies at the end of the war. Many of these younger men were able to return to universities, utilizing their educational skills to make their way into the professions. Most of them chose medicine or dentistry. The magazine *Shūkan Yomiuri* (1980:35-40) named 579 former Army officers who were involved in medicine in March 1980, 153 from all classes prior to 1944 and the remainder from classes which were scheduled to graduate in 1945-1948. Not only was age at work here; the surge in the number of former officers and officer-candidates in the universities prompted Occupation authorities to close public universities to them. This was particularly cruel to those who, by 1948, were returning from prisoner of war camps but could not even consider reeducation because of the purge.

Subsistence farming was, of course, one route open; a large number of men turned to it. This was not always as one might suspect, in family land, but quite open on "reclaimed" land. Irony is heavy in such descriptions as "farmed on a 'reclaimed' airfield" or "engaged in the farming of a military base." The landlords who had sent sons into the Army in substantial numbers in the prewar days were losing their holdings under Occupation land reform policies. This severly restricted the "agricultural option" of an officer. Many officers had gained valuable experience during the war overseas and were quite proficient in farming, having learned much from their men. One officer in particular became a specialist in berries and has been a bit of a nuisance with his constant requests to me for detailed information on the subject of the exportation of cranberry bushes from Massachusetts.

Some officers tried their hand at running their own businesses. Salt-making, clothing stores, printing shops and other enterprises requiring small capital outlay were among these efforts. Yet there seems to be something to the old phrase *bushi no shōhō* ("doing business like a samurai") for very frequently these ventures failed, or else did so poorly that the founder needed to start again in something else. One man, with a vast array of social connections stemming from his status as a member of the prewar peerage, opened a cosmetics shop on the Ginza which has gotten on famously!

More often than not the officer turned again to commercial companies, seeking ones with which he could form a direct, almost personal relationship. These efforts, sometimes marking an individual's third or fourth attempt to reestablish himself, were directed into areas where he had personal experience — e.g. as a specialist on Burma for a trading company — or where he could link into a reemerging network of personal connections. Often these were combined. Lacking the technical skills which could win a former Navy officer a position in companies manufacturing pumps or in building and designing ships, the Army officer was thrown on his chief talent, the assumed skill he had in human resources management, and on the common bond with his fellow officers.

The very values which had drawn an officer into the Army rather than the Navy (and the record is quite definite that many men chose the Army when both options were avaiable) were to hinder him in the immediate postwar era. One officer of the class of 1911 said that

145

he had never considered a naval career, for he thought it "better to have more opportunities to communicate with fellow men." Another stated, "I felt it better to spend my life among men rather than face machines." What this meant, however, was that after the war, advanced technology-related careers were more open to naval men than to Army men of equivalent rank.

In affiliating with a small company, or in organizing one, the Army officers frequently turned to their own Academy class, or ones close to it, for help. Small companies formed by a few officers, while they seldom grew to be major industrial enterprises, often survived. As they became stable, they began to more openly solicit business from former fellow officers. The magazine of the Army Officers' Association, Kaikō, is replete with advertisments from these companies. They offer products or services in wording determined, it would seem, to emphasize the graduating class number of the advertiser, which is always given. Classmate groups have come to be an important force in the officers' readjustment. Dozens of these associations now play a part in these men's family careers, for there are frequent requests for assistance in finding mates for one's children. They have evolved into a network of Cadet School Associations and Military Campaign Associations in a bewildering variety of permutations.

The experience of officers who were able to enter the larger corporations (especially if they started below the execuitve level, as most did) was almost universally undistinguished. Their employment records show little upward mobility; instead one reads of lateral movement from one satellite company to the next. The slot in the Japanese corporate structure that does seem to have evolved for men of the officer corps is that of "spiritual advisor." In the 1960's such careers opened to many former officers, men by then in their fifties or early sixties. Their function is to empart something of prewar spiritual education to today's youth. At least one former officer has built this into a lucrative business, now a full-time one, by taking young company employees on retreat to his camp in the hills and putting them through a regimented week, with only himself as instructor. The fee is quite substantial and more than paid for the *mugi-meshi* (the mixture of barley and white rice which formed a major part of the diet in military schools before the war) the men consumed. One university, the Kokushikan Daigaku (which might be translated as Patriots' University), has enough former military officers on its faculty and administration that the place resembles a Military Academy reunion.

146

Table 7.4. Postwar Occupational Distribution, in Percentages,
Among Respondents From Selected Japanese Military Academy Graduating Classes

| Employment Experience | Graduating Class and Year | | | | | | | |
|---|---|---|---|---|---|---|---|---|
| | (Percent of Respondents in Each Class Having Each Experience) | | | | | | | |
| | 23rd | 27th | 33rd | 36th | 40th | 44th | 48th | 56th |
| | 1911 | 1915 | 1921 | 1924 | 1928 | 1932 | 1936 | 1944 |
| | (N = 12 | 46 | 64 | 64 | 48 | 86 | 92 | 27) |
| | % | % | % | % | % | % | % | % |
| Business/Company | 67 | 67 | 62 | 98 | 96 | 65 | 94 | 85 |
| Private/Self-employed | 8 | 11 | 19 | 19 | 19 | 27 | 27 | 11 |
| Official/Government | 17 | 26 | 34 | 45 | 25 | 32 | 37 | 30 |
| Military/Defense | 0 | 0 | 2 | 3 | 10 | 41 | 49 | 15 |
| Education | 25 | 6 | 8 | 8 | 15 | 8 | 13 | 7 |
| Agriculture | 17 | 6 | 16 | 16 | 15 | 21 | 23 | 7 |
| Non-profit association | 25 | 22 | 20 | 20 | 15 | 9 | 9 | 4 |
| War criminal | 8 | 6 | 0 | 5 | 4 | 1 | 1 | 0 |
| Extended unemployment | 42 | 15 | 12 | 0 | 0 | 4 | 2 | 4 |
| Professional/Licensed | 0 | 0 | 0 | 3 | 2 | 2 | 2 | 4 |

Note: Totals come to more than 100% because of multiple responses.

By the mid-1950's, career shifts from company to company seemed to be a thing of the past for most men. They seem to have reached a point where they could once again assert themselves. They make specific reference, in their responses, to their status *shachō* (president), *jūyaku* (director), or *torishimari yakuin* (general manager). There might be only five employees (as is true of some of the printing companies I have seen) or it might be 50 and on rare occasions 500, but the post is an important one. This status consciousness may well be a reflection of Japanese society at large; or it may be a reassertion of the self-identification that for officers was so hard to find in the first decade after the war.

One side of the postwar experience which is of great interest is how a man sought to reintegrate his military "career" with his other life careers. Family needs and the problems of individual "subjective career" choices now intruded where little thought seems to have been needed or given before. The military officer's role — its stoicism, its frugality, its simplicity — had often substituted, as it were, maxims for choice in family relations. Wives were to support husbands in their role, children were to become officers or officers'

147

wives, and discipline was to be enforced by "presence." Suddenly the officer found that he had to assume the responsibility for his family's welfare — no institution would do it for him and no institution would support him in his former assumptions, either.

In the postwar years, officers who had at times been sublime in their separation from such mundane concerns, were thrown back on family resources. "We returned to my wife's family's home area and engaged in farming," "I went to my family's land to farm, but we were unable to support ourselves, so we went to my wife's home," and "I went to work for my brother's company" are common descriptions. One can speculate on the evolution in human relations between couples that may have occured. Certainly, the officers' wives I have met so far are more than just strong ladies.

One tragic group are the prisoners of war, especially the survivors of the Soviet camps in Siberia. These men often had to wait years before they could return to Japan and even for the youngest, men just out of the academies who might have redirected themselves relatively quickly, there was a long delay in the "lost years." They share a feeling, even more intensely than other officers (although it seems present in nearly all) that they were spared death for no apparent reason; and they show other signs of what Robert Lifton calls "survivor guilt." (1967: 35)

Quite a different experience was had by the Sugamo Prison "graduates." Eleven inmates of Sugamo completed my questionnaire; their attitude was expressed in statements such as these: "Sentenced to life imprisonment 1948/Became company president 1955," or "Served seven years in Sugamo, then became an official of the Japan Motorboat Association." There is certain defiance, though little real bitterness. The respondents seem to consider Sugamo to have been a stop on their progress through the years, but not as a gap.

The one career line which emerged in the postwar era, and which would seem at first glance to be a natural option for the former officers, was that of Japan's Self-Defense Forces. The National Police Reserve and the Self-Defense Forces, which slowly came into being following the outbreak of the Korean War, did open a career option to members of later Academy classes. Forty percent of the class of 1932 respondents and almost half of those from the 1936 class served in the Air and Ground Self-Defense Forces (SDF). Yet service in the SDF is a very different military career from that in the Imperial Army.

The Self-Defense Forces are not even openly recognized as an Army, a Navy, and a Air Force under the Constitution of postwar Japan. Service in the SDF, in contrast with that in the Imperial Japanese Army, carries much lower social status. In fact, the uniform of the SDF is not a matter of pride to many who wear it and there have been protests against the rule that officers must wear their uniforms at all times when coming from and going to work.

Former officers who applied to the National Police Reserves and the Self-Defense Forces had to openly profess their rejection of militarist ideology and they had to accept, nay, endorse the current ideological climate with sufficient enthusiasm to please their interviewer. Some men only gradually were able to overcome feelings of guilt at wearing the "enemy's uniform" or deserting the spirit of their dead comrades. Of even greater importance, a man entering the Self-Defense Forces, even if his former rank was restored, could not view what he was doing as a logical extension of his Imperial Army service. From the SDF's point of view, former Imperial Army officers were seen as a temporary necessity but they were really stopgap officers, except for the few who rose to the very top, who could hold the senior ranks until the Defense Academy's own graduates had matured. The Defense Agency, a civilian bureacracy, sits in control where before the Army took second place to no one. In the Ground Self-Defense Force it was years before one could call a tank a tank and a gun a gun.

However, despite this situation, a great many former officers jumped from civilian positions which seemed settled in order to once again put on the uniform. Whether this was out of a motivation to serve the country, yearning for the military career — however truncated — or malaise at their postwar life, or complicated permutations of these and other factors, it seems to me quite important that such a large number of former officers turned their backs on civilian life and opted again for a military career, even in an "antimilitaristic" military.

This gives rise to the question of how persistent their earlier training is, particularly their professional socialization into the idioms and thought patterns of the Imperial Army. Extensive contact with them, including men of different cohorts with wide divergences in background and experience, cautions me not to make any sweeping general statements. These are highly complex individuals. The very characteristics that helped them to achieve their childhood goals of entering the Military Academy and that had set them on a course which was clearly defined early in life; the pride and confidence with which they carried out their duties; and especially their consciousness of being members of an elite — a many-leveled awareness of being apart, but above, first as members of the Army, then as officers, and finally as reinforced by their achievements in rank, command, awards, and the respect paid them by their peers, all tied to their fundamental belief that their "career" motivation of national service was pure in contrast to the selfish motives of their contemporaries, all seem to be very much present among former officers today. Their talk of their careers in the past tense is full of pride. Speaking of themselves and their postwar experience, they often dwell on their military life.

Tsurumi Kazuko, in her thought-provoking and extremely sensitive studies of military education and the condemned war criminals, created a typology which has some utility here (1970: 144-145). One type is the "ever-committed," which she uses to denote acceptance of Japan's war aims (145), but I use to indicate acceptance of the military socialization process. One can see among the former officers an "ever committed" attitude of sorts even thirty years after the end of their Imperial military service. After all their postwar experiences, the majority emphasize over and over again how important their early socialization was. The career upheavals which they went through seem for many almost to have proved the worth of that socialization.

Many of the officers say of their early education and its pattern of life that although it is deficient in some "small ways" (usually they criticize technical matters rather than ethical or personal ones), they found it an excellent preparation for life. A member of the class of 1924, who served on the Board of Directors of five companies after the war, put it this way:

> I am really grateful for the spiritual education I received founded on the Imperial Rescript on Education and the Imperial Precepts for Soldiers and Sailors. I learned from this the spirit of sacrifice and a view of life which has become a conviction. I learned how to judge situations which has been a useful skill for me down the present day. Technical education was not deep enough, but was conducted in a broad range of subjects, sufficient for my duties, and even after the war this has been of assistance to me.

This commitment to the values of their military education is strongest among members of the earlier classes. A member of the class of 1915, who served as a member of his municipal committee in his home prefecture of Tochigi, and who worked in a nursing home, and later founded a hotel for the poor, wrote, "I received a disciplined spiritual and technical education. They were perfect and I am, even now, proud of having received that education."

Such views are often linked with what might be called an inability to separate the military career from prerequisite components in that career. A member of the class of 1924, who worked as a farmer until 1952, then as a security guard down to 1957, before becoming a manager of a spinning company, was able to state:

All the education in military schools was really perfect. I believe this even now. There is a Japanese proverb that says, "If you win, you are the government's army and if you lose, you are a rebel army." Of course military education is attacked because Japan lost, but under the circumstances, there was no other way of education.

It seems to me vital when looking at the postwar careers of former officers to think in terms of their commitment to their "first life." Colonel Shimanuki reminded me that his reasons for choosing the military career were really quite simple:

I wanted to follow my father, who was an officer, in the work most worthwhile in serving the nation. All five of my brothers entered the Cadet School and Military Academy. It was natural for me to become a *gunjin* (military man). At that time, *gunjin* were respected.

Military men adjusted to the changed circumstances after 1945, but a great many of them, whatever their postwar careers, still see themselves in terms of their "true" career.

## References

Baerwald, Hans H.
  1959  The Purge of Japanese Leaders under the Occupation. Berkeley and Los Angeles: University of California Press.
Cook, Theodore F., Jr.
  1978  The Japanese Reserve Experience: From Nation-in-Arms to Base-Line Defense, *In* Supplementary Military Forces: Reserves, Militias, Auxiliaries, Louis A. Zurcher and Gwyn Harries-Jenkins, eds. Beverly Hills: Sage Publications.
Elder, Glen H., Jr.
  1977  Family History and the Life Course, Journal of Family History, 2(4): 270-304.

Feit, Edward
1973    The Armed Bureaucrats. Boston: Houghton-Mifflin Company.
Hughes, Everett C.
1971    Cycles, Turning Points and Careers. *In* his The Sociological
        Eye. Chicago: Aldine.
LeVine, Robert A.
1978    Adulthood and Aging in Cross-Cultural Perspective. Social
        Science Research Council. Items 31/32(4/1), March 1-5.
Lifton, Robert J.
1967    Death in Life;   Survivors of Hiroshima.   New   York:
        Random House.
Shūkan Yomiuri
1980    Rikushi, kaihei shūshin katsurochū 2000 nin [Two thousand
        escaped Military and Naval Academy Graduates],   39(13):
        32-55.
Tsurumi Kazuko
1970    Social Change and the Individual; Japan before and after
        Defeat in World War II. Princeton: Princeton University Press.

*Part Four*

# WORK, FAMILY AND
# THE HANDS OF TIME

One of the great archetypes of our industrial age is that of the commuter, shuttling daily from home to workplace and back again. A fair number of adults may not fit the image, at least during part of their lives: many housewives do not, nor will the considerable number of people who are self-employed or are engaged in cottage industry (e.g., the Tachikui potters we meet in Chapter Ten). But most people, for much of their adult lives, move in the daily orbit of commutation. And whatever else the routine may do to us, perhaps it provides the benefits of segregation — by holding them apart, it allows us to manage the dissonant tempos of life imposed on us by family and by occupation.

For it is not just that home and office are two radically different social structures, they are radically different structures for the scheduling of lifecourse events. How people go along synchronizing these schedules, how they reconcile family plans with occupational ambitions, is a central issue in the study of adult human development. (On the academic scene, however, the issue tends to be obscured by a tug-of-war between family sociologists and industrial sociologists). It is a central theme in each of the next three chapters.

Each of these reports examines the issues of scheduling during a different phase of the domestic cycle. For James McLendon in Chapter Eight, it is the phase of mate-search, as he saw it in the lives of young "Office Ladies" in the corporation headquarters where he himself was employed. For Samuel Coleman in Chapter Nine, it is the phase of family formation, characterized by tough, intimate decisions about the timing and spacing of childbirths. For Jill

153

Kleinberg in Chapter Ten, it is the replacement phase, when one generation is recruiting and training its household (and in this instance, also workshop) successors.

Each of our authors points up a different aspect of the work/family tension. McLendon emphasizes how family goals shape an Office Lady's entire — and usually brief — career in the corporation. Coleman reverses the arrow of causation, showing how the tempo of working careers will raise sympathetic vibrations in the tempo of childbearing. Kleinberg, dealing with a cottage industry, sketches a rough balance of power between the "paired trajectories" of pottery enterprise and household descent.

A second theme — expectable enough when the subject is family — is that of intimacy, of how careers are adjusted to the demands of one's significant others. In Parts Two and Three, other people put in appearances from time to time, but mostly as work colleagues. They are nodes in one's network of sources for career information; they are examples for one to contemplate when forecasting his own career trajectory. But always there is an element of potential if not actual rivalry in the relationship.

In the family domain there may well be rivalries, too, but people also invest a heavy "developmental stake" in the lives of others. We can see this most readily for a housewife, whose personal career success will be measured not so much by what she does but by what others do — by how well her husband succeeds at work and her children at school. But the essence of family life is that it is a *community* of fate.

A third theme in these reports has to do with time consciousness, now viewed on a more complex level than earlier in the book. To the knowledge of organizational careers from Part Two and wider occupational paths from Part Three, Part Four adds an awareness of the domestic cycle and of the slow tides of turnover in the generations. Coleman, for example, shows how young marrieds carefully try to bunch and space childbirths, not just with regard to present demand-and-supply factors in labor for infant care but also with a view to the husband's probable career advancement and thus the family's capacity, a decade and more in the future, to provide support for two or more offspring simultaneously in college.

A key lesson to be learned from the lifecouse approach is this: not only do we need to investigate how behavior at one stage of the life cycle shapes a person's options at a later stage. We need to examine how clusters of people mutually shape each other's futures. As we do so, we need to keep in mind that much of the shaping is done by people in terms of their timetable consciousness of what, at various later stages, the consequences of a present act may be.

JAMES MCLENDON received his doctoral degree in anthropology from Harvard University in 1980; he is back in Japan conducting post-doctoral investigations of organizational careers. SAMUEL COLEMAN is Assistant Director of the North Carolina State Japan Center. JILL KLEINBERG is a Research Associate in Anthropology in the University of California, Los Angeles; she is now studying the careers of Japanese executives.

CHAPTER 8

# The Office:
# Way Station or
# Blind Alley?

JAMES MCLENDON

## Way Station or Blind Alley

Women make up about forty percent of Japan's labor force, a surprisingly large figure when compared with the minimal attention they receive in most studies of work organizations in Japan. On the other hand, the number of women whose careers fit the pattern of lifetime employment and promotion by seniority, usually offered as the standard wisdom on Japan, must be very small indeed. The majority of women leave the labor force after a few years — though the pattern is changing, as Karen Holden shows in Chapter Two.[1] Athough long-term employment — without, of course, any prospect of managerial responsibilities — is a thinkable option in some cases, a women is usually under great pressure not to exercise that option. When a young woman gets a job she is encouraged to think of the workplace not as the first stage of a working career but rather as a way station on the route to marriage.[2] For the women who do not find a marriage partner but go on working, the office becomes a blind alley. Their continued presence there serves only to remind them that they have failed to achieve their proper goal in life — marriage.

In this chapter I look at women's careers in a large general trading company (*sōgō shōsha*) — GTC for short — which I will call Yama Shōji.[3] While every organization has its unique features, I believe that the uncertainties and dilemmas female employees encounter in this company typify the career situation for women in most large Japanese organizations.

I worked as a full-time employee in Yama's Planning Department for two years, 1976-1978, while conducting research on the company's social organization. Prior to becoming an employee — the first non-Japanese ever hired by Yama — I had been informally affiliated with the company for three years and had conducted research there for three months in 1975. I returned to the company for three additional months of research in 1979 and have since then continued my association with the company. (For a good introduction to the GTC see Yamamura 1976.)

## Women at Yama and Elsewhere

Yama has approximately eight thousand employees, about half of whom are women. It is medium in size when compared to Japan's other eight GTCs.[4] Like them, and like other large Japanese companies, Yama does not assign its women to its overseas offices, of which there are about one hundred and fifty. So the actual proportion of women to men in the company's offices in Japan is considerably larger than employment figures would indicate. As in most Japanese white-collar organizations, men and women at Yama work together in Sections, work groups consisting on the average of eight to ten employees seated at a cluster of desks (for a description, see Rohlen 1975). Each is presided over by a Section Chief, who is usually aged 40 to 45 and — with a few conspicuous exceptions — male.

The GTCs differ from other large Japanese companies in the proportion of women to men and in the qualifications of the women hired. Compared to the GTCs, the proportion of women is larger in banks and smaller in manufacturing companies. The banks need a large number of young women to work as tellers at branches located throughout Japan. Most banks fill these positions with women who have just graduated from high school. These women, averaging only 18 years old when hired, can be expected to stay with the bank for at least five or six years before they get married and resign. In some cases banks with many branches in urban areas make special efforts to recruit women from rural areas and house them in dormitories operated by the banks in major cities. Coming from the countryside, they are thought to retain — better than their big-city sisters — the traditional feminine virtues of politeness, modesty, and obedience the banks prize in their tellers as part of a strategy for creating favorable customer attitudes in Japan's highly competitive banking sector.

157

A manufacturing firm's biggest personnel requirement is for production workers. Although some factories employ large numbers of women, most, particularly those in the heavy industrial sectors, hire more men than women. To meet their varied requirements, manufacturing companies recruit women from junior high schools for production-line jobs, from high schools for both production-related and clerical duties, from junior colleges for office jobs, and from universities a very few with technical or scientific training for research positions. These women come from both rural and urban areas.

The GTCs recruit their women almost solely from two-year junior colleges located in urban areas. Until about ten years ago women were hired from high schools, but the increasing complexity of international trade, it is said, has resulted in this raising of the educational qualfications required for entry. However, GTCs avoid hiring women who have graduated from four-year colleges for fear that these women will marry and resign after only one or two years of work.

Exceptions have been made at Yama in the past only where there was a specific requirement for a woman with skills in a language such as Chinese or Russian which is important in international business but rarely studied by men in Japanese universities. In 1982, for the first time and on a trial basis, a few female university graduates were hired as general, nonspecialized employees identical to those of junior college graduates entering the company. Women entering Yama must agree to live at home or with close relatives while working. This rule is intended — according to company men and women — to ensure that young single female employees live in a stable, secure environment in the big city. One effect of this rule is that almost all Yama women come from the urban areas of Japan.

## Why Women?

This study could have been written equally well about men in the company and about the ways in which they use the office as a place to find wives. In deciding which company to join, a young man takes into consideration its reputation for the beauty, charm, education, and personal cultivation of its women. During his first two or three years with the company, he may be more interested in going out drinking with his company chums than in seeking a wife. But by age 25 he is beginning to look at company women in terms of their suitability as marriage partners. Looking ahead, he begins to realize the importance of becoming a married man with family as a precondition for being recommended for managerial responsibilities in the company. The company is a marriage mart, then, for both men and women.

I focus upon the women because so little has been written about them. Furthermore, they offer possibly the most poignant demonstration of the inadequacy of the "groupist" stereotypes which have been so popular since the war in attempts to account for Japanese social behavior. For the women at Yama, in place of a communion of goals shared by the organization and its members, there is a complex symbiosis between, on the one hand, the organization using people for organizational goals and, on the other, people using the organization for their own personal objectives.[5]

Yama uses its women to do routine, low-skilled jobs at salaries lower than it would have to pay its men. The women, on the other hand, use Yama as a place to find husbands. Since they have almost no possibility of developing long-term work careers that would bring them into a closer identification with the organization's goals, women are primarily oriented to personal goals. The most important of these — the one in the pursuit of which they initially enter the company and in the achievement of which they hope soon to leave the company — is marriage.

### The Company Way to Marriage

Yama takes an active role in organizing social and recreational activities that allow company men and women to meet members of the opposite sex they would not nornally come into contact with in their daily work. In addition to the enjoyment for the participants and the benefits to the company in good morale, these activities play an important part in making possible the contacts that can lead to marriage.

From the point of view of a young woman, these activities are essential to her search for a mate and a major inducement to her joining the company in the first place. One way a women still in junior college finds out whether Yama has an active social life and attractive men is by talking to women from her school who have already graduated and entered the company.

Another way in which women students form opinions about which company to enter is by reading the magazines which specialize in informing young women about employment opportunities in large Japanese companies like Yama. The companies run advertisements featuring pictures of handsome, well-dressed young men together with young women taking part in company recreational activities or working in the office. The emphasis is upon the company as a place to meet young men and find husbands. Nothing is said about work careers for women. It is understood that marriage is the only appropriate life career for women, and these large companies portray themselves as ideal places to find desirable marriage partners.

## Marital Bliss, Japanese Style

The essence of marriage — as idealized and experienced by many men and women in Japan — is captured in a song written and sung by Sada Masashi, entitled Kampaku Sengen ("The Lordly Marriage Declaration"), that was one of Japan's top-selling records in 1979.

### KAMPAKU SENGEN

("The Lordly Marriage Declaration")

1. Before I take you as my wife,
   There's something I want to say;
   Some of my words may be rather harsh,
   But you better know what's on my mind.

   You mustn't go to bed before I do,
   And you mustn't get up after I do.
   Be a good cook and always look beautiful:
   Do what you can and it'll be okay.

   Don't forget that if a man can't do his work well,
   There's no way he can take care of his family;
   There are things only you can do,
   But aside from those, don't butt in:
   Just be obedient and follow me.

2. There's no difference between your parents and mine:
   Take care of mine as you would your own.
   Get along with my mother and sisters:
   It should be easy as long as you love them.

   Don't speak ill of people behind their backs,
   Don't listen to such talk,
   And don't give way to silly jealousy.

160

I won't be unfaithful,
Perhaps I won't be,
There's a good chance I won't be;
Well, anyway, get yourself a bit ready for such things.

Happiness is created by two people;
It is not something to be built through the pains of one alone.
You are coming to my place, casting your own home away,
So think that you have nowhere to return to:
From now on, I am your home.

3.  After our children are grown and we are old,
    You mustn't die before I do;
    Even one day later is okay,
    But you mustn't die sooner than I do.

    The only thing I'll need from you when I die,
    Will be for you to take my hand and shed some tears.
    and I will say I lived a good life because of you,
    I will definitely say it.

    Don't forget you'll always be the only women I love,
    The only woman I'll ever love,
    The only woman I'll ever love is you,
    The only one.

*Note:* My translation. Used by permission of the publishers of Kampaku Sengen, Free Balloon Company Ltd., and Free Flight Records Company, Ltd., of Tokyo.

A survey conducted by one of Tokyo's radio stations indicated that most young Japanese women regard marriage as described in the song as ideal. In talks with record shop employees in Shinjuku, I found that the record was being purchased primarily by young single women. Informal chats with friends — men and women of various ages and backgrounds — suggest that the song accurately expresses the prevailing idea of a desirable marriage: a strong husband who guides and takes care of his wife, who in burn supports her husband and is obedient. (On traditional husband and wife roles, see Pharr 1976: 305-308.)

## Women's Careers at Yama: The Marital Quest and the Pressure to Quit

Yama's career expectations, then, differ sharply for men and for women. The proper course for a man is to remain with the firm until retirement at age 58, or later if he becomes a Director. Upon for-

161

mal retirement, he can often continue to work in a subsidiary company well into his 60's. A woman, however, is expected to resign when she marries. If she does not marry during her mid-20's but chooses nevertheless to stay, or if she marries but continues to work, her co-workers tend to regard her as a burden. Though she has a right to job security until retirement age, just as a man does, she will have to stubbornly resist co-worker pressure in order to assert that right. (On male and female career tracks in Japanese companies, see Jones 1976-77 and Moloney 1978:2-3).

Women are well aware of this when they enter the company. So the chief source of uncertainty for a young company women is whether she will find a desirable mate before she has passed her period of marriageability *(kekkon tekireiki)*. If she is not married by the end of this period, the pressure on her to leave builds and intensifies. My purpose here is to examine how a woman copes first with this uncertainly and then — if she doesn't find a mate — with this pressure.

I sketch the career of a typical company woman. I follow her as she is recruited, trained, and then incorporated into a working Section of the organization. I examine her relationships with co-workers both inside and outside of the Section and indicate some of the ways in which she seeks personal cultivation. I look at strategies for mate-search; and I show what happens when the search fails.

The life of a woman in Yama Shōji can be thought of as consisting of two stages. The first covers her time of peak eligibility for marriage. The second stage begins after she had passed her prime, 30 being a pretty definitive dividing line, and ends with retirement at 58. Almost all women enter the company immediately after graduating from a two-year junior college at age 20. If they do not marry by age 26, chances decrease rapidly of their ever finding a husband who has a good job and who is not considerably older. By age 30, hopes for a normal marriage are considered to be almost nil.[6] Men who reach 30 as bachelors are similarly considered to be handicapped in finding a wife.

Gradual changes take place during both stages. The greatest and most rapid changes come, however, at some point between ages 28 and 30 when women begin to fear and then to realize that they will not easily find a husband either in the company or outside. In describing these changes, I use a simple schema which portrays the strivings of young women for self-realization through the pursuit of specific goals by means of shifting investments in three action domains.

162

By self-realization I mean the achievement of certain life goals upon which the society bestows value and from which the individual derives psychic satisfaction. The term self-fulfillment or the Japanese word *ikigai* ("purpose in life, meaning in life, reason for living") would equally well express my thought here. For company women, marriage is the most important source and measure of self-realization in the sense in which I use the term here.[7] For company men, by contrast, self-realization comes through work within the organization.

I use the term "investments" here to draw an analogy with a person seeking wealth through investments in three different sectors of the stock market, for example. In the same way that the wealth-seeker shifts his investments among market sectors and modifies his strategies in each according to his perception of what is called for in light of changes in business and the economy, the company woman shifts her investments and modifies her strategies according to her reading of what is required in order to maximize her chances of marriage — or if that no longer seems attainable, to seek self-realization in some other way — amidst the changing circumstances of her lifecourse in the company.

I identify three action domains: the personal, the interpersonal, and the impersonal. The *personal domain* refers to the personal cultivation of talents, skills, wisdom, and expressiveness. The *interpersonal domain* includes associations with family, intimates, and other persons known to the individual. The *impersonal domain* designates society at large as experienced most immediately through one's job-related activities in a work organization. In their pursuit of self-realization, individuals constantly reassess and reformulate their strategies and change their portfolio of investments in these three domains based on judgments of what changing circumstances require in order to achieve their goals.

The first and second "life-career stages" of company women can be thought of as being differentiated from each other by an intervening shift in goals and strategies that results when company women, between ages 28 and 30, reallocate their investments among these three domains in the light of their greatly reduced prospects for marriage.

Company women basically follow three career routes across these two stages; they get married and leave the company in their mid-20's; they leave the company without getting married, typically between ages 28 and 30; or they stay in the company, unmarried, until retirement. The first and second career routes end with the

163

first stage; I make no effort to pursue these ladies and observe their life careers after they leave the company. The third career route traverses both stages. The women who follow this third route entered the company with the purpose of making the company a way station on the road to marriage but, unable to find a mate, they find the company instead to be a blind alley. In following the women through their careers, I seek to show what meaning life in the company has for them during their time there — whether short or long.

## Joining the Company

A woman seeking employment with Yama Shōji comes to the company for a job interview in the middle of her second year in junior college, usually in September. (The Japanese academic and fiscal year begins in April.) She meets with a committee consisting of three men from the Personnel Department.[9] The factors that are given the greatest weight during the interview are the woman's personality and looks. She is asked general, open-ended, and sometimes intentionally vague questions to test her poise and resourcefulness in responding to a stressful situation, which the interview by design always is. For instance, she might be asked, "What did you think of school?" If she takes the question as a springboard to show her positive attitude toward hard work and cooperative effort, as in school clubs, she is considered suitable for employment. If, on the other hand, she candidly states her view that college was of little use in preparing her for life, although the interviewers might privately agree with her assessment of women's junior colleges, they would decide she has an attitude that would interfere with her functioning harmoniously and effectively in a work Section.

The committee also attaches importance to whether or not she is attractive. If she is beautiful, it is thought that she can help create positive client attitudes toward the company. Women are also considered to be a company morale factor. If young and pretty, they can create an atmosphere of feminine vitality and freshness which will inspire the men to give their best efforts to their work. Looks are valued, thirdly, because women entering the company are potential wives to company men.

A friend in the Personnel Department told of a weekend trip he took with a group of men and women from the company. When they arrived at an inn, the elderly lady innkeeper greeted my friend and said, "You are from a big company, aren't you?" "Yes, but how did you know?" "Your women are very beautiful. Big companies always have beautiful women."

Prior to the employment interview each woman takes a written examination evaluating her aptitude, general knowledge, technical knowledge, and personality. The examination is used merely to weed out those lacking the most basic qualifications, and very few fail; the interview is far more important.

Sometimes of even greater importance than either the examination or the interview, however, are the steps taken before the applicant's first visit to the company. These consist of recommendations from two sources: colleges attended by the applicant, and influential friends and relatives.

The recruitment process begins each summer when the Personnel Department announces to a number of women's junior colleges the quota of women Yama Shōji will accept from each college in the following April. If Yama asks for three women from Tokyo Jōshi Tanki Daigaku (Tokyo Women's Junior College), three women are sent for interviews. On occasion, Yama will turn down an applicant on the basis of an interview. The ties between Yama and the schools are, however, long-term and strong, and the schools have a pretty good idea of the qualities Yama wants in its company women. The rate of failure of college-recommended female applicants is, therefore, low.

The other main source of recommendations is the array of large companies with which Yama does business. A director from one of these companies can be of great assistance in helping a woman gain entrance to Yama. The director is usually a friend or relative of the woman's family, but in some cases he is a father trying to get his own daughter into the company. At a company entrance ceremony some years ago a Yama spokesman got somewhat carried away and talked in glowing terms of the close relationship being established with a major client firm now that the daughter of that firm's president was going to be working for Yama.

## Early Training

Training begins as soon as a woman receives official notice of her acceptance at Yama in October or November. From then until April she is required to submit on a monthly basis assignments that include essays written on themes relating to social responsibility, and instructional workbooks completed covering such skills as accounting, billing (*ukewatashi*), and business documentation.

The entrance ceremony on April 1st is attended by the newcomer men and women and by the company's directors. Parents do not attend; the new employees are supposed to realize that in entering the company they are now *shakaijin* (adult members of society) who should be responsible, self-reliant, and no longer dependent on their parents. The president gives a speech welcoming the newcomers and tells them of business conditions. Finally, he urges them to dedicate themselves to the company. The women, of course, know that these final comments are directed to the men — not to the women. About 120 women were admitted in April, 1979, and about 50 men. (See Rohlen 1974a: 35-40, for a description of the entrance ceremony at a bank).

During the following two weeks, the women receive their initial training under the supervision of the Personnel Department.[10] In addition to further instruction in business-related skills, the newcomers are taught how to answer the telephone and how to greet guests. Great attention is given to making sure that the women use the proper degree of politeness in speaking with customers and with men in the company. Other features of "women's work" are also emphasized, such as serving tea to the men in the Section at ten in the morning and at three in the afternoon, serving tea or coffee to guests whenever they visit the Section, and keeping the Section area clean and neat. (Newcomer training for men lasts six weeks and includes two weeks of "spiritual training" at a government training center and at the company's mountain lodge, both near Mount Fuji, and four weeks of lectures at the company.)

At the end of the two weeks the women are sent to their assigned Sections. The first six months in a Section continue to be a time of training. A senior woman, ideally one in her third or fourth year, is designated as a "junior adviser" to the newcomer and is responsible for introducing her to her duties. The adviser is often training her own replacement, as a newcomer normally is assigned to a Section in which one of the women has given formal notification of her intention to resign.

The adviser is expected to take her protégé out after work for dinner and drinks and to explain the ins and outs of social life in the company. Topics for discussion include how to behave toward senior women and toward men and how to deal with managers. The adviser rarely fails to give the newcomer an evaluation of each person in the Section and in the Department and to offer suggestions on how to get along with each. The skills required in relations with company men on a private basis outside the company are also discussed. The relationship between newcomer and adviser is never allowed to exceed six months. Though the dependency that develops during this period is believed to be valuable for instructional purposes, it is felt that the newcomer will not become an effective worker unless the relationship is terminated within a reasonable period of time. At that point the newcomer is expected to know how to perform her basic duties and solve her own problems. Thereafter, she is expected to get along by following the example of the senior women in the Section, and by trial and error. She is constantly under the eyes of others, and the pressure on her is compounded by the fact that she, being the most junior woman, is given a heavier burden of work than her seniors. The justification for this is that whe will learn the work of the Section best by doing it, and the more she does, the faster she will learn.

## Relations with Senior Women

During her first year, a woman depends upon the senior women in the Section for guidance not only in work tasks but also in the social ways of the company. Much of her time is spent with them performing "women's work." Lunch is almost always taken with them. The women often go to the cafeteria about five minutes before noon, eat quickly, and return to the Section area by 12:20. One or two of the men stay in the area during this time to answer phones. When the women return, the men who remained go to lunch. The women then gather at one of the areas that has a sofa and arm chairs and chat until work begins again at one o'clock. Sometimes women from two or three adjacent Sections will take part in these get-togethers, but the relations between senior and junior women in the same Section are regarded as the most important ones, for they are the basis for cooperation in the work of the Section.

The most senior woman in a Section — often no more than three or four years older than the most junior woman — is expected to play the role of housewife (*okusan*) for the Section by making sure that all of the men are provided with everything they need. She is the one who, without being asked to do anything, makes everything go smoothly. In the office, she orchestrates the work of the younger women; and she oversees the serving of tea, coffee, or other refreshments to Section men and guests.

167

JAMES MCLENDON

When the Section has a *bōnenkai* (end-of-year party; literally, "forget-the-year party"), *sōbetsukai* (farewell party), or other party out on the town, the senior woman positions the younger women strategically around the table so that every man is served by one of them. No man should have to pour his own drink or serve himself rice. If the waitress fails to bring enough bowls or chopsticks, it is the senior woman's responsibility to deftly rectify the error without creating a flurry or disturbing the gay atmosphere of the party. As the party reaches its close, she makes sure none of the men forgets coats or briefcases; and she herds the young women on their way home despite the urgings of the men to join in on a second party (*nijikai*) at a nearby club.

In short, the senior woman becomes a role model for the junior women. They are expected to develop the same sensitivity to every situation as it arises and to respond effectively and smoothly. A young woman arriving from junior college finds her powers of adaptability put to the test. In junior college, life was casual and she could be relatively independent. Of course, there were responsibilities associated with school clubs and homework assignments, but other people were not affected much by her actions. Suddenly, in the company, failure to do her tasks can have painful consequences for many other people. A woman newcomer's first challenge on entering the company is to learn how to function effectively in this environment. Senior women in the Section are the guides in finding the way through this new world.

Relations among women in a Section follow the *sempai-kōhai* (senior-junior) pattern and in this respect resemble relations among men. (Nakane 1970:25-35; Rohlen 1975:195-200). The younger women are to be respectful, and the senior women are to provide nurture and guidance. The absence of significant work tasks for the women and the implicit understanding shared by men and women alike that the women's association with the company is short-lived, however, results in a more rigid observance of seniority among women than among men. The men are all *tantōsha* (the person responsible for specific Section duties) and major contributors to the Section's work goals. They regard themselves as the inner core of the Section and share feelings of mutual confidence and partnership in their dealings with each other, regardless of age differences. These feelings are strengthened by the men's realization that they will be working together in the company until their late 50's or 60's. Women, on the other hand, perform only secondary, peripheral functions and are excluded from the inner core of the Section's relationships and work which are monopolized by the men.

The women, fundamentally, have only one common concern — indeed, they have come together in the company primarily in pursuit of one common goal — marriage. But to openly acknowledge this shared concern, particularly where it involves a specific man in the company, always runs the risk of engendering in the listener feelings of rivalry, jealousy, or envy more likely to destroy a relationship than provide a basis for building one. The women also know that any relationship formed between women is almost certain to be terminated as soon as one of them gets married, hardly a firm foundation upon which to build a relationship. In default of any alternative basis upon which to build their relationships, women in the company fall back on the seniority principle and enforce it much more rigorously in ordering their relationships with each other than do the men.

In departments or divisions where there are many women and few men, such as the General Affairs Division or the Billing Departments (*ukewatashibu*), these seniority ties among women often result in the formation of clique-like groupings of women that cut across several adjacent Sections. These groups frequently contain as many as 10 or 12 members and form under the leadership of a senior woman considered attractive in personality and appearance. Severe rivalries often develop among these groups, and a woman's social identity and standing in the company is sometimes defined more by her membership in such a group than by her position in her Section. Even in divisions where the balance of men and women is more even, such groupings of women, though on a smaller scale, are usual. To be left out of a group is to be an outcast of sorts. Among the more pathetic of such outcasts are the senior women who are at an age — 26 to 30 — where they would normally be group leaders but who lack the personal qualities. If these women stay in the company beyond age 30, their social isolation becomes all the more extreme. It is common knowledge among company women that getting along with company men is no major problem. The ones to worry about are the senior women, and it is their acceptance that must be won and kept if a young woman's life in the company is to be bearable.

These strict relations with seniors are, however, complemented by informal relations with peers or *dōki*: those who entered the company at the same time as oneself. (Nakane 1970:26-27). When the senior women have an appointment for lunch, the younger women get in touch with their *dōki* in other Sections. An invitation from a senior woman always takes precedence, but a young woman usually prefers to be with a *dōki*. Being with a senior is rarely a relaxed af-fair: the junior must be careful to observe the courtesies due a senior woman. Among peers, however, everyone is on an equal footing and can have a genuinely good time.

A young woman's first few years in the company are focused, then, upon learning the work and social requirements of her job. The personal, social, and work skills she acquires during this period are thought to be training not only for her job in the company but also for her career as a housewife. Her greatest concern during this period is with maintaining good relations with the senior women in the Section and in her more informal groupings.

## Shifts in Attention to Men

A woman must also develop cooperative relations with the men in the Section. During the first year, the senior women set an example and act as intermediaries between a young woman and the men. As she gains proficiency in her work, however, her direct interaction with the men increases. This becomes particularly true after the senior women standing between her and the men leave the company. She is expected to support the men in their work and to be so alert to their needs that she knows what they are before the men do. The initiative, however, must always be — or at least appear to be — with men. Regardless of what happens, she must try to keep a cheery disposition. Her proper work role is not very different from that of a Japanese younger sister, wife, or mother.

The men, for their part, are very careful in their work relations with the women, more so than with the other men. The Section Chief, particularly, must exert special efforts in his relations with the women. It is generally accepted that a man must be adept in the arts of human relations in order to become a Section Chief and that he must put these skills to their fullest use if he is to get his men to work for him wholeheartedly. (Rohlen 1974a:104; and 1975:204). For a Chief to gain the cooperation of his women, however, it is said that he must win their love. It is believed that a woman's behavior is more influenced by emotions than is a man's, and she is therefore not expected to be able to hide her feelings in the way a man can. A Chief must, according to company wisdom, be very gentle with his women workers and sensitive to their feelings. For a Chief to yell at a female subordinate for making a mistake, although an acceptable way to treat a man, is to risk reducing her to tears, casting himself as an ogre, and losing her cooperation. Particularly in Sections where women do much of the work — such as General Affairs or Billing — a Chief must play a role somewhere intermediate between that of an ardent suitor and a benevolent father, and at the same time take care not to excite jealousies.

The other men in the Section behave in an analogous manner, though relative age differences between the men and the women sometimes produce variations in the character of the relationship. Where the man is older, his role is similar to that of an older brother, husband, or father. Where the man is younger, however, problems sometimes arise. The man is thrown into a conflict of roles between that of man in the company — which naturally puts him in a dominant position with regard to women — and little brother or son, which places him in the position of a woman's dependent. In such cases, both the man and the woman must exercise great sensitivity and restraint if a cooperative relationship is to be preserved. One of the reasons why a woman is encouraged to marry and resign in her mid-20's is to avoid these sorts of complications in the work relations of the Section.

As a young woman gradually gains confidence in her ability and feels less pressure of work as the burden is gradually shifted to newly arrived juniors, she realizes that she must start to think more seriously about marriage. She begins to look at some of the men in the company more concretely in terms of their suitability as husbands, becomes more active in company clubs which have a large number of men (e.g., ski club, tennis club), and possibly even starts dating.

This shift is evident in another way. She attempts to make herself more attractive, both in appearance and in personality. She gives greater attention to cosmetics and hairstyle. She seeks to develop more poise and grace in her way of working and conducting herself. She starts to devote more time to flower arrangement and tea ceremony as part of a program of self-cultivation.

The company makes it known that women are expected to work for at least two years, and preferably for three or four, before they marry. When the Personnel Department recruits a woman who is exceptionally beautiful, intelligent, a graduate of a well-known junior college, and of attractive personality, the delight at having such a woman around is tempered with foreboding that her time may be too short for the company to get a return on the time and money invested in her. In one case, where Personnel's worst fears were realized, a woman entered the company in April and was almost immediately the object of hot pursuit by four bachelors in her own department and by several others from other departments.

171

In June she secretly started dating one of them, the man to whom she was the designated assistant. Their engagement was announced in October, she left the company in November, and the wedding was held in January. When the company magazine announced in May the birth of a son, the father got his share of razzing.

Such speed in marital matters is the exception. More commonly, a woman refocuses her attention gradually. During her first year she becomes an assistant to one of the men and sits at a desk beside his. If he has overtime work to do, she often will stay to help him. When the work is done, sometimes as late as 9 or 10 p.m., the man will, as a matter of course, invite her out for a cup of coffee and a snack to express his appreciation. Her circle of acquaintances among company men gradually expands through work, parties, club activities, and trips. These associations sometimes lead eventually to romance and marriage. Since men frequently work overtime and must travel one or two hours to reach their dormitories or homes, they have little opportunity to establish ongoing relationships with women outside the company.

When romantic relations develop between a man and a woman in the company, concealment is of the utmost importance. (Rohlen 1974a:237-238). In the example given earlier, because of my close personal relationship with the man, I was the only person in the company who knew that the two were dating before the marriage was announced. Their behavior during the day revealed not an iota of the deep personal feelings they had for each other. They had resolved that they would conceal the relationship until they had decided whether or not to marry. Once they made the decision to marry, the announcement elicited from others, as it always does, a mixture of surprise and of admiration at the skill with which the couple had conducted their secret romance.

Since the women in a Section are regarded as the "daughters" and "sisters" of the men, if it becomes known that a man and a woman in a Section are romantically involved, the fiction is shattered, and her usefulness as a member of the team is destroyed. She is also usually ejected from her women's group, especially if someone else in the group had been interested in the man. If a liaison is discovered before any announcement of marriage plans is made, the woman usually leaves the company immediately because of the speed with which social disapproval and gossip are mobilized to destroy her reputation and effectiveness. If no marriage takes place, the man will be regarded as irresponsible for having become intimate with a woman while having no intention of marrying her, and he will probably suffer damage to his career as a result. The woman is usually unable to get another job in a large company and must reconcile herself to employment in a smaller, less prestigious company. But the circumstances under which she left Yama may make it difficult for her to find another job she is willing to accept.

A woman's romatic relationships, of course, are not necessarily limited to company men. In fact, the longer a woman is in the company, the greater her attention is likely to turn to seeking a husband outside. The *omiai* (meeting with a view to marriage) is one of the most accepted ways of doing this. (Rohlen 1974a:238-240). Being a member of a large and famous company gives a woman an immediate advantage in an *omiai*: she has to some degree been preselected and given society's stamp of approval. Though the *omiai* is theoretically open to a woman at any age, once she gets to be 30 it becomes difficult to meet a desirable mate.

### Single and Turning 30: The Katatataki

If a woman reaches 30 and has no spouse, a radical change begins to take place. The optimism of her earlier years is replaced by anxiety and, sometimes, desperation bordering on panic. Fear of failure begins to affect both her self-image and her relations with her parents. A woman's mother particularly feels that her responsibility does not end until her daughter is married. The company woman's feeling of having let her parents down and being a burden upon them is often made worse by constant coaching from her parents about how to find a husband.

The frightening realization by the unmarried company woman as she approaches 30 that her chances of achieving marriage are now very small is constantly reinforced by the behavior of those around her. Men no longer treat her as they did a few years ago, and the younger women now regard her as someone belonging to another generation. By this age, almost all company men her age or older have already married. Since more than twice as many women as men are hired each year, the competition for company men as husbands is severe. When a woman approaches 30 and is still single, she knows that the chances of finding a husband in the company are practically zero.

Some women leave at this point. Their departure is often speeded if not compelled by pressure from other company members. One standard procedure is the *katatataki* (tap on the shoulder). The Sec-

173

tion chief or Department Manager typically comes up behind the woman working diligently at her desk and taps her on the shoulder, saying something like, *Mō yametara dō desu ka?* ("Isn't it time you resigned?")

Realistically, a woman of 30 cannot hope to be hired by another large and famous Japanese firm. She must take a job with a smaller, less well-known Japanese firm or with the Tokyo branch of a foreign company. The latter option is normally open only to those proficient in a foreign language and is usually chosen by women who do not dismiss as unthinkable the prospect of marrying a foreigner (though most male employees in these branches are Japanese). I do not know how much success these women have in finding a spouse after they leave the comnpany.

## The Obahan

Single women who assert their right to stay beyond what is regarded as a marriageable age enter upon the second stage of their careers in the company.[11] They are a small minority of the women who originally entered the company. Their reasons for staying are various. Many believe that they stand a better chance of marriage through *omiai* or other channels as long as they maintain a firm footing in a famous company. Most are also hesitant to lose their seniority, as reflected primarily in pay. Only a small number of these women ever get married, although they probably continue to have hopes. They try to meet eligible men through friends outside the company. Within the company they shift their efforts away from company social activities, where they increasingly encounter rebuffs and frustrations, to two other areas of endeavor — work and self-cultivation.

The meaning of these two areas of activity, however, changes radically. Previously, she had to prove herself in her work to show that she had what it takes to be a good wife. Self-cultivation, similarly, had previously been aimed at preparing herself to be a good wife and mother. Now these activities themselves come to replace marriage as alternate routes to self-realization. Before they had been the means to marriage; they are now unhappy substitutes for it.

Though there is little possibility for real growth in work responsibility for women in the years remaining until retirement, some women nevertheless seek meaning in their lives by devoting

174

themselves to their work. An infinitesimal number are rewarded with promotion to Section Chief. At the time I was in the company there were three such women, one in the President's Secretariat, one in Billing, and a third in the Steel Coordination Office. None of the three transacted business or had contact with customers, but they had actually achieved positions of responsibility. Some older women work as appointment secretaries to Department Managers or Directors; others have jobs of various sorts outside of the Sections. Only a very few are allowed to stay inside a Section as they get older. Many of them perform their jobs with perfection and dispatch, in spite of the lack of enthusiasm many of the men show about having to work with an older woman.

Most of the older men in the company are from the Kansai region, and they use the word from their native Kansai dialect, *obahan* instead of the standard Japanese word, *obasan* "aunt", in order to augment the sense of ridicule they wish to express toward these older women. Other disparaging terms used in reference to older women in the company are *isuwatchatta* ("she hung on to the bitter end," "she became a permanent fixture") and *ikazu goke* ("old maid," "spinster"). The original meaning of this second term is a widow who doesn't remarry. In the traditional ethics this was the virtuous course of action for a widow even if still young, attractive, and pursued by many serious suitors. In the company the term is used with cruel humor and disdain to refer to a woman who was eager to find a husband but was "forced to be virtuous" and stay single because she was unattractive and had no suitors. An invidious comparison is implied with the "normal" women who use their work in the company as a *koshikake* ("a temporary job," "stop-gap work," "a post occupied temporarily until the time comes to move to a more important post") while waiting for marriage.

The other route older single women turn to is personal cultivation. One older woman I know is an avid golfer, paints very well, and uses her vacations to take trips overseas. Another, probably in her early 50's, asked my advice about where to begin the study of English, as she had received her education when English was not taught in school. Her interest in learning English was both a form of self-cultivation and an effort to improve her job performance since she had just been transferred to a position where she would be having contact with foreign visitors. Several of the older women are accomplished in tea ceremony, flower arrangement, and calligraphy, as well as in other traditional arts.

175

These women also make great efforts to remain young-looking. Company women of all ages wear the same uniform, so clothes are no indication of age. The success of several such older ladies in disguising their age made a great impression on me. In one case, I saw a woman who had recently entered an adjacent Section and I assumed she was a newcomer. When I referred to her in these terms in talking with one of the men in her Section, he grinned broadly and told me she was almost 30. He thereafter informed her of my error, and she became my great friend. An even more startling case involved a woman who worked in another adjacent Section. By her girlish manner, young hairstyle, trim figure, and submissive air, I had assumed for over a year that she was still in her late 20's. You can imagine my shock when I learned she was in her early 50's.

Some women continue to work after they are married. The company has no rule requiring that women quit when they marry, but most Sections prefer not to have married women because marital duties interfere with overtime work and with participation in Section outings and weekend trips. There are notable exceptions, however. There is even one case of a married woman being hired. The China Trade Office has a woman who lived and worked in China for many years with her Chinese husband. Her knowledge of China and of the language made the company eager to hire her even though she was at the time in her 40's, married, and the mother of three. In 1981 she was promoted to Section Chief, thus joining the select group of three or four women of managerial rank in the company.

There is a different psychological quality to be found in older women who are married as compared to those who are single. It's possible that the company allows only the most able married women to continue working, but married women clearly have more self-assurance and ease in interacting with others. Older single women sometimes exert frantic efforts to win approval of others, as if the company were everything for them. The married women, on the other hand, seem to have greater self-confidence and inner calm arising from their secure position as wives and mothers. Since this is generally accepted by Japanese society as the proper career for a woman, these older married company women regard themselves — and are regarded by the company — as successes in life. As a result, they are spared much of the open disdain and ostracism the older single women must endure. Whether married or single, however, these women are, generally speaking, not welcome in the company. Most employees would like to see them replaced by fresh young women just graduated from junior college.

With the slowdown in the Japanese economy, career uncertainty for older women in the company and the pressure for them to quit has increased in the last few years. In addition to decreasing the number of recruits hired each year, the Personnel Department has been encouraging older women to retire early. In exchange they are offered full payment of all retirement benefits they would normally receive at age 58. Personnel eliminated 800 women from the payroll by these means during 1977-1978. This is about a one-fifth cut in the size of the company's female work force. Younger, lower-paid women take over the duties of the older, higher-paid women who leave. What little security older women in the company once enjoyed is now being further undermined.

## Conclusion

During most of a woman's first career stage in the company, ages 20 to 28, there is a steady shift in her investments away from the impersonal (job) domain to the interpersonal (relationships) and personal (self-cultivation) domains in her search for a marriage partner. It is important during the first couple of years that she not only become competent but also be regarded as such by others. Her reputation for being a diligent and effective worker can influence her marital prospects. While being trained in her job, close ties with the senior women in her Section are essential; once she has learned her job, however, her attention turns toward associations with men as the way to meet a marriage partner. She also directs more of her energies to making herself attractive and developing her talents.

For those who are successful in their mate-search during this first stage, company life ends and "self-realization," as the term is being used here, is achieved through marriage. For those who are not successful, desperation begins to set in between age 28 and 30. The women who at this point do not marry and do not leave the company to seek a mate elsewhere begin what I consider to be the second stage in a company woman's career.

As she reaches 30, she begins to withdraw — or, more correctly, to be excluded — from the associational activities of both men and women. In many cases, the job again becomes important to her as it was during her first two years with the company. Personal cultivation in arts or skills frequently acquires an even greater emphasis than it did in her mid-20's. But this shift in investments is part of a shattering upheaval in a company woman's whole understanding of life and of what it has to offer.

As marriage, the all-important goal, becomes unattainable, the very meaning of the quest for fulfillment changes. Originally, strategies were pursued in the impersonal, interpersonal, and personal domains with the hope of winning the crowning reward of marriage; later, with the loss of such hope, strategies in the three domains become activities aimed at escape from despair rather than means to fulfillment. To return to the analogy of the investor on the stock market, the woman is no longer seeking wealth: she is now merely trying to limit her losses. She must reinventory her life, and find new goals around which to reorganize it. She has 28 to 30 more years to go before formal retirement. During these years of vitality — but underutilization by the company — she must struggle to find new avenues for life expression and fulfillment.

I have looked to the women of Yama to carry the burden of my argument because I believe they can do it more ably than can the men. The women, shaped by Japanese society, come to the company with a personal purpose — namely, marriage and early retirement from the company — which is far removed from organizational goals. The women in their relationship with the company demonstrate the simple truth that organizations and people, in Japan as elsewhere, are in a symbiotic relationship in which each side uses the other and in which organizational and personal goals become entangled in a complex manner.

The relationship between the company and its women — whereby the company uses the women during their youthful days for menial, routine, dead-end jobs at low salaries while the women use their youthful days in the company to prepare for marriage and to find a husband — does not offer the women at Yama the opportunity to pursue meaningful work careers. This pattern is not unique to Yama; it is found in almost every Japanese company. The lack of opportunity for women to develop work careers in companies reflects the attitudes of the society at large.

Changes are taking place. The young women at Yama in the early 1980's are more varied in their interests and life plans than they were in the late '70's. One young woman who entered the company in 1981 is hoping to persuade the company to send her to the United States to study for two years, at company expense, in the same way that men are sent each year. Though she has little chance of succeeding in this effort, her plan shows a remarkable change in expectations among young company women, and it will be largely through such shifts in attitudes among its employees and among Japanese in general that the company itself will change.

An even more startling indication of change is Yama's decision in 1982 to hire a young American woman with a Master's degree from a leading American university as the company's third non-Japanese employee — the successor to my own successor. She was selected from 30 candidates, both men and women, through interviews conducted at locations throughout the United States. In 1976 it was almost unthinkable to hire a non-Japanese; the company has now actively recruited a person who is not only non-Japanese but also a woman to do the work normally done by a man.

Other signs of change are evident. The report in mid-1982 of the Women's and Young Workers' Problems Council, an advisory panel to the Ministry of Labor, calling for an end to sexual discrimination in employment is one such sign. (*Japan Times*, 1982:2) But fundamental changes in women's work careers in Japan will proceed only as fast as changes occur in attitudes in the larger society concerning the proper roles of women in the home and office. And these changes are likely to occur slowly.

Dedicated to the women of Yama Shōji —
wherever they may be now . . . .

## Notes

1. Molony (1978:3-4) also sees increased opportunities for Japanese women to pursue work careers outside the home.

2. Jones (1976-1977) found this idea expressed by a manager of an electrical company, interviewed by *Asahi Shimbun*, who said that "women employees do little more than serve tea and perch on their chairs until marriage. Marriage is a woman's true happiness, and all women can do is to keep house and rear children."

3. Yama, meaning "mountain," is the name I have made up for the GTC where I worked. "Shōji" is commonly used in company names and in such cases can best be translated as "Trading Company." So the English name of my company, were it to exist, would be "Mountain Trading Company."

4. The figures given for Yama are intentionally altered to prevent easy identification of the company. These changes, however, are unlikely to result in any serious misrepresentation of the company's size, character, or operations.

Japan's Big Nine GTCs, in descending order of size by total sales, are Mitsubishi Corporation; Mitsui and Co., Ltd.,; C. Itoh and Co., Ltd.; Marubeni Corporation; Sumitomo Corporation; Nissho Iwai Corporation;

Toyo Menka Kaisha, Ltd.; Kanematsu-Goshō Ltd.; and Nichimen Co., Ltd.

5. I am indebted to Solomon Levine and Susan Pharr for their help in arriving at this formulation of the relationship.

6. Bandō (1977:15-16) notes that "the desire among women to get married increases with every year of age after they turn 20. It reaches a peak when they are 25, and thereafter suddenly decreases. In particular, the decrease generally becomes more marked when they pass 30, and, on the contrary, there is a marked increase in the number of those who state they have no desire to marry."

7. Vogel (1979) indicates the importance of marriage to Japanese women when she says that "the role of the housewife is *the* socially expected and socially approved role for women," that "marriage in Japan is a woman's life-time employment," and that it is "her mothering, her caring for her family that gives a housewife her self-definition and her *ikigai* (her purpose in life)."

8. Brown (1974:185-186) describes the way in which Japanese men shifted their sense of identity and personal worth from family to government ministry and economic enterprise during modernization, with the result that "a man's worth, his character, or his status is determined by the extent of his firm's participation in the economic life of the nation." Given the continued belief that a woman's proper work is in the home, the word "man" here should be taken literally, that is, as referring specifically to men, not generally to humans.

9. Carter and Dilatush (1976: 78) discuss the selection process for women at another *sōgō shōsha*. Rohlen (1974a:63-73) presents the selection process for men and women at the bank he studied.

10. Rohlen (1974a:192-211) details the training for both men and women at his bank. Carter and Dilatush (1976:78) point out that women in offices "receive training only in specific job skills like telephone operator duties and things related to their hostessing-type work."

11. On the problems of older single working women in Japan see Shiozawa and Shimada (1976).

## References

Bandō Mariko.
    1977    The Women of Japan: Past and Present. About Japan Series No. 5 Tokyo: Foreign Press Center.
Brown, William.
    1974    Japanese Management: The Cultural Background. *In* Japanese Culture and Behavior, Takie Sugiyama Lebra and William P. Lebra, eds. Honolulu: The University Press of Hawaii.

Carter, Rose, and Lois Dilatush.
 1976 "Office Ladies." *In* Women in Changing Japan, Joyce Lebra, Joy
   Paulson, and Elizabeth Powers, eds. Boulder: Westview Press.
Clark, Rodney.
 1979 The Japanese Company. New Haven: Yale University Press.
Cole, Robert E.
 1971 Japanese Blue Collar: The Changing Tradition. Berkeley and
   Los Angeles: University of California Press.
Doi Takeo.
 1973 The Anatomy of Dependence. Tokyo: Kodansha International.
Dore, Ronald.
 1973 British Factory — Japanese Factory: The Origins of National
   Diversity in Industrial Relations. Berkeley and Los Angeles:
   University of California Press.
Japan Times
 1982 Panel says Japanese Firms Should End Sex Discrimination.
   May 9:2.
Jones, H. J.
 1976-1977 Japanese Women and the Dual-Track Employment System.
   Pacific Affairs 49 (4, Winter): 589-606.
Lebra, Joyce, Joy Paulson, and Elizabeth Powers (eds.)
 1976 Women in Changing Japan. Boulder: Westview Press.
Lebra, Takie Sugiyama.
 1976 Japanese Patterns of Behavior. Honolulu: The University
   Press of Hawaii.
Molony, Barbara.
 1978 The Ephemeral Work Force: Female Temporaries in a per-
   manent Employment System. Paper prepared for the Associa-
   tion for Asian Studies Annual Meeting, Chicago, April.
Nakane Chie.
 1970 Japanese Society. Berkeley and Los Angeles: University of
   California Press.
 1974 Criteria of Group Formation. *In* Japanese Culture and Be-
   havior, Takie Sugiyama Lebra and William P. Lebra, eds.
   Honolulu: The University Press of Hawaii.
Pharr, Susan J.
 1976 The Japanese Woman: Evolving Views of Life and Role.
   *In* Japan: The Paradox of Progress, Lewis Austin, ed. New
   Haven: Yale University Press.
 1981 Political Women in Japan: The Search for a Place in Political
   Life. Berkeley and Los Angeles: University of California
   Press.
Rohlen, Thomas P.
 1974a For Harmony and Strength: Japanese White-Collar Organiza-

tion in Anthropological Perspective. Berkeley and Los Angeles: University of California Press.

1974b Sponsorship of Cultural Continuity in Japan: A Company Training Program. *In* Japanese Culture and Behavior, Takie Sugiyama Lebra and William P. Lebra, eds. Honolulu: The University Press of Hawaii.

1975 The Company Work Group. *In* Modern Japanese Organization and Decision-Making, Ezra F. Vogel, ed. Berkeley and Los Angeles: University of California Press.

Shiozawa Miyoko, and Shimada Tomiko.

1976 Documentary on Postwar Women Living Alone. Japan Quarterly 23 (4, Oct.-Dec. 363-377.)

Vogel, Suzanne.

1979 The Professional Housewife. *In* Proceedings of the Tokyo Symposium on Women. Tokyo: International Group for the Study of Women.

Yamamura Kōzō.

1976 General Trading Companies in Japan: Their Origins and Growth. *In* Japanese Industrialization and Its Social Consequences, Hugh Patrick, ed. Berkeley and Los Angeles: University of California Press.

CHAPTER 9

# The Tempo of
# Family Formation

SAMUEL COLEMAN

One theme in this volume is the fit between public careers and private lives in present-day Japan. This chapter examines some of the events that constitute critical points in private life: marriage and the creation of a new family. Demographic statistics indicate the proportion of Japan's adult population that is likely to marry and when, as well as when and how many children will result. The figures contrast with those of other industrialized cultures in a number of respects: marriage occurs at a relatively late age in Japan, but only a small proportion of the population remains unmarried; the country's fertility rate is quite low, but so also is the proportion of couples who remain childless; only a minute percentage of all births take place outside of marriage, and childbearing is concentrated in a narrow age range among Japanese women.

Such features of marriage and fertility are typically analyzed in terms of economic variables, historical trends, or social factors such as education. There is, however, yet another dimension that may be of value in understanding the extent and tempo of nuptiality and natality, namely the culture of marriage. This may be defined as the functions and meaning of family life for husbands and wives. Unlike many of the economic and social variables that have been applied to the study of marriage and fertility patterns, the factors that emerge when conjugal life becomes the object of analysis are difficult to measure, particularly as one moves toward the more psychological functions of marriage such as companionship and sexuality. The application of these considerations to such hard classes of data as age at marriage is still a tentative exercise. Their refinement could prove worthwhile, however, because they can be used in a framework that integrates the social and economic facts of public careers with the texture of private life, resulting in a more comprehensive picture of how marriage and childbirth patterns are determined.

My own view of the Japanese family is based on observations made in the course of field research on family planning in the Tokyo-Yokohama conurbation between August 1974 and January 1977. The data include numerous interviews and discussions with Japanese specialists in family issues and family planning; a self-administered questionnaire survey distributed to patients at eight obstetrical hospitals and clinics that yielded 635 valid responses; and intensive interviews with 22 married couples. (See Coleman 1982 for a description of research methodology.) These data and the observations that resulted from participant observation in daily family life have been supplemented by the results of research conducted by Japanese social scientists and medical specialists.

Central to my analysis is the question of how husbands and wives interact. In sharp contrast to the emphasis on shared activities and emotional compatibility seen in the United States, the Japanese marriage operates in a deeper sex-role division of household activities and responsibilities, de-emphasizing compatibility. (Japan and the United States could well be at opposite ends of the continuum among industrialized cultures in this regard.) The Japanese pattern results from centrifugal pulls from the husband's workplace and the wife's commitment to childbearing.

## I. Marriage

Marriage in Japan displays a pattern unique among developed countries: only a small proportion of the adult population never marries, but marriage takes place at a late age. The United States, by contrast, has traditionally witnessed relatively early marriage among a broad part of the population, as have many Eastern European countries. A third pattern, late age at marriage combined with a large proportion of individuals never marrying, prevailed in some Northern European countries until the postwar period (Glass 1976). Table 9.1 compares Japan and other developed countries in terms of the proportions of never-married men and women in different age groups, and provides mean ages at first marriage for men and women under age 50.

The numbers in the table suggest that the three patterns were still evident as of the mid-1970's, despite a trend between 1950 and 1970

Table 9.1. Proportion of Males and Females Not Yet Married, by Age, 1970/1975, and Average Age at Marriage, 1974, Japan and Other Selected Developed Countries

| Country | Year | Men | | | | Women | | | | Male-Female Difference in Average Age at Marriage (1974) |
|---|---|---|---|---|---|---|---|---|---|---|
| | | 15-19 | Never Married 20-24 | 45-49 | Average Age at Marriage (1974) | 15-19 | Never Married 20-24 | 45-49 | Average Age at Marriage (1974) | |
| | | % | % | % | | % | % | % | | |
| Czechoslovakia | 1970 | 99.0 | 66.4 | 5.7 | 23.5 | 92.2 | 34.9 | 5.0 | 20.9 | 2.6 |
| Denmark | 1974 | 99.8 | 81.6 | 9.4 | 25.8 | 97.6 | 56.2 | 6.3 | 23.2 | 2.6 |
| England & Wales | 1974 | 98.1 | 64.8 | 10.1 | NA | 92.2 | 41.9 | 7.2 | NA | NA |
| Federal Republic of Germany | 1975 | 99.5 | 77.6 | 5.6 | 24.9 | 93.9 | 46.7 | 8.3 | 22.0 | 2.9 |
| France | 1972 | 99.5 | 72.9 | 10.9 | 24.2 | 95.3 | 50.1 | 8.0 | 22.1 | 2.1 |
| German Democratic Republic | 1975 | 99.0 | 63.5 | 2.4 | 23.3 | 94.2 | 34.9 | 8.2 | 21.2 | 2.1 |
| JAPAN | 1975 | 99.5 | 88.0 | 2.4 | 26.8 | 98.6 | 68.8 | 4.8 | 24.5 | 2.3 |
| Norway | 1975 | 99.5 | 75.5 | 12.0 | 24.8 | 95.2 | 50.3 | 6.4 | 22.3 | 2.5 |
| Sweden | 1975 | 99.9 | 91.0 | 13.5 | 27.0 | 98.7 | 75.2 | 7.1 | 24.6 | 2.1 |
| United States | 1975 | 97.4 | 59.9 | 6.3 | 23.3 | 90.7 | 40.3 | 4.6 | 21.2 | 2.1 |

Note: Average age at marriage computed from 1974 data in *United Nations Demographic Yearbook 1976* (UN, 1977) for men and women under age 50.

Source: United Nations (1977).

185

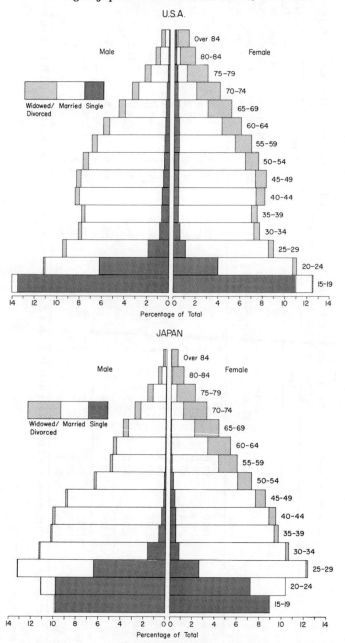

*Figure 9.1*: Marital Status by Age Distribution of Males and Females, in Percentages, Japan and the United States, 1970-1975

U.S.A.

Male

Female

Widowed/ Married Single
Divorced

Over 84
80-84
75-79
70-74
65-69
60-64
55-59
50-54
45-49
40-44
35-39
30-34
25-29
20-24
15-19

14  12  10  8  6  4  2  0 0  2  4  6  8  10  12  14
Percentage of Total

JAPAN

Male

Female

Widowed/ Married Single
Divorced

Over 84
80-84
75-79
70-74
65-69
60-64
55-59
50-54
45-49
40-44
35-39
30-34
25-29
20-24
15-19

14  12  10  8  6  4  2  0 0  2  4  6  8  10  12  14
Percentage of Total

Sources: Computed from the 1970 Census of the United States and the 1975 Census of Japan.

186

among Western women to marry earlier and in increasing proportions (Blake 1974). The population pyramids for the United States and Japan (Figure 9.1) also show the early/late contrast.

*Factors in the Extensiveness of Marriage in Japan*

The great majority of men and women in modern societies marry; what requires explanation is the margin of people in Japan who might have remained single if left to their own predilections. Certain aspects of the culture of marriage in Japan might explain how the balance tips in favor of marriage among these people.

Marriage for Japanese men is not subordinated to occupational career goals: it is integrated with them as a supportive element. One very strong theme portrays the married man with a family as more responsible and trustworthy; he has left youth behind and has become socially accountable, a true adult. A popular expression, literally "to solidify one's postion" *(mi o katameru)* not only reflects the sentiments, but is commonly used as an explanation of why men marry. "Social stability" as a motive for marrying ranks very highly in opinion surveys among single Japanese men who claim that they intend to marry (Fujin Chōsakai 1974:33; Yuzawa 1971).

These themes are not alien to the West, but they take on a greater significance in Japan because they appear to be strongly related to men's workplace status. Informants believed that men who either do not marry by age 30 or who become divorced suffer a distinct disadvantage in promotion. One interviewee, a 36-year-old college graduate in a managerial postion for a heavy equipment sales company, recounted his reasons for marrying:

> At that time I was nearly thirty. I really didn't care to get married at that time, but once you're past thirty and not married your clients can't trust you. My manager from a job I'd had in my college days at a department store kept telling me I should marry soon, and he kept trying to find a partner for me.

The importance of marriage to on-the-job functioning is suggested by the interest in subordinates' marriage plans often displayed by workplace superiors. The groom's supervisor figures prominently in the wedding banquet, and his dinner table speech is bound to include praise for the groom's workplace performance and the hope that the new bride will be an ideal helpmate.

The married state in Japan does indeed provide tangible elements of support for the working man in the form of domestic services.

187

When asked about domestic chores, husbands often replied that they took part if their wives were ill or exceptionally tired. Some explained their nonparticipation by saying that their work left them too tired to do anything after returning home, or that domestic tasks should be performed by women only. In an 11-nation time use study, Japanese men ranked lowest in average weekly time spent on household tasks and errands.[1] When men do participate in household tasks, these are very simple brief activities.

There are also indications that wives in Japan are more heavily involved in housework tasks than their counterparts in other industrialized countries. The same survey found that, unlike women in the other countries studied, Japanese wives who were not employed had less time for sleep then their husbands and their sleeping time was found to be almost one hour less than the average for European housewives (Keizaikikaku-chō 1973:64). Another revealing figure concerned wives' Sunday housework; in contrast with a decrease from weekday housework time in the West, the Japanese wife's time devoted to housework actually increased (Keizaikikaku-chō 1973:60; an exception is the category of childless housewives who are not employed). The group conducting the study interpreted this phenomenon as the wife's desire to "demonstrate" her diligence in housework to her husband, but an alternative interpretation more in line with my own observations is that it reflects the women's domestic service role or "self-sacrificing custom" (Fujin Chōsakai 1974:353). On Sundays, husband and children are home, and the wife spends more time seeing after their needs, in particular serving them meals and snacks.

Perhaps this additional domestic service feature of marriage attracts a portion of those men who would otherwise remain single. Young Japanese men stated that the domestic services provided by a wife are an attraction of married life; family sociologist Yuzawa Yasuhiko sums the prevailing view of marriage among young men as "an instrumentality for daily life" (1971:51).

Strong peer pressure to marry is also a noticeable part of the motivational equation, although the reasons for friends' and acquaintances' urgings are far less evident than employers'. It is enough to observe that the single man entering his 30's experiences disapproval from male workmates and former school classmates if he shows no interest in marrying. As their ultimate weapon, acquaintances might even accuse the bachelor of homosexuality.

The elements in Japanese social organization that encourage marriage for women appear even more compelling than those for men.

The "social stability" of marriage for women means a degree of economic security far superior to the livlihood offered by a single existence; the paucity of women's professional career pathways and the financial independence that they could offer is particularly noteworthy. Female labor in Japan is still used mainly as auxiliary work, and is treated as a temporary labor force in contrast to the permanent male labor force (Akamatsu 1969; Rōdō-shō 1975:13). Women's labor is thus concentrated in unskilled forms of work with little opportunity for job skill development or advancement (Rōdō-shō 1975:12,13). Since the employer has little or no investment in the woman employee's job skills, high turnover does not run counter to management interests.

The result is that relatively few women in Japan have occupations that could lead them to forego domestic and reproductive roles; for example, women occupy about 5.8 percent of administrative positions in Japan, as opposed to 18.7 percent in the United States and 11.9 percent in France (calculated using figures in International Labour Office 1975; cf. also Fujin Chōsakai 1974:81). Even in the field of education, where well over half of all primary and secondary school teachers are women, only 2.7 percent of all assistant principals and 1.1 percent of all principals are women (Fujin Chōsakai 1974:81).

Influence from workplace superiors may also serve as an incentive to marry. Since managerial policies that encourage women to leave their jobs for marriage are technically illegal in Japan, surveys of personnel policy toward female employees would be of little value for assessing pressure from superiors on single women to marry. Given the nature of Japanese women's labor participation, however, with its low investment in skills, employers probably welcome a higher turnover of female employees as well as their shift to part-time status upon marriage in order to minimize increased wages paid on the basis of seniority. Then, too, of course, a woman's marriage provides the indispensable counterpart to marriage for men: to the extent that married men become more desirable employees and colleagues, encouragement goes to women willing to marry and assume a supportive role.

Another factor that encourages marriage for women is the promotion of childbearing. As we shall soon see in more detail, the relationship between getting married and having children is strong enough, both in popular thinking and in actual practice in Japan, to be labeled synonymous.

The female employment pattern makes motherhood by far the

most accessible channel for self-development, recognition as a contributing member of adult society, and the opportunity for displaying skill and expertise. Childbearing is the touchstone of feminine identity. An author in the prestigious women's magazine, *Fujin Kōron,* neatly summed the prevailing sentiment:

> How does a women change when she marries and gives birth to children?..... This statement of the problem itself is fundamentally imprecise. It is not how a woman changes, but the fact that through marriage and childbirth she becomes a woman for the first time (Kurahashi 1972:60).

Unmarried women in their late 20's are particularly conscious of the relationship between childbearing and femininity, and complain that they are made to feel "as if you aren't a whole women unless you have babies," an observation made by a number of informants.

The best known source of interpersonal pressure on a young Japanese women to marry is her parents, particularly her mother. Parental persuasion typically begins as the daughter enters her early 20's, and intensifies as she approaches her late 20's. The pervasive threat is to be left behind, to be branded as undesirable — and, with that, a feeling of being abnormal and unfeminine.

## Age at Marriage

Why is marriage postponed if it is such a desirable state? Age at marriage is determined by a number of considerations that interact in a complex fashion. The culture of Japanese marriage itself deserves special attention, however, because its ramifications may be particularly far-reaching, exerting both direct and indirect effects on age at marriage.

The theme of the husband's capacity as economic supporter of his family receives considerable emphasis from both spouses. Husbands interviewed who used sex role ideals to justify shunning domestic tasks typically went on to emphasize the man's role as breadwinner and point out that they were providing the support for their families. Both husbands and wives tend to evaluate the man's performance as husband primarily in terms of his dedication to his work and his ability to support his family. A study of family role expectations conducted by Koyama Takashi and colleagues found Japanese wives' strongest expectations toward their husbands to be "enthusiasm for work"; the converse, wives' cooperation in economic matters, is lowest among husbands' expectations (1967:102-103).

Workplace demands diminish the Japanese husband's participation in domestic life, an observation that appears in the classic studies of urban life in postwar Japan (Dore 1958; Plath 1964; Vogel 1963). These commitments affect the husband's home life most directly through the number of hours that he devotes to this job. In the time use study mentioned previously, Japanese men ranked highest in hours spent at work (Keizaikikaku-chō 1973:54-55).[2]

The workplace may also take precedence in numerous ways that are less quantifiable. Gestures of involvement with wife and family are definite liabilities to the man's workplace reputation, the classic issue being whether or not the husband notifies his wife in advance of late arrival home from after-hours socializing with colleagues or overtime work. A weekly newspaper's informal survey investigating the wife's common complaint of "Why don't men say when they're coming home?" elicited this response from a 32-year-old bank employee:

> Unless you're a newlywed, something like an indiscreet phone call gives the mistaken impression to co-workers and superiors that "He doesn't have his house in order." What's more, if I called regularly, then they'd probably get all the more suspicious about my behavior. (*Sankei Ribingu* 1976).

Similarly, in an instance I encountered, a 28-year-old college graduate employed by a business consulting firm called home only when he was sure he could not be overheard by fellow emloyees.

The emphasis on maternity also encourages role segregation. Just as the husband's commitment to the workplace reduces his part in shared domestic tasks, the wife's commitment to childrearing accentuates her unique domestic role and diminishes task interchangeability. One expression of the focus of childrearing responsiblity on Japanese wives is their noticeable reluctance to rely on baby-sitters. This means that the couple with children is even more limited in time spent alone together than in the West; a survey of couples in Japan and then other countries (six of which are industrialized) ranked Japan lowest in the percentage of couples reporting that they go out for recreation together without their children (Sōri-fu 1973:23).

Shared leisure occupies a very small part of Japanese marital life. The kinds of leisure activities chosen by Japanese men and women may allow a common locus, but they are not typically shared activities. In general, a larger part of free time is spent in television viewing and resting than in other industrialized countries (Keizaikikaku-chō 1976:109-110). Sunday housework, in which increased effort is devoted to serving husband's and children's needs, also makes an important statement about the quality of the couple's shared leisure activities. The couple may be in the same place, but only the husband is enjoying leisure.

The prevailing sex role division of labor and leisure patterns provides a context for understanding the emotional content of Japanese conjugal life. The strength of these themes — of husband as breadwinner and wife as mother — imposes a high level of uniformity on couples, submerging individual personalities. When I asked spouses what they liked most about their partners, the wives consistently made reference to their husband's dedication to work and his dependability in that capacity much more than to shared interests or personality traits that they found appealing. More often than not, husbands referred to their wife's homemaking skills and ability to handle domestic matters smoothly. Typical of such husbands is a 38-year-old section chief at a major corporation, who said "I can just leave the whole household to her and she'll take care of things well." A few husbands made reference to their wife's personality traits, a favorite term being *akarui* ("bright" or "cheerful"). However, these men were unable to elaborate or to give specific examples of the expression of the trait; basically, they seemed to look to their wife for a pleasant and relaxing atmosphere at home, free from interpersonal problems.

Another typical theme for both spouses is the absence of a negative trait, the propensity to express dissatisfaction. The 33-year-old wife of the section chief (like her husband, a college graduate) said, "I like it that he doesn't gripe." A husband will say of his wife that she is "not bothersome" (*urusakunai*). Or he is apt to say of his wife's cooking, "I eat it all and never complain." When asked about household chores, one 35-year-old housewife (a junior high school graduate) replied that her husband did none, saying "In return for not complaining to me, he doesn't give me any help." These responses bespeak a high degree of emotional autonomy — if not a certain kind of emotional territoriality.

Japanese marital life style also affects sexuality: in part because minimal demands are placed on compatibility, sexuality as a source of mutual attraction is a weak theme. Despite a considerable decrease in the number of children born to Japanese couples in the postwar period,[3] a new ethic emphasizing sexuality for the sake of the couple's relationship has not arisen to replace sex for reproduction.

The primacy of occupational commitments for men also

downplays sexuality as a dimension of family relationships. Men's occupations are linked to male sexuality — as the widely displayed recruitment poster for the Tokyo Metropolitan Police Department proclaims, "A Man's Got His Job" *(Otoko wa shigota da)*. When workplace demands or work-related sociability take precedence over interaction with members of the opposite sex, it is an affirmation and not a denial of male identity. A man is praised if he treats romantic matters indifferently and concentrates his attention on work (or studies, if he is a student). It is said that he is "serious" *(majime)* or of "sound, staunch" character *(shikkari shita;* see also observations made on dating and other association with members of the opposite sex by Rohlen 1974).

Characteristics of the Japanese woman's identity also hamper a more positive approach to marital sexuality. Sexual inhibition is marked among Japanese females, who have far less latitude in matters of sexual expression and activities than do males. Since sex for the sake of pleasure is the male's domain, because it implies aggressiveness and self-gratification, the kind of sexuality that is the most emotionally comfortable for the Japanese woman is sex for the sake of reproduction (Coleman 1982).

This description of Japanese marital life is of course one of degree than of fundamental differences: Sex role divisions of domestic labor have not disappeared from Western households, Japanese couples are not devoid of emotional interaction, and sexuality is an element common to couples in nuclear families regardless of the culture. Consideration of the contrasts, however, can help us to understand why Japanese young people marry when they do.

Since compatibility plays less of a part in the functioning of the family unit, the social channels for pairing up marriage candidates in Japan do not incorporate the extensive exposure between the sexes so familiar to the United States, where prospective partners explore one another's personalities and tastes. The young are not encouraged to cultivate social skills for dealing with the opposite sex. The general rule for boys and men is "work first"; among students, preparation for entrance examinations requires a near-monastic existence. Although the public schools are coeducational, recreational activities are sex segregated, as are many activities at the workplace that would otherwise provide contact. One of the more noticeable examples is the company cafeteria, where males typically sit on one side of the room and females on the other.

The result is that Japanese youth are far less likely to have friends of the opposite sex than are their counterparts in other industrializ-

193

ed countries. An international study of youth conducted in 1972 found just that: only 17 percent of Japanese youth claimed close friends of both sexes, in contrast to a range of 47 to 72 percent among the youth of six European countries and the United States (Sōri-fu 1973:110-111).

The educational system evidently does not provide the opportunity for meeting prospective marriage partners in Japan that it does in the West. In the United States, increased education, together with the trend toward more cultural homogeneity, has helped lower age at marriage (Ryder 1974); and a similar combined trend of increased education for women plus lower age at marriage occurred in Europe between the 1950's and 1970's (Blake 1974). The educational process — in the United States, at least — promotes marriage in part through increased exposure to members of the opposite sex of the same age and similar intelligence and class background. Not so for Japan, however: Despite increasing participation in education for both sexes in the postwar period, age at marriage has not declined, as Figure 9.2 shows.

*Figure 9.2.* Average Age at First Marriage, Japan 1910-1977

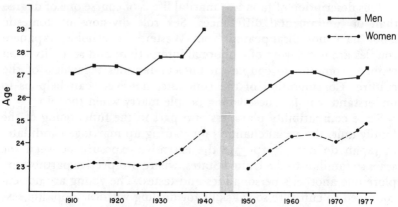

Note: Figures to 1940 are based on age at marriage registration
Figures for 1950 to 1977 are based on age at marriage ceremony
Source: Kōsei-shō 1979.

One reason is because Japanese education channels men and women who enter higher education into separate institutions. Whereas 86 percent of students in junior colleges in 1975 were female, women only accounted for 21 percent of students at four-year colleges and universities (calculated from figures in Monbu-shō 1976:221).

Because unmarried young people in Japan have fewer opportunities to meet, it takes more time to find an appropriate marriage partner. One indication that such lags exist emerged in a study conducted in Tokyo in 1968; the reason for not marrying earlier that respondents between age 30 and 34 mentioned most often was simply that there was no one who was a desirable marriage partner (Yuzawa, 1973:74-75).

The difficulty of finding an eligible person is probably the most important reason for the persistence of arranged marriages, which accounted for about 37 percent of new marriages in 1973 (calculated from figures in Kōsei-shō 1974). Granted, arranged marriages may constitute a political or economic strategy among property-owning families, but such cases are clearly only a small proportion of present-day Japanese marriages. Some parents insist on the chance to investigate the other party's background and then exercise the authority to approve or disapprove, but neither function is intrinsic to an arranged as opposed to a love match marriage. The critical feature, as Japanese social scientists define it, is whether the young couple meet one another on their own or are introduced by a third party. Arranged marriages are more likely to occur among older individuals, after they have failed to find an appealing prospect on their own. Average age at marriage is higher for arranged marriages among both men and women (Kōsei-shō 1968, 1973), and the proportion of marriages that are arranged increases steadily with each year of age among those marrying (Kōsei-shō 1968, 1973); there is a slight increase in the proportions of lovematch marriages among women marrying in their late 20's, however).

The amount of time required to find a suitable mate can be lengthened by changes in the relative sizes of adjacent age cohorts, because men are most likely to marry women from a younger age group; thus, a shrinking population means fewer eligible women per man, and an expanding population, the reverse. The population pyramid in Figure 9.1 illustrates the relationship between successive cohorts. Since the high-water mark for absolute number of births in Japan was between 1946 and 1950, a deficit of women in the most marriageable age group has occurred between 1975 and 1980; at those two points there are about 1,200 men between the ages of 25 and 29 for every 1,000 women aged 20 to 24. This discrepancy might well inflate the time period for finding a marriage partner more than the same ratio would in the West, and may thus explain the recent slight upturn in age at marriage that appears in Figure 9.1. The narrowing gap in husbands' and wives' ages at first marriage might also mean that men are more willing to marry a woman closer in age than wait for someone younger.

Other factors in Japanese social organizations also play an important part in determining age at marriage, among them the structure of the labor market, including the wage scale. Wages and salaries for Japanese men in their youth are uniformly low regardless of educational background and company size but rise considerably with age (Keizaikikaku-chō 1976:173-174; Clark 1970:143-144). Many younger men feel that they do not have an income adequate to support a family, and opt to wait for an increase in earning power. Then too, employers are apt to prefer that the new employee become adapted to company life before marrying — another instance of molding private family life to workplace career — which means that superiors may discourage marriage in the first few years of workplace life and then subsequently promote it. (See, for example Rohlen 1974).

Employment practices for women may also discourage marrying at an early age. When a women employee marries, or has a child, she is either dismissed or her status is changed from that of regular employee to "temporary". Her hours of work may be nearly the same, but she is cut off from the annual salary increases that are a part of full-time employment, as well as from many company benefits. Income statistics for women working in the manufacturing sector of Japan's economy show an increase in income with age up to age 29, with a subsequent decrease (Rōdō-shō 1976:3). Where marriage means a shift from regular employee status, the woman who wants to maintain her earning power must refrain from marriage.

Economic preparation for marriage is an important incentive for premarital employment. When a newly married Japanese couple sets up housekeeping, they begin with a wide array of brand-new household essentials, including electrical appliances. One study suggests that the bride's family's contributions to the new couple's household furnishings play an important part in determining the bride's status vis-a-vis the husband and his family, which in turn affects her authority in domestic matters. Her own savings account is also important to the degree of independence she enjoys (Perry 1976).

Another consideration in delaying marriage is the change of life style that a bride experiences: New responsibilities restrict her

196

freedom, and many of her social contacts become attenuated. Marriage means the end of relatively carefree days. Parents may also oppose early marriage on the grounds that the young couple lacks economic self-sufficiency.

Should it happen that a young couple decide to set up housekeeping, the greatest challenge before them is to remain childless until they have adequate economic resources. And in this their culture offers little assistance. Aside from showpiece pilot projects, there are no programs for sex education in Japan's schools. Nor is there an extensive program of family planning services and ready access to the most effective methods of contraception (Coleman 1982). The point here is that a lack of effective family planning itself may be an important factor in late age at marriage. This stands as one more expression of the subordination of the conjugal pair to the reproductive function of marriage.

## II. Childbearing

Japan poses interesting contrasts with other industrialized countries regarding relationship between marriage and childbearing. In a word, the connection between the two is remarkably tight. First, very few women give birth outside of marriage. Japan's low illegitimacy rate poses an interesting exception to the general rule that the later a country's age at marriage, the higher its illegitimacy rate. Second, very few women remain infertile within marriage. Although childbearing is nearly-universal in Japanese marriages, the childbearing period is remarkable compact, as Figure 9.3 reveals.

### Childbirth before Marriage

Japan's low levels of illegitimacy rival those of the Middle Eastern countries (Hartley 1971). Table 9.2 presents the rates for selected industrialized countries, along with a few of the highest and lowest recently known figures, to provide some idea of the range. Japan's illegitimacy rate has not always been so low; the postwar period witnessed a sharp drop to 0.9 percent of all births, a rate of one-tenth of that during the latter half of the Meiji Era (1868-1912) (Yuzawa 1973:124). From 1969 to the mid-1970's, the rate has remained below one percent (Kōsei-shō, 1977:67).

The rapid postwar decline has been attributed to fewer common

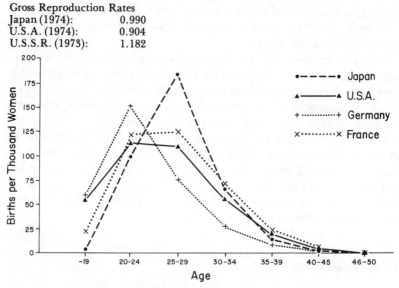

*Figure 9.3.* Birth Rates per 1,000 Women in Japan, 1974;
United States, 1974; and Soviet Russia, 1973.

Gross Reproduction Rates
Japan (1974):       0.990
U.S.A. (1974):      0.904
U.S.S.R. (1973):    1.182

Source: Coleman 1982

law marriages *(naien)* and the availability of induced abortion
(Yuzawa 1973:124). Among present-day Japanese youth, however,
an even greater reason may lie in sanctions against premarital sex
for females, and in the low level of interaction between the sexes.
Virginity is still an important requirement for prospective wives
(Asayama 1975:101; Kon 1973:166). Japan has one of the industrialized world's lowest proportions of youth experiencing
premarital intercourse for both males and females (Asayama 1976).
By contrast with the United States, where about a fourth of unmarried white women have experienced intercourse before the age of 20
(1971 figures from Kantner and Zelnik 1972), a study of women
within the same age group in Japan found fewer than 7 percent
reporting coital experience (Nihon Seikyōiku Kyōkai 1975). Nor are
the young the primary contributors to illegitimacy. In 1976, only
about a fourth (26.5%) of births registered as illegitimate were born
to women under 25 years of age (Kōsei-shō 1977:67).

Social sanctions against the unwed mother are particularly stringent. Young women are stigmatized by an illegitimate birth;
under Japan's family registry *(koseki)* system, all births are recorded
in the mother's family register regardless of whether or not the child
is adopted out. The legal machinery for paternity suits exists, but
the cost and the stigma prevent all but a very small number of

Table 9.2. Proportion of All Live Births Registered as Illegitimate,
Japan and Other Selected Countries, 1972-1974

| Country | Year | Illegitimate Births |
|---|---|---|
| | | % |
| St. Kitts-Nevis-Anguilla | 1974 | 82.8 |
| Sweden | 1974 | 31.4 |
| United States | 1972 | 12.4 |
| United Kingdom | 1973 | 8.6 |
| France | 1972 | 7.8 |
| Federal Republic of Germany | 1973 | 6.3 |
| Hungary | 1974 | 5.7 |
| JAPAN | 1974 | 0.8 |
| Egypt | 1973 | 0.0 |

Source: United Nations (1976).

women from resorting to that option. In addition, winning a recognition battle is no guarantee of subsequent child support, which could require further litigation.

## The Timing of First Births

Japanese couples are likely to begin childbearing quite soon after marriage. The average period between marriage and first birth in the mid-1970's was about 1.7 years, and couples did not appear to deviate much from the average; about 40 percent of all first births were to couples in their first year of marriage, and another 40 percent to those in their second year (Kōsei-shō 1976b:64). By contrast, the two-year period after marriage accounted for 53 percent of all first births to white women in the United States from 1970 to 1974 (U.S. Bureau of the Census 1978:81; the figure excluded premarital births).

It is hard to know the extent to which premarital conceptions pull down the average length of time between marriage and first birth. Japanese vital statistics reports do not provide information on the proportions of births conceived before marriage. Present-day youth are more inclined than the last generation to condone sexual relations when the couple plans to marry (Sōri-fu 1971:7,16).

Nevertheless, the present social structure militates against premarital conception for the same reasons illegitimacy rates are low: a low degree of exposure to conception, coupled with the availability of induced abortion. Weddings involving men who have impregnated their partners but otherwise would not marry them are

199

rare, in large part because women lack the political leverage to exact marriage from such men.

A premarital conception is a social stigma in present-day Japan. I encountered stories of wedding dates being moved up, and gynecologists reported women requesting induced abortions in order to avoid appearing pregnant at their wedding ceremonies. Even so, it is not the emotion-laden topic that it is in the United States, mainly because it rarely results in marriage but also because childbearing occurs so soon after marriage that some cases of premarital conception can be obscured. Many couples experience conception immediately after marriage, for which the popular expression "honeymoon baby" (*hanēmūn bebii*) was coined. A large marriage hall in Tokyo proudly advertises that "50 percent of our brides have babies in the first year of marriage."

A large proportion of Japanese newlywed couples want to begin childbearing immediately. A 1973 government survey found 52 percent of newly married husbands and 45 percent of their wives desiring a childbirth "as soon as possible" (Kōsei-shō 1974:22). In addition to the aura of romanticism attached to having a baby soon after marriage, there is a widespread preference among women to confine childbearing to their younger years. Some husbands are also conscious of the economic crunch that would occur if they had dependent children at the time of their retirement at age 55, when income drops sharply (see Keizaikikaku-chō 1976:174). One other factor may be the nature of domestic life for a bride who is unemployed; while she might want to remain childless for awhile, if she is living in a new and unfamiliar location, isolation could make having a child more desirable (Perry 1976).

The timing of first births may also be influenced by the degree of control that newly married couples have over preventing conception. This situation results from both the unavailability of contraceptive methods and the couple's inability to coordinate using them effectively. Some of the most effective contraceptives are difficult to obtain; to procure them, Japanese couples have to exercise more initiative and spend more of their income than is the case in the United States (Coleman 1982).

The problem is exacerbated by the young couple's inexperience in negotiating in such an intimate area. In contrast to the well-defined allocation of domestic duties by sex in the Japanese culture of marriage, there is no designation of responsibility for contraception. (In actual practice in the United States, the responsibility falls to women; see Luker 1975.) Despite the young woman's concern, she risks her husband's displeasure if she displays knowledge of a topic so worldly as birth control. The young man is more free to be sexually assertive, but he too has no access to information, and if he does not share his wife's concern about avoiding pregnancy, such latitude does the couple little good. There are no indications that Japanese men are especially cooperative in contraceptive matters (Coleman 1982).

The result is that Japanese couples who postpone their first birth through effective contraception are in a minority. Although newlyweds appear able to communicate on the number of children they desire, the issue of when to begin may be left unstated. When I asked if they discussed when to start having children, the most common response I heard from husbands was, "No, but I wanted a child soon and I knew she did too." In the United States 57 percent of white wives between the ages of 25 and 29 in 1970 reported contracepting before their first pregnancy, in contrast to only 29.5 percent of Japanese wives in the same age group in 1971 (Westoff and Ryder 1977:58; Muramatsu n.d.:5).

Some couples do have reasons for wanting to postpone birth. The reasons are most often economic: The wife works and her income is important to the couple, or they are restricted by housing that does not allow children. Then, too, there are couples who just want to enjoy one another's company. Of those who contracept, the great majority use condoms, often in alternation with a rule-of-thumb rhythm method to avoid condoms when possible.[4] The combination is both difficult to use and unreliable.

Reliance on condoms is a reflection of their widespread availability rather than of any intrinsic preference for them. Condoms are the most inexpensive method in Japan (aside from coitus interruptus and rhythm), and they are sold door-to-door and in supermarkets, as well as through pharmacies. Because conjugal sexuality is deemphasized, people find it difficult to take the initiative to find more effective and easier-to-use methods, particularly early in marriage when the couple is least able to discuss such matters, and when wives have not culturally validated their sexuality by bearing children.

Whether or not to abort their first pregnancy is a particularly difficult emotional issue for those who want to postpone childbearing. The media, representatives of the medical profession, and family planning counselors all express strong opposition to the practice. They argue that abortions of first pregnancies are more likely to produce harmful side effects like sterility (see, for example, Yamashita 1974), an assumption that may be correct but as yet lacks scientific substantiation. Two of the most typical reasons for wanting to abort a first pregnancy — the wife's wish to continue working and the couple's desire to remain a twosome for a while — do not receive support as socially acceptable reasons for procuring an abortion. (Housing regulations forbidding infants, by contrast, are likely to be regarded as a lamentable but unavoidable motive.) the husband who wants to preserve the companionate element in his mariage by terminating a pregnancy is particularly vulnerable to criticism for being selfish; in the words of one family planning counselor, he is "trying to monopolize his wife."

The proportion of all induced abortions that happen to those Japanese married couples who want to postpone their first live birth is not negligible. In my questionnaire survey I found that 20 percent of the 184 reported marital abortions took place before a first birth or were among recently married wives who nevertheless desired having children. This percentage probably exceeds the contribution of newlyweds to Japan's total abortion rate because the sample over-represented younger women who are still completing their families. A five-year Tokyo hospital study of 1,284 abortion recipients had even more striking results among patients drawn from all age groups. About half (49%) of the married abortion recipients had had no previous live births (Miyamoto 1976:8).

*Childless Marriages*

Childless couples constitute a very small proportion of Japan's married population. In 1974, only 4.7 percent of ever-married women between 30 and 34 years of age had not given birth to at least one child (Kōsei-shō 1976b:16), in contrast to 10.5 percent of American women in the same category in 1976 (U.S. Bureau of the Census 1977:34). In terms of expressed desire, an even smaller proportion of Japanese women claim they intend to remain childless; among both married and unmarried women, the figure ranges from 1 to 3 percent (Kōsei-shō 1978:43; Mainichi Shimbun 1979:10; Yuzawa 1971:50). Such results are to be expected, given the heavy emphasis placed on childbearing for women.[5] A comparable figure for women under age 35 in the United States in 1976 would be 10 percent (U.S. Bureau of the Census 1977:14), although this does reflect a recent rise in the number of American women intending to remain childless.

The onus of infertility traditionally fell upon wives in Japan, as reflected in the classical quote, "The bride leaves if she cannot produce a child in three years." In the postwar period of reform, however, infertility was removed as legitimate grounds for divorce, and the media have promoted the knowledge that male reproductive disorders are implicated in roughly half of all cases of infertility. Infertility specialists in the Tokyo area have observed that husbands are generally cooperative when the couple cannot produce a child. Nevertheless, the point at which a childless couple adopts a child may be strongly influenced by the husband's career cycle. Tado Shizu, a medical social worker with extensive experience in counseling infertile couples, observes that husbands around 30 years of age are eager for children, but their lives are soon after caught up in pursuing promotions or guiding their self-owned businesses through a time of expansion. All of these take more time away from the family. As the husband enters his late 30's, the desire for children once again emerges, inspiring open communication on the subject. This depiction fits well with data on couples adopting children: most are childless couples that have been married between six and 10 years (Yuzawa 1973:140-141).

Childless Japanese couples do not appear to rely on adoption of infants and young children as much as their Western counterparts.[6] There is also another form of adoption, in which people adopt an adult male directly, or give him their family name when he marries their daughter. The practice is motivated by the desire to perpetuate the family line. Although this form outnumbers cases of adoption of minors (Yuzawa 1973:135), it appears to be the province of families owning productive property. Present-day Japanese couples are not apt to cite continuity of the family line as an important reason for having children (Dore 1958:144-145; Fawcett et al. 1974:13, 36-38; Kōsei-shō 1973:93-101).

My informants typically expressed the conviction that an adoptive relationship with a child was undesirable because somehow the mother's lack of a "blood tie" (chi no tsunagari) made effective discipline of the child difficult. Such an opinion fits with the emphasis placed on motherhood and the childbearing experience. Nevertheless, Tom Paton, a missionary active in adoption issues in Japan, has identified social structural reasons that in the long run are probably more important in not adopting a minor.

Contrary to popular Japanese belief, there is no lack of either homeless children or couples wanting to adopt — at least not in the Tokyo area. Biological parents whose identity is known are reluctant to release their institutionalized children for adoption, however. They may hope that at some point they will be able to take their children back or they fear mistreatment of their children, a legacy of the old foster parent system where children were taken into a family to be used as labor (Paton 1974).

The situation is exacerbated by the way in which the family registration system handles adoptive status. As already mentioned, children born out of wedlock are permanently recorded on the mother's family register. The price of a permanent stigma must intensify a woman's hopes to eventually reunite with her child. In addition, Japanese adoption law requires entry of the biological mother's name (and the father's name if available), the child's original family name, and a notation of the child's adoptive status. Paton (1974) observed that this system sometimes prompts their family members to try to dissuade the would-be adoptive couple, out of the desire to maintain purity in the family lineage.

Illegal adoption is another alternative, and it is conducted in a manner that serves to strengthen the marriage-reproduction bond. Since delivering physicians or midwives provide the legal forms for birth registration, they have sole authority in identifying the infant's mother. One practice is to persuade young unmarried women seeking late abortions to deliver instead, and pass the infants over to couples who are unable to conceive. In that way, both parties avoid stigmatized family registers.

Although it is practically impossible to determine the frequency of the practice, illegal adoption could be extensive — perhaps extensive enough to help explain the low percentage of childlessness. The practice became a cause célèbre in 1973 when an obstetrician in northeastern Japan openly announced that he was performing such illegal adoptions at the rate of about ten a year (Kon 1973:128-29). During my field work, a Tokyo area gynecologist told me that he was aware of the practice among local practitioners, and that he had only recently conducted a secret adoption himself. (He had instructed the unmarried pregnant woman to tell her friends that her distended abdomen was an ovarian cyst that would require surgery.) There were also instances reported of adopting women preparing by wearing pillows under their clothing when in public in order to appear well along in pregnancy.

### Reaching Desired Family Size

Japanese women who have not completed childbearing generally expect to have two children; expressed as an average, couples' expectations are around 2.2 children, a figure which matches the completed fertility (children ever born) of currently married women between the ages of 40 and 44 (Nohara 1979). There is nothing intrinsically inconsistent about a society in which a relatively short childbearing career exists side by side with the intensive promotion of parenthood. Then too, the prevailing sentiment in Japan in the mid-1970's was that, "If economic conditions were to permit it, we'd have more children." Two of the most salient motives for limiting fertility have been increased expenditures for the new array of consumer goods and for children's education (see, for example, Yamamura and Hanley 1975). My informants often mentioned economic limitations, particularly the cost of housing. As for the number of children that married women would *ideally* like — that is, if there were no economic or physiological obstacles (Nohara 1979:17) — the three-child family has predominated in surveys up until 1979 (Kōsei-shō 1976b:132; Population Problems Research Council, The Mainichi Newspapers 1978:23; *Mainichi Shimbun* 1979:10).

The tempo of childbearing has been described as a "bunched birth pattern," in which the desired family size is reached soon after marriage (Yamamura and Hanley 1975:115ff; Jinkō Mondai Shingikai 1974:117). If birth rates of various countries are graphed by age groups, a particularly sharp peak results for Japanese women in their late 20's, as figure 9.3 shows. The pattern probably results from the large proportion of women who marry in their mid-20's and commence childbearing soon thereafter. The rapid decline from the late 20's peak reflects the small number of children desired by Japanese parents, coupled with the availability of induced abortion for limiting family size. The sharp peak in births is not, however, the result of an extremely rapid succession of births among individual wives; there may be only a brief period between marriage and first childbirth, but the average intervals between first and second births and between second and third births in the mid-1970's were three years and 3.3 years, respectively (Kōsei-shō 1976b:66). This is slightly longer than the intervals of 2.7 and three years seen among United States women for such births between 1970 and 1974 (U.S. Bureau of the Census 1978:11). Given these intervals, a Japanese woman marrying before the age of 25 could have three children and still complete her childbearing before reaching age 33.

The preferred length of time between births can be affected by many considerations, and one way to examine them would be to separate the more future-oriented reasons from those operating at or near the time of a subsequent birth. Among the Japanese, the

205

most prominent long-run consideration is the desire for the last child to complete college before the father's earning capacity drops due to retirement (Yamamura and Hanley 1975; Jinkō Mondai Shingikai 1974:117). Another consideration may be the mother's concern about reentering the labor market after her child enters school (Jinkō Mondai Shingikai 1974:117). A few informants mentioned that children born three years apart would place considerable stress on the family budget when the older child enters high school, since it would be the same time that the younger child enters middle school — an occasion demanding a considerable outlay for school supplies and uniforms for both children, as well as the stress of entrance examination preparations for both children at once.

Despite the eminent rationality of these considerations, the mothers in my interview sample who had children under school age — and hence were closest to the issue of birth spacing — talked about much more immediate reasons. They were most likely to say that three years or "two to three years" were preferable, and their reasons centered around the effort involved in childraising. The energy demands of care for infants not yet toilet-trained were expressed vividly, and the possibility of children born within a year of one another (for which there is a term in Japanese, *toshigo*) was roundly rejected as "horrendous." (The word typically heard was *taihen*, also meaning "awful" or "immense.") Wives were also concerned that children spaced too far apart (over four years) would be unable to relate to one another as siblings, which would in turn increase the burden of parental attention. Another theme was the desire to avoid prolonging the most difficult years of childraising by waiting more than three years.

Husbands tended to give figures for child-spacing that were shorter than their wives'. Men's responses strongly suggest that they were not able to recognize the undesirability of another conception within two years of childbirth. Fewer husbands than wives mentioned the work demands, and their reasoning typically lacked detail. In the case of one couple with a child 20 months old, the husband (a 29-year-old college graduate) said he had no reasons for the birth interval that he gave except that he knew it was his wife's opinion. The more explicit men's answers involved the effects of nearness of age on the children's relationships as siblings. Wives were also concerned about siblings' relative ages, but they were much more likely to talk about such personality development problems in terms of their significance as extra-parental childraising demands.

The differences between husbands' and wives' opinions on spacing births are probably generated by conjugal role segregation that separates men from childraising tasks. Few men are present at the hospital when a wife gives birth; they are either at work or at home (presumably resting for work, given the late hour of some births) when they are given the news.[7] It is also common practice for the wife to return to her family of origin and remain with them for six to twelve weeks after giving birth in order to recuperate and receive infant care help from her own mother (husbands are not expected to help by assuming a larger share of household chores).

A substantial portion of induced abortions accrue to couples with children who have not ended their childbearing careers. The abortion rates reported by age group in 1975 suggest that such is the case: Although the highest rate (38.3 per thousand female population) appears among women between 30 and 34 years of age, wives who have probably completed their desired family size, it is followed closely by the rate for women between 25 and 29 years of age (34.3) (Kōsei-shō 1976a:23; cf. Figure 9.3). This contrasts sharply with the United States, where the rates decline sharply for women over 24 years of age (Tietze 1979:49). Although my questionnaire data come from a sample biased toward young couples still completing their families, the extent to which these couples have relied on induced abortion before attaining desired family size implies a major role for abortion in helping maintain the desired interval between births. Over half of the induced abortions reported were followed by a live birth.

Exhaustion from infant care figures prominently as a reason for induced abortion among Japanese wives. Most wives interviewed who had had induced abortions stated that caring for an infant made them too tired or weak to undergo the birth of another child. Medical social workers also observed that this is a major reason among wives for seeking abortions.

The extent to which Japanese couples rely on induced abortion is more than an issue of public health; it also stands as a testament to the difficulties of adjustment between young husbands and wives in a culture that does not encourage sophisticated contraceptive practice. For most of these couples, ineptness in family planning in the early years eventually gives way to more careful contraception. The necessity of limiting family size is even more stringent than the need to put space between births (and perhaps gets more cooperation from husbands, involving as it does family economics), and the couple has come to learn more effective contraceptive practice through their own trial and error experiences. Then, too, parenthood gives many Japanese women a sense of legitimacy in pursuing contraception they can control. In the questionnaire sample, use of female-controlled medical methods (almost entirely the pill and the IUD) is concentrated among wives married six years or more, in contrast to a nearly-universal reliance upon condoms (or condoms and rhythm) among those in their first years of marriage. The women who use female methods have higher educational levels and husbands with higher incomes; one could surmise that these wives have found condoms unsatisfactory and possess the means to acquire more effective methods, a sequence that is borne out by interviewed couples' histories. Nevertheless, the switch to more effective contraception takes place only after the couple has undergone the most difficult years of marital adjustment and the experiences of poorly timed pregnancies.

## A Final Word

The modern Japanese family poses problems for the assertion that emotional interdependence between husband and wife is a — if not the — major source of perpetuation of the family in industrialized societies today (see Ryder 1974). What I have suggested is that the emphasis on other family functions in Japan overshadows conjugal emotionality, and that the resulting pattern can in turn influence demographic phenomena such as age at marriage.

The relationships presented here offer themselves as variables for predicting trends in family demography in Japan. To the extent that public careers command so much of men's lives and energies — and so much less of women's — the functional priorities of the Japanese marriage should survive in their present form. The concomitants, such as widespread marriage at a late age along with low levels of childlessness should also persist. The result would be the persistence of what we have seen in the 1970's: a number of interesting exceptions to the trend of convergence in demographic patterns among modern societies.

## Notes

Field research was funded by the Social Science Research Council. My thanks to Key Kobayashi of the Library of Congress for his kind responses to my many requests for Japanese documents, and to Ronald Rindfuss

(Carolina Population Center) and Eleanor Westney (Yale University Department of Sociology) for their helpful comments.

1. Japanese men averaged 24 minutes of weekly time spent in household tasks and errands as opposed to an overall average of 83 minutes for men in each of the other countries investigated. As a ratio of women's housework, this represents one hour for every 10.8 hours of women's housework time, in contrast with ratios ranging from 2.3 to 5.4 for the other countries studied (calculated using figures in Keizaikikaku-chō 1973:60). Data for the ten Euro-American countries in the study — the United States, West Germany, France, Belgium, Hungary, Czechoslovakia, Yugoslavia, Poland, Bulgaria, and the Soviet Union — were gathered in 1965-1966; Japanese data were gathered in 1972.

2. Japanese men averaged 7.2 hours of work daily for a seven-day week, a figure matched by Hungary but well above the mean of 6.4 for the average of all other countries in the study.

3. The total fertility rate (an estimate of how many children each woman bears in her lifetime based on the current reproductive record of all women of child-bearing age) for 1947 was 4.5 children; by 1970, it had sunk to 2.1.

4. About 90 percent of newlywed contraceptors in the questionnaire sample were relying on condoms alone or with rhythm, a result corroborated by surveys of newlyweds in which between 72 and 87 percent reported using condoms (Ogino 1976:35; Kon 1973:114).

5. Japanese infertility specialists commonly assumed that 10 percent of all couples are infecund (see, for example, Iizuka et al. 1972:19), although fewer than 10 percent of American couples within some subgroups are childless (U.S. Bureau of the Census 1973:138. Much smaller percentages of infertile couples are known; among the Hutterites, a highly fertile religious community, only 2.4 percent of couples married over 20 years are childless; Tietze 1957).

6. In 1962 the absolute numbers of adoptions of minors in Japan and the United Kingdom were nearly identical, but the number of adoptions of minors in Japan in the 1960's actually decreased, despite an increase in the number of married couples, in contrast to an increase of over 70 percent in the United Kingdom in the same period (Yuzawa 1973:134-135).

7. See, for example, Murayama 1976; in a study of 210 husbands of women delivering in a Niigata Prefecture hospital, only 26.2 percent were present at the hospital when their children were born, almost all of the rest being either at work or home.

## References

Akamatsu Tadashi
   1969   Women Workers and Retirement after Marriage. Japan Labor
          Bulletin 8 (5, May): 6-8.

Asayama Shin'ichi
1975   Adolescent Sex Development and Adult Sex Behavior in Japan.
       Journal of Sex Research 2 (2, May): 91-112.
1976   Saikin seishōnen no seikōdō — wagakuni no tōkei shiryō ni
       arawareta tokushoku [Recent Youth Sexual Behavior — The
       Special Characteristics of Japan Revealed by Statistical Data].
       Presentation before the Japan Association for Sex Research,
       Tokyo, April 24.
Blake, Judith
1974   The Changing Status of Women in Developed Countries.
       Science 231 (3 Sept.): 137-147.
Clark, Rodney
1979   The Japanese Company. New Haven: Yale University Press.
Coleman, Samuel
1982   Japanese Family Planning: Traditional Birth Control in a
       Modern Urban Culture. Princeton: Princeton University Press.
Dore, Ronald P.
1958   City Life in Japan: A Study of a Tokyo Ward. Berkeley and
       Los Angeles: University of California Press.
Fawcett, James T., et al.
1974   The Value of Children in Asia and the United States: Com-
       parative Perspectives. Honolulu: East-West Center Press.
Fujin Chōsakai (abbreviation for Fujin ni Kansuru Shomondai Chōsa
       Kaigi).
1974   Gendai Nihon josei no ishiki to kōdō [Attitudes and Behavior
       of Present Day Japanese Women]. Tokyo: Ōkura-shō Insatsu-
       kyoku.
Glass, D. V.
1976   Recent and Prospective Trends in Fertility in Developed Coun-
       tries. Philosophical Transactions of the Royal Society of London
       275 (928, March 4): 1-52.
Hartley, Shirley F.
1971   Contributions of Illegitimate and Premaritally Conceived Legit-
       imate Births to Total Fertility. Social Biology 18 (2, June):
       178-187.
Iizuka Rihachi, Ōno Toranoshin, and Kawakami Seiji
1972   Jinkō jusei no rinshō [The Clinical Practice of Artificial Insem-
       ination]. Tokyo: Kanehara.
International Labour Office
1975   1975 Year Book of Labour Statistics (25th Edition). Geneva.
Japanese Organization for International Cooperation in Family Planning
       (JOICFP)
1977   Fertility and Family Planning in Japan. Tokyo.
Jinkō Mondai Shingikai
1974   Nihon jinkō no dōkō [Trends in the Japanese Population].
       Tokyo: Ōkura-shō Insatsu-kyoku.

Kantner, John F., and Melvin Zelnik
1972   Sexual Experience of Young Unmarried Women in the United States. Family Planning Perspectives 4(October 4: 9-17).

Keizaikikaku-chō
1973   Seikatsu jikan no kokusai hikaku chōsa [International Comparative Time Allocation Survey]. Shiryōhen [Data Volume]. Tokyo.
1976   Shōwa 51 nenpan kokumin seikatsu hakusho —kurashi no naka no atarashii teiryū [1976 Edition, White Paper on Life in Japan: New Undercurrents in Living]. Tokyo: Okura-shō Insatsu-kyoku.

Kon Yasuo (ed.)
1973   Shōwa 49 nendo boshi hoken kazoku keikaku nenpō [1974 Year Book of Maternal Health and Family Planning]. Tokyo: Nihon Kazoku Keikaku Kyōkai.

Kōsei-shō
1968   Shōwa 41 nendo jinkō dōtai shakai keizai men chōsa hōkoku: kon'in [1966 Vital Statistics, Social and Economic Aspects Survey Report: Marriage]. Tokyo: Kōsei-sho Daijin Kanbō Tōkei Jōhōbu.
1973   Shōwa 47 nendo jittchi chōsa dai 6 ji shussanryoku chōsa hōkoku, sono 1: gaiyō oyobi shuyō kahyō [1972 Field Survey, Sixth Fertility Survey Report, Part 1: Summary and Tables of Principal Results]. Tokyo: Jinkō Mondai Kenkyūjo.
1974   Shōwa 48 nendo jinkō dōtai shakai keizai men chōsa hōkoku: kon'in [1973 Vital Statistics, Social and Economic Aspects Survey Report: Marriage]. Tokyo: Kōsei-shō Daijin Kanbō Tōkei Jōhōbu.
1976a  Shōwa 50 nen yūsei hogo tōkei hōkoku [1975 Eugenic Protection Statistics Report]. Tokyo: Kōsei-shō Daijin Kanbō Tōkei Jōhōbu.
1976b  Sekai shussanryoku chōsa hōkoku [World Fertility Survey Report]. Tokyo: Kōsei-shō Daijin Kanbō Tōkei Jōhōbu.
1977   Shōwa 51 nen jinkō dōtai tōkei jōkan [1976 Vital Statistics, Volume 1]. Tokyo: Kōsei-shō Daijin Kanbō Tōkei Jōhōbu.
1978   Shōwa 52 nendo jitchi chōsa dai 7 ji shussanryoku chōsa hōkoku — gaihō oyobi shuyō kekka hyō [Seventh Fertility Survey of 1977 General Report and Tables of Major Results]. Tokyo: Jinkō Mondai Kenkyūjo.
1979   Shōwa 52 nen jinkō dōtai tōkei jōkan [1977 Vital Statistics, Volume 1]. Tokyo: Kōsei-shō Daijin Kanbō Tōkei Jōhōbu.

Koyama Takashi (ed.)
1967   Gendai kazoku no yakuwari kōzō: fūfu. Oyako no kitai to genjitsu [The Structure of Roles in the Present-Day Family: Husband-Wife, Parent-Child Expectations and Actuality]. Tokyo: Baifūkan.

Kurahashi Yumiko
1972    Shussan to onna de aru koto no kankei [The Relationship between Childbirth and Being a Woman]. Fujin Kōron 675 (August): 60-65.
Luker, Kristin
1975    Taking Chances: Abortion and the Decision Not to Contracept. Berkeley and Los Angeles: University of California Press.
*Population Problems Research Council* The Mainichi Newspapers
1978    Summary of Fourteenth National Survey of Family Planning. Tokyo.
Mainichi Shimbun
1979    Shosan no keikō ni hakusha: dai 15 kai kazoku keikaku seron chōsa [Spurs to the Low Birth Trend: Fifteenth Family Planning Opinion Survey]. (July 19): 10-11.
Miyamoto Junhaku
1976    Background Considerations on Induced Abortion. International Journal of Fertility 18: 5-12.
Monbu-shō
1976    Shōwa 50 nendo wagakuni no kyōiku suijun [1975 Edition: The Level of Education in Japan]. Tokyo: Okura-shō Insatsu-kyoku.
Muramatsu Minoru (ed.)
1967    Japan's Experience in Family Planning — Past and Present. Tokyo: Family Planning Federation of Japan.
n.d.    Conventional Contraception in Japan. Reference Materials for Seminars in Population/Family Planning. Tokyo: Japanese Organization for International Cooperation in Family Planning.
Murayama Ikuko
1976    Ninshin shussan ni fusei wa dō kakawarieruka [How Can We Involve Fatherhood in Pregnancy and Birth?]. Josanpu Zasshi 30 (1): 15-21.
Nihon Seikyōiku Kyōkai
1975    Seishonen no seikōdō: wagakuni no kōkōsei daigakusei ni kansuru chōsa hōkoku [Youth Sexual Behavior: Report of a Survey of Japanese High School and College Students]. Tokyo: Shōgakkan.
Nohara Makoto
1979    Gendai Nihon ni okeru shussanryoku yosoku no kanōsei [The Usefulness of the Intended Number of Children for Fertility Predictions in Japan]. Jinkō Mondai Kenkyū 149: (Jan) 16-31.
Ogino Hiroshi
1976    Shinkonsha no hinin jisshi jōkyō [The Use of Contraception among Newlyweds]. Rinshōka no Tame no Seiigaku 3 (9, Sept) 34-37.
Paton, Tom
1974    The Unwanted Pregnancy in Japan. Japan Christian Quarterly 40 (2, Spring):93-102.

Perry, Linda L.
1976    Mothers, Wives, and Daughters in Osaka:  Autonomy, Alliance
        and Professionalism.  Ph.D. dissertation, University of Pitts-
        burgh.
Plath, David W.
1964    The After Hours:  Modern Japan and the Search for Enjoyment.
        Berkeley and Los Angeles:  University of California Press.
Rōdō-shō (Fujin Shōnen-kyoku)
1975    Shōwa 50 nenpan: fujin rōdō no jitsujō [Women's Labor, 1975
        Edition].  Tokyo:  Okura-shō Insatsu-kyoku. (Daijin Kanbō
        Tōkei Jōhō-bu)
1976    Saikin no chingin kōzō no dōkō [Latest Trends in Wage Struc-
        ture].  Rōdō Tōkei Chōsa Geppō 28 (3, March): 3-14.
Rohlen, Thomas
1974    For Harmony and Strength:  Japanese White-Collar Organiza-
        tion in Anthropological Perspective.  Berkeley and Los Angeles:
        University of California Press.
Ryder, Norman
1974    The Family in Developed Countries. Scientific American 23 (3,
        Sept.): 123-132.
Sankei Ribingu
1976    Otoko wa naze...kitaku jikan wo renraku shinaika [Why Don't
        Men Say When They're Coming Home?]. 238 (Oct. 30): 8.
Sōri-fu
1971    Seishōnen no sei ni kansuru ishiki chōsa [Survey of Youth At-
        titudes toward Sex].  Tokyo:  Seishōnen Taisaku Honbu.
1973    Sekai seinen ishiki chōsa hōkokusho. Sokuhōhen [World Youth
        Attitude  Survey  Report,  Preliminary  Edition].    Tokyo:
        Seishōnen Taisaku Honbu.
Tietze, Christopher
1957    Reproductive Span and Rate of Reproduction among Hutterite
        Women. Fertility and Sterility 8 (1, Jan./Feb.): 89-97
1979    Induced Abortion: 1979. Third Edition. New York: Population
        Council.
United Nations
1976    Demographic Yearbook 1975.  Twenty-Seventh Issue (Special
        Topic:  Natality Statistics).  New York.
1977    Demographic Yearbook 1976.  Twenty-Eighth Issue (Special
        Topic:  Marriage and Divorce Statistics).  New York.
U. S. Bureau of the Census
1973    Census of Population: 1970.  Women by Number of Children
        Ever Born.  Subject Reports PC(2)-3A.  Washington, D.C.:  U. S.
        Government Printing Office.
1977    Fertility of American Women: June 1976.  Current Population
        Reports, Series P-20, No. 308 (June). Washington, D.C.:  U. S.
        Government Printing Office.

1978 Trends in Childspacing: June 1975. Current Population Reports, Series P-20, No. 315 (Feb.). Washington, D.C.: U. S. Government Printing Office.

Vogel, Ezra
1963 Japan's New Middle Class: The Salary Man and His Family in a Tokyo Suburb. Berkeley and Los Angeles: University of California Press.

Westoff, Charles, and Norman Ryder
1977 The Contraceptive Revolution. Princeton: Princeton University Press.

Yamamura Kōzō and Susan Hanley
1975 Ichi hime, ni tarō: Educational Aspirations and the Decline in Fertility in Postwar Japan. Journal of Japanese Studies 2 (1): 83-125.

Yamashita Akira
1974 Hataraku josei no ninshin: bunben to ikuji [Working Women's Pregnancy, Birth and Child Raising). Tokyo: Nihon Boshi Eisei Joseikai.

Yuzawa Yasuhiko
1971 Gendai seinen no kekkonkan, kateikan [Modern Youth's View of Marriage and Family]. Gekkan Ekonomisuto 3 (March):50-55.
1973 Zusetsu kazoku mondai [Family Issues Illustrated]. Tokyo: NHK Books.

# CHAPTER 10

# Where Work and Family Are Almost One: The Lives of Folkcraft Potters

JILL KLEINBERG

Recent studies of careers in Japan perpetuate what is, according to Kanter, the common position on work and family in the social sciences. This is the myth that "in a modern industrial society work life and family life constitute two separate and nonoverlapping worlds, with their own functions, territories, and behavioral rules" (1977:8). Many studies of occupations analyze work totally independently from the family sphere (Abegglen 1958, 1973; Cole 1971, 1979; Whitehill and Takazawa 1968). Dore (1973), in a comparison of industrial relations in British and Japanese factories, and Rohlen (1974), in an ethnography of a Japanese bank, recognize the ties between work and family but give limited insight into the dynamic connections.

The analyses of occupations cited above concern persons whose livelihoods rest on employment in modern, large-scale enterprises. While work and family careers should be viewed as mutually interlinked in this context, the linkages are more clearly defined in the context of smaller-scale enterprise.

Japan's dual economic structure includes innumerable small and medium businesses (Broadbridge 1966; Cole 1971; Dore 1973; Hollerman 1972). Here, the lines of a person's working life and family life, if they never totally fuse, nonetheless often overlap extensively.

In this chapter, I look at the "enterprise household" in Japan, the setting in which, more than any other, occupational and domestic roles inform each other. I draw on data gathered during a field study of Kami-Tachikui, a hamlet in Western Japan in which the majority of households specialize in the production of folkcraft pottery. I give special attention to how, in such a household, people maintain the linkages among their work and family career trajectories within individual life cycles, and how they replicate these linked roles as generation succeeds generation.

## Framework of Analysis

The framework within which I view the work/family careers of potters in Kami-Tachikui borrows largely from the lifecourse approach to describing and interpreting human experience. It is an approach that social scientists and family historians increasingly find useful (Elder 1977; Modell, Furstenberg, and Hershberg 1976; Hareven 1977, 1978).

One fundamental concern of the lifecourse perspective is a person's location in time. For my purposes, this time reckoning encompasses individual time, family time, and historical time. Location in social space is a second concern, particularly where this involves affiliation with a distinctive subgroup or community, as Kami-Tachikui clearly is. Variables of time and place directly bear on the distribution, sequence, and timing of transitions from one reference point to another along career lines. They affect the prospects for career continuity as well. Roth's definition of career underlies the lifecourse-oriented literature. In Roth's words, a career is:

> a series of related and definable stages of a given sphere of activity that a group of people goes through in a progressive fashion (that is, one step leads to another) in a given direction or on the way to a more or less definite and recognizable end-point or goal or series of goals. This means that there m_st be a group definition of success or attainment of a goal. (1963:94)

Advocates of a lifecourse perspective variously emphasize its inherent interactionalism. Abeles and Riley (1978:4-5) set the general tone. They stress the interaction of different processes — in this case biological, psychological, and social — and the impact of this interaction on the lifecourse of age-related cohort sets. They recognize a second interactional dimension in positing that events of earlier life stages have consequences for later stages.

However, Roth brings the human actor to the foreground of the interactional arena. For example, he considers bargaining over timetables to be integral to the structuring of careers that involve a service or authority relationship. This aspect of career construction is particularly relevant to the study of potters in rural Japan. To paraphrase Roth, the objectives, criteria of progress, and ideas of proper timing are different for each party concerned. Therefore, unless bargaining and accommodation occur, the relationship cannot continue (1963:107-108).

I will look at the coordination of work and family careers by members of four separate cohorts whose adult lives unfold in Kami-Tachikui. The object is to explore differences among the cohorts in the distribution, timing, and sequencing of transitions along each of the two trajectories. The reasons for differences mainly are sought in the demographic, social, and historical factors that give each cohort its own distinctive pattern of individual and family life cycles. Such changes as have occurred affect the dynamics of coordinating linked career lines.

Although we may talk about cohort-specific patterns, Roth's discussion of timetable bargaining reminds us that these patterns evolve from numbers of individual dramas. I will cite examples from actual life histories to show that individuals in Kami-Tachikui actively try to create the best possible position for themselves within existing constraints. In doing so, they help effect changes in role expectations and patterns of behavior. The study of enterprise households points to ways of transcending the all-too-prevalent perception that the Japanese are bound by prearranged, scripted roles.

## The Enterprise Household

In describing the enterprise household, we are essentially talking about the *ie*, the basal socioeconomic unit of premodern Japan. Historically the concept of *ie* has varied from social class to social class and, for all classes, has been influenced by successive legal codes (Fukutake 1967; Koyama 1961; Nakane 1967; Nakano 1966). Nonetheless, the Japanese have articulated the tenets of their "family system" (*ie seido*) purposefully and didactically, blending them with a Confucian morality that minimizes individualistic goals. DeVos and Wagatsuma elaborate on the theme:

> The social philosophy of Confucianism tended to deemphasize the individual as an end in himself and to emphasize instead the network of *particularistic* obligations and responsibilities that the individual

217

assumed as a member of his family and his community. Living in accordance with one's prescribed role within the family and within a political and social hierarchy was the ultimate basis of moral values, subjectively sanctioned by one's own conscience and objectively reinforced by the informal sanctions of the community and the legal codes of the state . . . . In traditional Japan, the self-awareness of a Japanese was fused with some conception of expected role behavior, often idealized in his mind as a set of internalized standards or directives. (1973b:12)

Kami-Tachikui potters' behavior regarding work and family must be measured against the social and psychological parameters of the *ie* construct which reifies a notion of "role." I take patterns of behavior and belief characteristic of commoners as the basis of the ideal-typical *ie*. It was the samurai household pattern that was promulgated in the Meiji Civil Code of 1898, but commoner patterns remain vital in many domestic settings today.

*Ie* is translated here as "household," or as "house" in the sense of a social unit. Ideally it is an enduring corporate entity — managing agricultural, commercial, or artisan activities — that brings both production and reproduction within the framework of family life. It is normally formed around a stem family composed of nuclear units affiliated through parent-child relationships. Sons and daughters outside the main line of succession enter other households. However, the *ie* is given flexibility by its capacity to incorporate a wide range of kin as well as nonkin (Ariga 1956; Nakane 1967; Nakano 1962, 1964, 1966).

Relations among members are regulated by gender and age differences and by a person's position in the supergenerational flow of *ie* existence. A bias toward males and toward seniors is clear in formal decision-making and prestige. However, the principle of "position" (Bachnik 1978; Kitaoji 1971; Nakano 1962, 1966) frequently modifies the principles of gender and age. Nakano uses the term *"ie* line" to refer to the unending succession of (male) household heads and their spouses, who together carry major responsibility for ensuring household continuity. Representatives of the *ie* line distinctly outrank other household members.

Household headship is the paramount status. The head is steward over *ie*-owned assets, overseeing the internal affairs of the group and representing it in civic and business activities. Although *ie* ideology favors primogeniture, headship may pass to a junior son if the eldest is considered unfit. Or, where there are only daughters, one daughter may marry a man (*mukoyōshi*) who comes to her house as heir and adopts her family name.

*Ie* ideology embodies two fundamental tenets: The household should exist over generations and each of the generations should strive to maintain and, if possible, expand the house's economic assets (Kawashima 1957; Nakano 1959). Japanese Confucianism ties these principles to devotion toward superiors, expressed in "vigorous and continuous performance with respect to the collective goal" (Bellah 1957:39-40). But in addition it teaches that one's duty to parents (*kō*) is conditioned or mediated by one's "right" to anticipate reciprocity (*on*) (Bennett and Nagai 1953).

The structure of the *ie* can be extended to embrace a multi-house organization widely known in sociological writings as *dōzoku* (Nakano 1958, 1966). The *dōzoku* is a hierarchical federation of households composed of a "main house," or *honke*, and one or more "branch houses," or *bunke*, usually situated in the same community. Ideally, a house creates a *bunke* by apportioning part of its property to one of its members who stands outside the *ie* line, most frequently a nonsuccessor son. The basically inferior status of a branch house derives from its founder's exclusion from the *ie* line of the main house. In addition, a branch typically holds a diffuse indebtedness to the main house for its patronage. It is characteristic of such dependency relations that, once initiated, responsibility and obligation continue over a long time period — as the *dōzoku* is conceptualized, forever. But in practice a *bunke's* degree of subordination is shaped by the extent to which it depends on the main house for its livelihood.

## Pottery-Making in Kami-Tachikui

The hamlet of Kami-Tachikui nestles in the mountains of southwestern Hyogo prefecture. Along with its neighboring villages, it is the historic focal point of Tamba pottery production, Tamba being the ancient name of the region. Archeological evidence dates Tamba pottery as a regional specialty to at least the beginning of the Thirteenth century. From then until the 1920s, Tamba potters supplied utilitarian ceramics to farmers, merchants, and middlemen within a relatively narrow geographical range. It is likely that the production of storage jars, sake bottles and, after the turn of the Twentieth century, flowerpots, arose in this area to provide supplementary income for farmers in the land-poor mountain villages.

There were some technological and stylistic innovations during these years. Notably, around the year 1600, wooden kickwheels replaced hand-turned potter's wheels; long wood-burning kilns of adobe-like construction replaced small kilns hollowed out of the mountainside; and the use of glaze was introduced. However, the basic Tamba style remained unchanged. Pots continued to be thick-walled, unsymmetrical, and somber in color.

After the mid-1920s the demand for Tamba pottery dropped precipitously because of a national economic slump as well as the growing popularity of glass as a material for sake bottles and other containers. A number of Kami-Tachikui houses gave up pottery at that time and this trend accelerated in the 1930s as Japan mobilized for war. By 1940, when Japan was well into the early stages of World War II, only about 26 percent of Kami-Tachikui's households had pottery workshops, compared to 64 percent in 1920. Production in other Tamba hamlets had all but ceased.

Although a few houses resumed making pottery after the war, sluggish market conditions extended into the 1950s. Inexpensive, mold-made acid containers and flowerpots comprised the bulk of production. By the late 1950s, however, national prosperity nurtured a movement to revive traditional Japanese folkcrafts, commonly known as *mingei*. (The movement originated in the early 1920s but had attracted only a small group of artists and philosophers.) Pottery was chief in importance among crafts that a large, affluent urban middle class was coming to value.

Kami-Tachikui felt the impact of the folkcraft boom around the early to middle 1960s. Workshop owners responded by reviving traditional techniques and styles. Many also began making tea ceremony ware and dinner ware in much greater quantities than previously. "Folkcraft" pottery, a term which by common usage includes the mundane to the uniquely beautiful, as long as the pottery has a rustic, sedate quality, has gradually replaced other lines of production. The use of electric wheels and gas and electric kilns allows higher productivity, so that today the picturesque wood-burning kilns which appear on travel posters are reserved for firing a potter's most artistic wares. With growing financial and social rewards, more houses have regenerated defunct shops or have initiated pottery production anew.

When I studied the community in the early 1970s, 31 out of 72 houses owned ceramic enterprises. Five of the enterprises were *dōzoku*-based; members of a branch house worked in the main house shop. By 1978 five additional household enterprises had begun operating. In all but one case, the new shop was run by a branch house whose members earlier had been potters for the main house enterprise.

## The Pottery Enterprise Household

The tight interconnection between work and domestic roles gains clarity when we look at who works in pottery and at a potter's general attributes. If you ask in a ceramic shop which members of the house do pottery-related work, you will find that the typical pattern resembles that shown in Figure 10.1. Ordinarily, it is only representatives of the *ie* line who are potters. In Figure 10.1, the workshop head and his wife are active potters, as are the successor and his wife. The head's father is shown as an active potter but not his mother: this reflects the fact that women tend to retire from pottery work earlier than men.

*Figure 10.1.* Household Enterprise Model,
Kami-Tachikui Pottery Workshops

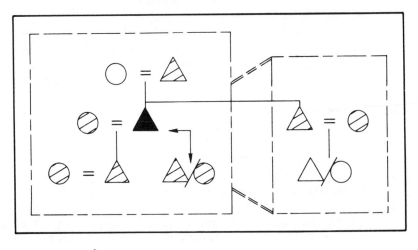

▲    Workshop head

△○    Active worker

◭◑    Retired adult;
pre-work age child

⌐ ¬    Household unit

☐    Workshop

⫽    Ie—genealogical tie

⌐↓    Apprenticeship tie

Men and women who are responsible for household continuity will contribute to the house enterprise out of duty, although of course many enjoy pottery work. Other family members might *choose* to participate in the pottery enterprise, but usually are under no moral pressure to take it up as a vocation. Younger brothers or junior sons of heads most commonly work alongside potters from the *ie* line. (The head's younger brother in Figure 10.1 already has established a separate branch house.) A daughter is not thought of as a source of pottery labor unless she is expected to marry a *mukoyōshi* and remain in the household.

Apprentices join an enterprise house without difficulty and participate in most of its social and ceremonial activities. Since the *mingei* boom, young men and, recently, women too have arrived in Kami-Tachikui in growing numbers in order to learn pottery skills. In the early 1970's twenty apprentices lived in the hamlet, divided among twelve of the workshops. Most apprentices stay a year or two and then move on to another pottery center.

Persons shown in Figure 10.1 are "core" workers. These workers devote the longest hours to pottery production, have the most skill, and/or have managerial responsibility. Rarely are persons outside the household, except branch house members, counted among the core potters. Moreover, most enterprises are so small that they include few besides core workers.

## Pottery and Domestic Careers

The traditional *ie* paradigm builds on a formalized progression of statuses for men and women in the line of succession. Household heir (*atotori*) and junior wife (*yome*) become, respectively, head (*shūto*) and senior wife (*shūtome*), then retired head and retired senior wife, and ultimately come to rest among the venerated ancestors of the house. Masuda (1975) vividly illustrates how these gender-specific statuses are integrated and how, at each stage of the paired progression, male and female roles are broadly defined. This well-enunciated progression fits Roth's definition of career. However, I want to distinguish analytically among the various role-associated activities that a "career" in an *ie* entails for men and women in Kami-Tachikui, so that we can more easily view role as process.

As Figure 10.2 shows, I analyze a person's *ie*-centered life course in terms of two career trajectories: domestic activity and pottery activity. The choice of nomenclature for the first of these requires explanation, particularly since recent writing about gender roles uses the term domestic more narrowly than I do here. "Domestic" according to Rosaldo, "refers to those minimal institutions and modes of activity that are organized immediately around one or more mothers and their children." "Public," in opposition, "refers to activities, institutions, and forms of association that link, rank, organize, or subsume particular mother-child groups" (Rosaldo 1974:23). Rosaldo explains sexual asymmetry by the fact that women, bound (not by biological necessity) to the domestic domain, lack access to the prestige and authority that accrues to actors (men) in the public domain.

By my definition, a domestic career encompasses all social activity that maintains the *ie* over time. Career events such as marriage and

*Figure 10.2.* Articulation of Domestic and Pottery Careers
in Kami-Tachikui Enterprise Houses

A.  Members of the ie – line

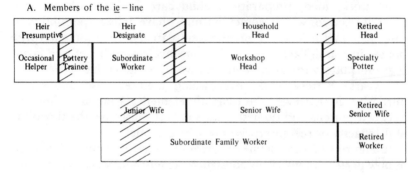

B.  Members outside the ie – line

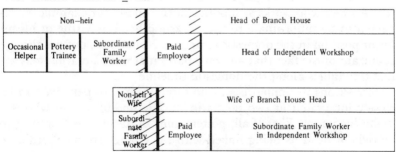

Note:    = points of potential tension between roles.

the birth of children involve men and women equally; they mark progress, and may constitute reference points, as one passes through household time. In Part A of Figure 10.2, stages along the domestic trajectory coincide with the formal succession of *ie* statuses. The domestic trajectory illustrated in part B diagrams the status sequence of family members who eventually form a branch house.

One's domestic career in an enterprise house concerns the public as well as private domains. A household head, particularly, is propelled into the public sphere, for example through his participation in the hamlet assembly. Association among women also may be "public" in that it links domestic groups; participation by the wife of a household head in the local women's association is a prime example. Nevertheless, such participation neither symbolizes nor enhances women's prestige and authority the way "public" activity does for men. "Sexual stratification," to use Morgan's (1975:134-170) term, is intrinsic to the enterprise house paradigm.

In this chapter I concentrate on the work of pottery production. Housework, food, preparation, child care — the work of social reproduction for which women normally have daily responsibility, is discussed in the context of domestic careers. In most enterprise houses in Kami-Tachikui, production involves both wet-rice farming and pottery-making; their relative importance has varied over the years. Pottery work, over which men exercise undisputed authority, is, however, the dynamic element. Analysis of linkages between pottery and domestic careers best illustrates the flexibility and tenacity of the enterprise household model.

In Figure 10.2 the scheme of career stages reflects my observations of how potters interactively construct a career course. Although they do not name the stages in a pottery career line, potters recognize a relationship between their domestic career and their work role that tends to emphasize the determinative influence of the domestic factor. An heir who works as a potter in the house, for example, is expected to be subordinate to the workshop head by virtue of his inferior position in the domestic structure. Nonetheless, potters also are cognizant of the fact that an heir's particular work situation may affect timetables along the domestic timeline.

Transitions in domestic and pottery careers are perceived to be closely integrated at two points in the lifetime of a man who is a main-line potter. First of all, potters think of the change from heir to household head as being linked with the change from subordinate potter to workshop head. Secondly, they consider the transition from house head to retired head to be linked to the transition from shop head to "specialty potter." (Retired shop heads often concentrate on specific tasks, unlike younger male potters whose work is diffuse.) In an ideal world the trajectories would mesh smoothly. But tension between paired career trajectories is especially likely around these two transitions. It is due to structural dissonance, stemming from questions as to when to allocate formal status and authority.

Men in the line of succession may experience tension between paired career courses at an earlier point as well: when the heir-to-be is deciding on an occupational career. This too might quality as structural tension. If a young man chooses a career other than pottery-making, he and/or his family may well reevaluate his status as heir.

Women, those in the line of succession and wives of junior sons, do not experience structural dissonance with regard to linked careers. Conflict between domestic and pottery roles does not stem from questions of how and when to allocate authority. Instead, it arises from competition between careers for women's time. Role conflict is especially likely during years women are giving birth and caring for young children.

A non-heir son tends to feel considerable frustration during the few years before he establishes a branch house. The structure of the *ie* makes frustration at this time, and later, all the more inevitable. Although being a subordinate potter is compatible with the status of non-heir, the aspirations of an adult junior son are incompatible with long residence in the parental home. An enterprise house can defuse tension for a time by making a non-heir head of his own household but retaining him as a paid pottery employee. However, there may be a further conflict when the branch house head acts to establish his own workshop. The establishment of an independent pottery career is consonant with a junior son's new domestic career course.

The enterprise household presents its successive generations with a static structure. An unchanging sequence of social positions must be filled in both the domestic and pottery career lines; successor to workshop head, workshop head, and retired shop head are less formalized counterparts to the progression of domestic statuses. But persons who pass through this structure face different sets of problems and opportunities. The following section describes the particular conditions that affect different cohorts of enterprise house potters. Not only does conflict between linked careers differ qualitatively among cohorts but the prospects for career continuity vary, for individuals as well as households.

## Career Continuity in Four Cohorts

My cohorts are defined broadly. They include both husbands and wives, and spouses may vary widely enough in age to have been shaped by different values and experiences. But because men have been the lead actors in maintaining pottery as a household specialty, for convenience I characterize each cohort by the attributes of the men who are in it. All hamlet men of a given age group are included, so long as they were born into a pottery enterprise house.

The oldest cohort, which I call Kimaro's, had its values shaped and its opportunities largely defined during the late Meiji (1868-1912) and early Taishō (1912-1926) years. Kimaro and the other two men in the cohort ranged from age 65 to 67 when my field data were gathered. Their wives were aged 61 to 64. Persons in Dentarō's cohort were born during early Shōwa (1926-    ). At the time of fieldwork, these six men were between 40 and 42 years of age, while their wives were between 35 and 41. This cohort's situation was greatly colored by World War II. Men in each of these cohorts began their domestic and work careers as successors in the *ie*. As a third cohort I will consider four men who started their careers as junior sons. This is Mitsuhiko's; the same male and female age parameters as in Dentarō's cohort describe husbands and wives, respectively. Finally, there is Sei'ichi's cohort, seven men between 22 and 24 years old. Only one was married when I left Kami-Tachikui.

The specific age parameters were selected because, while still narrow enough to have analytic meaning for each (male) cohort, the particular groups they isolate give the best longitudinal view of social process. All three persons in Kimaro's cohort have a son in Dentarō's. Men in Mitsuhiko's cohort are among the first junior sons affected by the folkcraft pottery market. And Sei'ichi's includes the youngest of the potters for whom the *mingei* boom opened new vistas.

The framework for examining linked careers in each cohort is suggested in a study of transitions to adulthood by Modell, Furstenberg, and Hershberg (1976:12-13). *Timing* refers to the typical points in the lifecourse when (status) transitions in a career occur: Timing is measured by the distribution of ages at which a cohort makes a particular transition. *Spread* refers to the time interval it takes a cohort to accomplish a particular transition. Timing, spread, and *prevalence* — the proportion of the cohort that experiences a given transition — all refer to properties of single status transitions. Two additonal dimensions concern the interrelationship of status transitions. *Age congruity* measures the degree to which the spreads of two or more transitions overlap. The measure is based on aggregate age distributions for cohorts, not the closeness of timing at the individual level. The *integration* of the same transitions also can be measured; the concern here is the degree to which one status transition is contingent upon another for individuals in a cohort.

Several sources supply the data I use. Detailed information gathered during personal interviews covers the work histories of men and women who comprise the cohorts. Knowledge of other individual lifecourse events, such as marriage, parenting, succession to headship, and becoming a branch house head, also come from personal interviews. Whenever possible, facts learned through interviews were cross-checked with information from records kept at the town hall. The same data that illuminate individual lifecourse patterns, viewed another way fill out the pattern of family (*ie*) lifecourse in Kami-Tachikui.

## Kimaro's Cohort

In order to assess career patterns for each cohort, we must look first at the point at which, ideally, young men begin pottery work. The primary identity of an individual in rural Japan traditionally rests in his or her affiliation with a household. In Kami-Tachikui, potting houses and their members are known by the shop name (*yago*) of the enterprise. Even today, the *ie* is equated socially and emotionally with its enterprise — in the present, in the past, and in the future. The very existence of the *ie* as a continuing entity may hinge on continuity in the enterprise. Therefore, the time when successors choose their life's work can be an uneasy one for enterprise houses.

Small doubt existed that heirs in Kimaro's cohort would carry on the *ie*'s economic specialty. For one reason, local conditions offered little alternative to pottery making as a means of providing the cash income needed to supplement farming. More conjecturally, parental teaching very likely reflected the heritage of the Tokugawa value system in which the family was a microcosm of the larger society. In the premodern framework, occupation *(shokubun)* "is not nearly an end in itself but a part of society. One's occupation is the fulfillment of what one owes to society, it is the part one plays which justifies one's receiving the benefits of society" (Bellah 1957:115).

Men in Kimaro's cohort began working on pottery for their *ie* at about age 13, near the end of the six years of school typical for hamlet residents then. The transition was gradual. While still in school, boys helped out around the shop. My informants said that no sense of apprenticeship characterized their first years of full-time pottery work. Nonetheless, *if* we consider marriage to be a significant milestone in the transition to adulthood, congruent with greater initiative in work, the youthful, preparatory phase of linked domestic and pottery careers lasted 10 to 13 years for Kimaro's cohort.

Marriage almost certainly signified an heir's acceptance of his role as successor. In this respect, the "adult" phase of linked careers began when men in the cohort were 23 to 25 years old. The birth of his first child, in all cases within a year after marriage, confirmed the successor's position. Ideally men could anticipate that for the next twenty years or so their life would be regulated by the daily rhythm of pottery-making, under their father's direction. Wives would help with pottery work. Primarily, women helped carry pots to the hillside kilns, helped bundle pots for delivery, or peddled pottery to nearby farming hamlets. Unless they grew up in a pottery house where occasionally they would have done chores related to the pottery, their pottery careers started when they married into their husband's house. Women's domestic career, however, could be expected to monopolize most of their years as junior wife. Each woman in this cohort gave birth to four or five children who lived. Childbearing was spread over some fourteen years, when women were between 20 and 34 years in age.

To use Harold Wilensky's (1968) characterization, Kimaro's cohort has experienced "orderly" domestic careers but generally "disorderly" work careers. Only one man worked continuously at home throughout the years of local economic stagnation. The others interrupted their work in the household pottery two or three times between 1928 and 1959. They worked as day laborers for some of the more stable pottery workshops in the hamlet. Interruptions cut an average of 15.5 years out of each man's ideal work trajectory. Since the first career reverse began just before or after the men had married, career disorderliness plagued most of their years as adult successors and probably their early years as household head. The house shops of both men ceased production during at least part of their absence. Figure 10.3 illustrates the extent to which prewar and

*Figure 10.3.* Production Histories of Pottery-Making Houses in Kami-Tachikui, 1849-1972

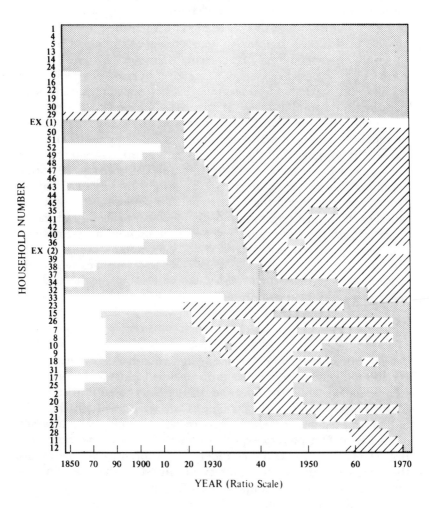

Source: Survey of Kami-Tachikui houses made in 1972.

signifies pottery production activity.

'////, signifies no pottery production.

'blank' signifies the house is not yet established or, in conjunction with "Ex", that the house is extinct.

Houses 5 and 31 co-own a workshop.

229

early postwar economic conditions disrupted household ceramic production throughout Kami-Tachikui.

Several deceased men who could have been part of Kimaro's cohort never resumed household pottery-making after the long slump in the local industry. Like so many men their age, they were too old and lacked training to compete successfully for urban industrial employment. As I reconstruct their work histories, men in this position experienced frequent turnover in low-paying jobs in the hamlet and its vicinity: employment in pottery workshops, pottery peddling, and mining rocks for gardens.

The uncertainty of work for men in Kimaro's cohort undoubtedly affected the timing of major transitions in linked domestic and work careers. It is known that the men who had disorderly pottery careers each assumed workshop headship around 1946 (at age 39), upon resuming household pottery-making after an extended break. Nonetheless, I lack other data that are essential for knowing whether the transition from subordinate potter to shop head was integrated with the transition from heir to household head for any of the men in the cohort. More can be said about timing in their passage *out* of formal authority positions. However, because the successors to these three men are located in Dentaro's cohort, details regarding retirement are presented below.

*Dentarō's Cohort*

Dentarō's cohort came of working age around 1945 when markets for Kami-Tachikui pottery were in decline. Outside opportunities were equally scarce, though, and all the heirs to enterprise houses found pottery work in the hamlet. They were about fifteen years old, having completed eight years of school. Only two, however, gained their first pottery experience in their own house shops. The first years of work were not considered an apprenticeship period for these men either. In fact, pottery produced at the time only required mastery of very simple skills compared to pottery made initially by Kimaro's cohort.

Although one man continued wage employment for 23 years, the others changed to their house enterprises after three or four years. Since age 18, then, their household pottery career has been orderly. Counting all their experience, these men were engaged in pottery for about the same number of years (10 to 14) as Kimaro's cohort before marrying. Marriage came later — between age 25 and 29.

The later age of leaving school, combined with delayed entry into the household labor force, possibly affected the age of marriage. The pairs of husbands and wives in Dentarō's cohort have each been a close team in the ceramic shop. Even though the first child was born soon after marriage, this cohort typically had just two children. The aggregate spread between first and last child shortened to five years, affecting women between the ages of 23 and 30. Child care clearly has made fewer demands on a junior wife's time than in the past.

Women in Dentarō's cohort, in fact, devote nearly as many work hours as their husbands to the house enterprise. Senior wives, who retired comparatively early from pottery work, perform a large share of the household chores. Nonetheless, women's labor is perceived differently from men's. Men and women both say that women's work consists of odd-job tasks (zatsueki). And with few exceptions, women are limited to such tasks as loading and unloading kilns, glazing, packaging, and fetch-and-carry work. Such tasks have proliferated as enterprises increasingly emphasize folkcraft ceramics. Whereas men, particularly the skilled potters, think of their work as a career that has a developmental course of its own, women view their pottery labor as an extension of their household chores.

The "public" aspect of men's work enhances the concept of a developmental career. As the skilled wheel-throwers, men alone can build a personal reputation for the product of their labor. Also, as men gradually achieve responsiblity in the work group, they increasingly represent the workshop in primary transactions with buyers and suppliers. Growing responsiblity culminates in the privilege of representing the shop in the local ceramic cooperative.

Timetable bargaining among Dentarō's cohort focuses on this particular privilege. The systems of prestige and political influence in Kami-Tachikui revolve around the ceramic industry. The Tamba Ceramic Cooperative Association, composed of workshop heads, is the primary extra-household group for men. Therefore, the decision to relinguish one's authority over the house enterprise does not come easily for aging men.

We get an indication of how timetable norms may evolve when we consider succession to enterprise headship in Dentarō's cohort. The point at which a father's and sons's lifecourse intersect seems to influence the timing of the transition. In three of our cases, sons were aged 33, 41, and 42 and their fathers were 63, 65, and 65, respectively, at the time of transition. The spread of ages in each generation is close enough to suggest that a general timetable norm exists, based on the paired ages of each father and son. I was able to observe some of the bargaining that underlay the latter two transitions in formal shop authority.

The houses concerned were headed by the men from Kimaro's cohort whose pottery careers had suffered disruptions. Both successors actually had managed daily production for several years. Yet their fathers were skilled and active potters who could not be pushed aside easily. The reasoning that clinched the status transmission was this: The fathers were the oldest in the hamlet to still retain workshop headship, and their sons were the oldest in their age group not to exercise headship. Because men from the two houses were friends, discussion in one house influenced the drift of discussion in the other house. Retirement did not bar the older men from positions of prestige in their enterprise or the pottery community. Rather, it freed them to concentrate on "specialty" work. The specialty of one man, for example, was enormous hand-thrown platters that few others in the hamlet could make.

Circumstances regarding succession to workshop head differed markedly where a fourth man from Kimaro's cohort was concerned. He was 50 and his heir 23 when the transition occurred. At the time (1955), the low demand for local pottery did not warrant the full-time labor of two men. The father preferred to earn income by making rock gardens. The remaining heirs in Dentarō's cohort became head of both shop and house atypically early because of their fathers' deaths.

The pattern of timing in succession to house headship even more strongly suggests the operation of a timetable norm. Heirs in Dentarō's cohort became head at ages 40, 41, 41, and 42. Their fathers retired from headship at ages 67, 72, 65 and 65 respectively. (The latter three cases include men from Kimaro's cohort.) All four transitions occurred during 1972. Therefore, there is hardly any age-congruity between this domestic status transition and its counterpart along the pottery trajectory which occured over a 17-year spread (1955-1972). (Based on Modell, Furstenberg, and Hershberg's scheme, the degree of age-congruity is 0.11 where a value of 0.00 indicates complete incongruity and 1.00 indicates complete congruity.) In only two cases were transitions along linked trajectories completely integrated.

The differences in timing of transitions to status that are generally thought to be occupied simultaneously may be interpreted as the result of household members' bargaining for a satisfying niche in life. By continuing to serve as household head after retiring as leader of the workshop, a man can retain a sense of importance. He may continue to be, or become a leader within the civil hierarchy (the *buraku sōkai* or Hamlet Association). The generational division of formal status in domestic and work domains also has an economic function. Men who headed both the pottery shop and the house during my field study in fact complained that their civic duties interferred with pottery work.

### Mitsuhiko's Cohort

Men in Mitsuhiko's cohort initially stayed in Kami-Tachikui because of a dearth of opportunities outside the hamlet. The parental houses did not actively recruit their labor for the then-undynamic enterprises. (Other nonsuccessors in this age grup, from both pottery and nonpottery houses, did however emigrate.) Having settled into a pottery routine, these junior sons lost the mobility to enter the urban labor market when it improved miraculously in the late 1950s. In time they became key figures in the economic expansion of parental house enterprise.

In certain ways, patterns characteristic of Mitsuhiko's cohort parallel Dentarō's. Men went to school for eight years. They began pottery work immediately after leaving school. They also married when they were within the same age spread, and had the same number of children within the same number of years. In other important ways, however, the lifecourse of junior sons and their wives sharply diverges from the life course of age-mates in the line of succession.

The length of time spent as a family potter is similar for each man in the cohort. Three started out in the family enterprise; the fourth joined his house shop after only a year of paid employment elsewhere. Men worked nine to thirteen years while still living in their parental house. They made the transition to branch house head, and consequently "branch house potter," between the ages of 25 and 29. The transition to these integrated domestic and work statuses was highly age-congruous (0.75) with their transition to married life. Branch house formation was in fact contingent upon marriage and generally accomplished within a year of marriage.

The work role of branch house potters differed from earlier periods, in that men now received a monthly salary instead of an "allowance." Branch house wives were no less obligated to work at

233

the pottery than wives living under the main house roof. They worked full-time in main house shops once child care required less of their time. Nevertheless, only one women in this cohort ever was paid directly for her pottery labor.

How much responsibility a man acquired in the main house shop depended on the production strategy of the enterprise. The transition to branch house potter spread over the three years between 1958 and 1960, years when Kami-Tachikui potters were just beginning to contemplate the potential of folkcraft ceramics. Some enterprises encouraged branch potters to improve their skills so they could develop a folkcraft pottery line. The first potter to apprentice outside the hamlet was among this cohort. In shops following this strategy, fathers and older brothers continued the bread-and-butter production that required less skill. Therefore, a division of labor in both physical and managerial activity evolved in some workshops.

In 1966 the first couple in Mitsuhiko's cohort embarked on independent pottery production. The transition to enterprise house status was yet to be finished 12 years later (1978) when I last interviewed potters from Kami-Tachikui. One couple still worked for its main house. Therefore, this cohort spent from seven to 18-plus years as branch house potters. The *ie* construct embodies the ideal that a main house should help its branch achieve economic independence. But the timing of independence, as well as the terms, are matters to be negotiated. These matters are critical to a dōzoku-based enterprise.

Branch house potters generally feel the greatest urgency to become independent around the time their children reach school age. Partly they are thinking of a patrimony for the succeeding generation. With growing children, they keenly feel the constraints of their comparatively low salaries as well. Folkcraft specialists, particularly, believe they can do better financially on their own. Furthermore, they chafe at being denied formal status in the pottery community when their efforts have been so instrumental in promoting the community's well-being.

However, the timing of a branch house's independence depends most on conditions in the main house enterprise. Can the enterprise sustain the loss of core potters? Does the main house have the collateral to underwrite loans the branch will need in order to open a workshop? Where the main house is in *its* family cycle often determines the answer to the first question.

When families in Mitsuhiko's cohort established an independent shop, the oldest children were ages 7, 12, and 20. Successors in the main house were 18, 20, and 22; they either worked in the house shop already or planned to do so after finishing ceramic training. Speaking about specific cases, potters voiced the opinion that the break in economic interdependency should be timed so role conflict between the older branch potter and the main house successor is avoided. This concern unquestionably enters into construction of a timetable norm. But I believe that the main house's ability to compensate for losing a veteran potter's labor is more decisive. The branch head who still worked as a paid employee in 1978 had overlapped with his brother's successor for seven years. It had taken the successor that long to transform a shop that made flowerpots into one that specialized in folkcraft ceramics.

*Sei'ichi's Cohort*

Today the houses that include men of Sei'ichi's cohort face a complex set of challenges and incentives, paralleling the growing complexity of postwar and post-industrial Japanese society. The stability of the house is threatened not only by the increase in new occupations but also by the diffusion of new ideas regarding work, family, and life style.

The postwar educational and legal systems, with their emphasis on democratic and individualistic ideals, give less support to the web of human obligations implied in the enterprise household. The *ie* has come under attack as a "feudal" institution. In its stead, the nuclear family has been pushed as the ideal for a modern, democratic society. The postwar civil law, in fact, abolished the lineality of the *ie* system by abrogating the supreme authority of the household head, declaring husband and wife to be equal, giving sons and daughters the right to choose their own spouses, and calling for equal inheritance for all children (Ariga 1956; Nakano 1962).

Unlike their parents, most young people in Kami-Tachikui today complete high school, and since around 1970, the number who go on to college has risen markedly. Sons and daughters in pottery enterprise houses are more likely to attend college than youth from other houses. What impact, then, have these changing values and opportunities had on Sei'ichi's generation?

Despite legal abolishment of the *ie* and national attitudinal changes downplaying succession, practically every Kami-Tachikui house has secured heirs in the postwar decades. It is interesting, however, that the houses that *have* become defunct since World

War II, and the three or four in which succession was in question in the early 1970's, all lack an economic specialty. Heirs in the nonceramic houses with very few exceptions have entered the urban labor force. They tend to find jobs either as white-collar workers or as bus, truck, or taxi drivers. Commuter jobs pay better than jobs on the local scene. In fact, more often than not, the annual earnings of a nonenterprise house have equalled or exceeded those of most pottery houses.

But the general picture is that heirs in Sei'ichi's cohort are tying their occupational career to their domestic career and to the future of the household enterprise. Two men who tried nonpottery work after leaving school returned to the family fold after several years. The other men took up pottery careers from the first. Many factors quite apart from the moral obligation of kinship draw these successors to the household specialization.

People perceive the market for folkcraft ceramics to be an expanding one that promises ever greater rewards. Pottery-making furthermore offers a potential for personal satisfaction beyond that gained from earning a good livelihood. The challenge of workshop management, and the broadened social and economic networks that ownership brings, obviously excite many present and potential enterprisers in Kami-Tachikui. Through the tourist trade, potters form connections with government dignitaries, wealthy businessmen, newspapermen, and other persons of a sort once far removed from the experience of rural craft producers. In addition in the postwar years it has become common for prospective potters to take training outside the area. Trainees return with new ceramic techniques and new outlets for marketing and exhibiting their wares.

The folkcraft movement has restored the status of *shokunin* or "artisan" to potters of Kimaro's cohort. It has, in addition, opened the way for younger potters to aspire to become *sakka* or "artists." The recognition that a pottery career can bring, so elusive for persons who pursue more ordinary occupations, may add further incentive to the idea of continuing an enterprise house in Kami-Tachikui. In short, "traditional" as the enterprise household may appear, it can help its young members of working age pursue the "modern" individualistic goals of personal career development and fame.

Conflicts between personal goals and collective welfare are more likely when household continuity hinges on the cooperation of a daughter who agrees to marry a *mukoyōshi*. The growing popularity of love matches obviously complicates the prospects of successful negotiations for a *mukoyōshi*. Events touching a house called here by the shop name Yamanaka illustrate the problems that may arise when a house lacks a natural male heir.

Of the four Yamanaka daughters, three married partners of their own choosing and settled outside Kami-Tachikui. Yoshiko, who is in the same age group as the men in Sei'ichi's cohort, told me she too had ideas of making a love match and leaving the hamlet. However, after considerable moral suasion, she compromised her wishes for the welfare of Yamanaka. Yoshiko actually went further to meet her house's needs than had any other village women in the same position. She quit junior college in order to attend ceramic training school in Kyoto, after which she returned and began working as a potter full-time. In the early 1970's she was the only woman in the hamlet who regularly worked on the potter's wheel.

When it came to deciding whom Yoshiko would marry, however, personal preference won out. Her family openly hoped she would marry a man willing to learn the pottery business. One such young man from a neighboring hamlet proposed to Yoshiko; however, she rejected him as well as a number of other candidates who turned up during months of searching by her family and relatives. So the Yamanaka task became one of finding a man she would accept rather than one who would take over the pottery enterprise.

Yoshiko eventually married Tadashi, a man who already had established a career outside the hamlet. It is conceivable that under extreme circumstances he would give up his city hall job for household pottery work. Yoshiko's father, himself adopted, had had a career with the National Railways before his marriage. However, upon the early death of his father-in-law, he quit the job in order to manage Yamanaka. The fact that Yamanaka was not a thriving enterprise at the time supports the contention that the continuity of a household craft is valued for more than its economic contribution alone. The pressure on Tadashi to involve himself in the family business was lightened by persuading the husband of one of Yoshiko's older sisters to train for a position of responsibility in the business. This brother-in-law was bored with the routine, low-paying company job he held. And the small city where he and his wife live is close enough to Kami-Tachikui so that he could commute daily.

So far, the pattern of linkage between work and domestic careers among Sei'ichi's cohort differs significantly from patterns that characterize other cohorts of successors. Men have joined house enterprise later and have brought greater skills to the enterprise.

Everyone in the cohort finished high school and one man graduated from college. Five men left the hamlet to attend a ceramic training school and/or to apprentice with a master potter after they completed their regular education. The training period for each lasted two or three years. Sei'ichi's cohort made the transition to household potter over a six-year period (1968-1973). Men ranged between ages 20 and 25 when they began working at home.

While it commonly is considered to be the right of a successor to share management responsibility (Nakane 1967:2) it is also common for conflict to develop when the successor controls superior skills or more "modern" knowledge than the household head (Fukutake 1967:54). Most men in Sei'ichi's cohort were the only potters in the house enterprise who had the sophisticated marketing and production techniques that involvement in the folkcraft market requires. I did not hear about open conflict between a father and son. But I did observe that several heirs virtually managed the shop while they were still in their middle 20's. In one house, the head and his wife make ordinary flowerpots, and the successor and his wife make folkcraft ceramics. A separate workshop was built for the successor and he was given total control over his own production and finances. It is likely that timetables for granting an heir de facto (if not de jure) control of a workshop prior to his succession to household head generally are being pushed ahead. Two fathers of men in Sei'ichi's cohort who had "retired" from the daily management of the shop, focussed their energy instead on the arena of hamlet or township (chō) politics.

The age at which men marry could be as late as in Dentarō's and Mitsuhiko's cohort. My impression was that, in general, men in Sei'ichi's cohort wished to build a steady clientele for their pottery before they married. The one man who had married had met his wife as an apprentice in Kyoto. She is a ceramicist who specializes in painting calligraphic designs on bisque ware.

The junior wife's work role showed little similarity to that of her mother-in-law. Rather than do miscellaneous work, she concentrated on her own specialty. While she deferred to her husband in both work and domestic roles, she nonetheless viewed her pottery work from a developmental perspective. Moreover, her pottery role was considered so important to the house that the senior wife, contrary to custom, performed the major share of the household tasks. The emphasis on the junior wife's pottery career continued at least until 1978, as the couple (by design) still had no children.

I do not know whether or not this young couple represents the

238

ideal for others in Sei'ichi's cohort. Making a love match; maintaining spatial separation between one's work place and that of one's parents; having a wife who could gain recognition for her own pottery work — even if these seem like ideal conditions, they are difficult to realize within the constraints of an enterprise house. Yoshiko, for example, had two children very early in her marriage; she all but discontinued her pottery career, at least for a time. But the couple does provide a model that people from other houses can point to when they are struggling with generational or gender-based role conflicts in their own lives.

## Discussion

The pottery industry in the hamlet of Kami-Tachikui rests on the paradigm of the enterprise house. Traditional concepts of role provide the broad outline for the sequence of major statuses one will hold along both family and pottery-making career trajectories. Yet familial (ie-based) role prescriptions of a general nature cannot strictly define the context of a household potter's life course. Behavior will reflect as well an individual's experience outside the household, and his or her response to historical events and socioeconomic trends. Pottery work and domestic relations are differentially affected by these events and trends. But the domains are so inextricably bound that adjustment in one may have tremendous impact on behavior in the other. For these reasons, when we view cohorts of household successors passing through family time at different historical times, we see that a unique balance between linked careers unfolds for each.

Since the Second World War, Japanese scholars of the family have been concerned with the impact of constitutional changes and trends such as prolonged life expectancy, declining fertility, growing occupational and demographic mobility, and a higher standard of living. Those who have delineated family life cycle stages and analyzed the nature of human relations at each stage (Ishihara 1977; Morioka 1967, 1973, 1977) address issues closely related to my investigation. Ishihara (1977), for example, has analyzed the allocation of authority within stem family households in two villages near Tokyo. Comparative data were gathered in 1965 and 1975. By focusing on five indices of power — representation of the household, management of assets, management of commodities, management of agriculture, and management of nonagricultural enterprise —

Ishihara demonstrates that decision-making involves the complex interaction to all house members.

Ishihara's conclusions complement mine on several points. For one, he finds a strong correlation between where a house is in its family cycle and the degree of authority held by members in various age- and gender-based positions. He constructs his analysis around four stages based on the composition of the household: nuclear family, generationally linked nuclear families, father and heir's nuclear family, mother and heir's nuclear family. To cite an example, a senior wife loses considerable authority if her husband dies. Especially interesting is Ishihara's conclusion that in both 1965 and 1975 the development of the older nuclear family influences power transfer more than the development of the heir's nuclear family. That is, *except* with regard to agriculture, the primary source of income. The timing of succession to house headship and workshop headship among Dentarō's cohort seems to reflect this same principle.

Ishihara, in addition, gives a longitudinal picture of timing in the transfer of authority from head to successor. Based on informants' recollections, he compiled a table (1977:197) showing the average age of fathers and sons when different privileges and responsiblities changed hands. Transfer of authority began and was completed later in the life cycle of fathers and sons after the war than before the war. However, the range of delay was greater between 1946 and 1960 than between 1961 and 1975. I think that if the data were more complete, a similar pattern would be found among pottery enterprisers. Dentarō's cohort probably acceded to authority later than Kimaro's, mainly because of the longer life expectancy of their fathers. Conditions of the local and national economy, however, will accelerate accession among Sei'ichi's cohort.

Methodologically, Ishihara's study is instructive because it emphasizes that a status transition may be multidimensional. My treatment of household headship and workshop headship in Kami-Tachikui, for example, focusses on the privilege to formally represent the house or shop. But each status has other dimensions, which may or may not be transmitted from head to successor at the same time as the power of representation. Tied to the framework of collective family stages, however, Ishihara's study tells us little about family variations based on differential timing and sequencing of power redistributions. Recent critiques of the family cycle as the prevalent analytical construct in family studies, have centered on the static, snapshop-like analyses it tends to generate (Elder 1977;

Hareven 1978). The critics argue instead for a lifecourse approach to family studies, because the lifecourse "encompasses both individual and collective family development, and the problems that arise from their synchronization" (Hareven 1978:2). Ishihara (personal communication), in fact, intends to incorporate the factor of individual life course into his continuing research on the allocation of power within the family.

One may wonder whether the pattern of interconnected careers in Kami-Tachikui is similar for persons engaged in other kinds of family enterprise in Japan. Possibly not. For one reason, the setting is a comparatively isolated community whose houses are interrelated by consanguineal and affinal kinship. Kinship underlies the idiom of personal relations. Moreover, Japanese society places a high value on the community's product, is willing to pay well for it, and accords producers considerable prestige.

Weavers in Nishijin, an artisan quarter in Kyoto, provide an interesting comparison. As Haak (1973, 1975) describes Nishijin weavers, men and women integrate family life around production of a traditional item (mainly *obi,* the sashes for kimono). Unlike the work lives of those in Kami-Tachikui, however, house weavers are controlled by commercial wholesalers known as *oriya.* These commercial companies provide weavers with designs and often rent them looms. Weavers are paid piecework wages for the *obi.* Under such conditions, a house head is prevented from expanding his own business and from gaining individual recognition as an artisan. Although today two generations of weavers may live and work in a house, the prospects of reproducing family labor in the next generation, according to Haak (1975) are declining. However, Haak's account (1973) suggests that *oriya* enterprises, in contrast, are built on an expansive, kin-based structure similar to the *dōzoku* cooperation found among potters in Kami-Tachikui.

Enterprisers in Tokyo's Arakawa ward are probably more characteristic of Japan's small producers. As DeVos and Wagatsuma (1973a; Wagatsuma 1975) describe the area, numerous house factories, most of which have fewer than nine workers, produce items of daily use such as clothing, furniture, toys, and pencils. For the most part, they subcontract for medium-sized or large manufacturers. Bankrupty is common when shifts in demand occur or conditions of recession prevail. The case studies of pencil-makers that Wagatsuma and DeVos present indicate that kin-based cooperation beyond household boundaries can be important. A house may help a son or son-in-law establish his own small enterprise, usually in an

241

aspect of pencil manufacture that complements the specialization of the parental house. The accounts do not tell us whether *dōzoku* nomenclature characterizes relations between interdependent houses; even if it does not, the principle of cooperation is the same. Nonetheless, mutual obligation and dependency probably are seldom as intense as between a main and branch house in Kami-Tachikui during the time they are working in pottery together. Moreover, it seems likely that generational continuity in house-based enterprises in Arakawa is much less certain than in Kami-Tachikui or, until recently, Nishijin.

Whether merged with strong *ie* consciousness or not, potters, weavers, and pencil-makers have in common an entrepreneurial outlook. Several scholars propose that a highly rated goal among Japanese is to achieve independent entrepreneurial status. Nakano (1966) attributed the hard work and loyalty of premodern merchant apprentices to this goal of theirs, and Pelzel (1979) notes its primacy among workers in the metal and machinery industry during the 1950's. Wagatsuma (1975:374) not only observes it in pencil manufacturing, but stresses that the desire to become an entrepreneur is as characteristic of the lower class as it is of the middle class in Japan.

According to Pelzel and Wagatsuma, the psychological rewards arising from self-employment justify certain sacrifices, usually in the direction of low standards of living and extended work schedules. Furthermore, despite the milieu of intense competition that spells bankruptcy for many, in Wagatsuma's view the small enterpriser maintains his visions of independence and success:

> He feels that if he works sufficiently hard he can somehow beat out nearby competition. He keeps the sustaining hope that he himself can somehow escape the destiny of failure he witnesses as occurring to others. He does this by competing better — by somehow devoting more time, energy, and dedication to his work than that given by his unsuccessful neighbor. And most important, perhaps, he does enjoy living by the old Chinese dictum, "Keitō to narumo gyūbi to naru nakare" (It is better to be the head of a chicken than the tail of a cow), very commonly used in Japan. (1975:375)

Dore (1967:193) points out that historically there are two paths to social mobility in Japan, "the individualist's route via commercial or industrial skill and the dependent employee's route via advancement within a bureaucratic organization." Because the latter path received government encouragement from the Meiji period on, we tend to overlook the vitality of the entrepreneurial alternative.

Although I am not able to cite evidence (it is a topic that attitudinal surveys have not covered), I detect mounting dissatisfaction with employment conditions in Japan. Almost all the apprentices in Kami-Tachikui, for example, had given up other occupations in order to turn to pottery. Their reasons partially reflect their inability to realize the salary-man ideal. They voiced boredom with their uncreative low-level jobs in large enterprise, saying they foresaw only slow promotion. Cole (1976) and Rohlen (1979), discussing the consequences of recession, slow growth, and an aging labor force, predict that increasing numbers of Japanese will feel alienated from work. The intensifying struggle for promotions and for higher wage increases, and the growing possibility of relocation and early retirement, run counter to the commonly held perception of industrial paternalism.

But the young people who seek a new career in Kami-Tachikui also reflect skepticism of the work style implied in the salary-man ideal. It is paradoxical that the dominant postwar ideology of work and family offers little opportunity for individual-centered growth through work, in spite of the individualistic values that postwar education to some extent has fostered. Dore's (1973) portrayal of work in a large Japanese factory and Rohlen's (1974) ethnography of work in a bank each make us keenly aware of how narrowly the seniority system channels individual initiative. Even more relevant to my point, both studies show that, for most workers, employment in a large enterprise neither requires nor allows the mastery and refinement of a particular expertise. Pottery apprentices were searching for a life-work that ultimately links mastery of skills with autonomy in the application of these skills. The premodern concept of work is, in fact, more consonant with these aspirations than the currently predominant views.

Obviously, the enterprise house cannot offer everyone the same opportunities that potters in Kami-Tachikui enjoy today. But it may allow a man more personal autonomy than most work situations. The benefits are not so clear for women. At least in Kami-Tachikui, if a woman is interested in "career" development, she will find it more readily outside of the family enterprise, despite the general sex discrimination in employment. In pot-making, even when a woman performs tasks that generally are done by men, her work is not evaluated in the same way. The exclusion of women from public

243

roles in Kami-Tachikui does much to perpetuate the view that their labor is subsidiary to men's and of less value.

In terms of domestic arrangements, both men and women of the postwar cohort are apt to find the enterprise household suffocating. Recruitment of a successor, and of a wife for a household heir, is a problem if traditional role definitions are adhered to strictly. However, the enterprise house is as flexible here as in the organization of work. Wimberley (1973), for example, describes the emerging practice of segregating the living space of older and younger couples in merchant houses in Kanazawa. This enables each couple to pursue its own tastes and reduces tension between the generations. But if privacy is scarce in enterprise houses, in Kami-Tachikui anyway, I felt that the quality of personal relations between husbands and wives is richer than in houses where work and family life are separated. The important economic contribution of women is recognized by all in pot-making houses and spouses exhibit a camaraderie generally lacking in other Japanese houses.

## References

Abegglen, James C.
  1958  The Japanese Factory. Glencoe, Ill.: Free Press.
  1973  Management and Worker, The Japanese Solution. Tokyo: Sophia University and Kodansha International
Abeles, Ronald P., and Matilda W. Riley
  1978  A Life-Course Perspective on the Later Years of Life: Some Implications for Research. In Social Science Research Council Annual Report, pp. 1-16.
Ariga Kizaemon
  1956  The Contemporary Japanese Family in Transition. Transactions of the Third World Congress of Sociology, pp. 215-221. London: International Sociological Association.
Bachnik, Jane
  1978  Inside and Outside the Japanese Household (Ie). Ph.D. dissertation, Harvard University.
Bellah, Robert
  1957  Tokugawa Religion: The Values of Pre-Industrial Japan. Glencoe, Illinois: Free Press.
Bennett, John W., and Michio Nagai
  1953  The Japanese Critique of Benedict's 'Chrysanthemum and the Sword'. American Anthropologist 55:401-411.
Broadbridge, Seymour
  1966  Industrial Dualism in Japan: A Problem of Economic Growth and Structural Change. London: Frank Cass.

Cole, Robert E.
  1971 Japanese Blue Collar, The Changing Tradition. Berkeley and Los Angeles: University of California Press.
  1976 Changing Labor Force Characteristics and Their Impact on Japanese Industrial Relations. *In* Japan: The Paradox of Progress, Lewis Austin, ed. pp. 165-213. New Haven: Yale University Press.
  1979 Work, Mobility, and Participation: A Comparative Study of American and Japanese Industry. Berkeley and Los Angeles: University of California Press.
DeVos, George, and Hiroshi Wagatsuma
  1973a The Entrepreneurial Mentality of Lower-Class Urban Japanese in Manufacturing Industries. *In* Socialization for Achievement, G. DeVos, et al., eds., pp. 201-219. Berkeley and Los Angeles: University of California Press.
  1973b Status and Role Behavior in Changing Japan: Psychocultural Continuities. *In* Socialization for Achievement, G. DeVos, et al., eds., pp. 10-60. Berkeley and Los Angeles: University of California Press.
Dore, Ronald P.
  1967 City Life in Japan: A Study of a Tokyo Ward. [Original edition 1958] Berkeley and Los Angeles: University of California Press.
  1973 British Factory — Japanese Factory, The Origins of National Diversity in Industrial Relations. Berkeley and Los Angeles: University of California Press.
Elder, Glen H., Jr.
  1977 Family History and the Life Course. *In* Journal of Family History 2 (4): 279-304. Reprinted in Transitions; The Family and the Life Course in Historical Perspective, Tamara Hareven, ed. New York: Academic Press.
Fukutake Tadashi
  1967 Japanese Rural Society. London: Oxford University Press.
Haak, Ronald
  1973 Nishijin Weavers: A Study of the Functions of Tradition in Modern Japanese Society. Ann Arbor, Mich.: University Microfilms.
  1975 The Zesty, Structured World of a Weaver. *In* Adult Episodes in Japan: David W. Plath, ed., pp. 42-50. Leiden: Brill.
Hareven, Tamara K.
  1977 Family Time and Historical Time. Daedalus 106 (2): 57-70.
  1978 Introduction: The Historical Study of the Life Course. *In* Transitions; The Family and the Life Couse in Historical Perspective, T. Hareven, ed., pp. 1-16. New York: Academic Press.
Hollerman, Leon
  1972 Changes in Japanese Small Business. Japan Quarterly 19 (2): 211-217.

Ishihara Kunio
   1977   Setai shusaiken kara mita life cycle to kazoku hendō [Life
          Cycle and Domestic Change as Seen Through Generational
          Power] *In* Gendai Kazoku no raifu Saikuru [Life Cycle of the
          Modern Family], Morioka Kiyomi, ed., pp. 180-205. Tokyo:
          Baifūkan.
Kanter, Rosabeth Moss
   1977   Work and Family in the United States: A Critical Review and
          Agenda for Research and Policy. New York: Russell Sage Foun-
          dation.
Kawashima Takeyoshi
   1957   Ideorogii to shite no kazoku seido [The Family System as Ideol-
          ogy]. Tokyo: Iwanami Shoten.
Kitaoji Hironobu
   1971   The Structure of the Japanese Family. American Anthropologist
          73 (5): 1036-1057.
Koyama Takashi
   1961   The Changing Social Position of Women in Japan. Paris:
          UNESCO.
Masuda Kōkichi
   1975   Bride's Progress: How a Yome Becomes a Shūtome. *In* Adult
          Episodes in Japan, David W. Plath, ed., pp. 10-19 Leiden:
          Brill.
Modell, John, Frank Furstenberg, Jr., and Theodore Hershberg
   1976   Social Change and Transitions to Adulthood in Historical
          Perspective. Journal of Family History 1 (1): 7-32.
Morgan, D. H. J.
   1975   Social Theory and the Family. London: Routledge & Kegan
          Paul.
Morioka Kiyomi
   1967   Life Cycle Patterns in Japan, China and the United States.
          Journal of Marriage and the Family 29 (3): 595-608.
   1973   Kazoku shūki ron [Essays on the Family Cycle]. Tokyo:
          Baifūkan.
Morioka Kiyomi (ed.)
   1977   Gendai kazoku no raifu saikuru [Life Cycle of the Modern
          Family]. Tokyo:Baifūkan.
Nakane Chie
   1967   Kinship and Economic Organization in Rural Japan. New
          York: Humanities Press.
Nakano Takashi
   1958   Honke to bunke [Main House and Branch House]. In Nishioka
          Toranosuke, Ōba Funao, Ōfuji Tokihiko and Kiuchi Nobuzō,
          eds., Kyōdō kenkyu kōza, dai 3 kan: Ie [Lectures on Col-
          laborative Research, Vol. III: Households]. Tokyo: Kadokawa
          Shoten.

1959   Ie no ideorogii [Ideologies of the Ie]. In Kōza gendai shakai shinrigaku [Lectures on Modern Social Psychology] 8: 100-118. Tokyo: Nakayama Shoten.
1962   Recent Studies of Change in the Japanese Family. International Social Science Journal 14 (3): 527-538.
1964   Shōka dōzokudan no kenkyū [A Study of Merchant Houses]. Tokyo: Miraisha.
1966   Merchant Dōzoku of Japan: Process of Their Change from the Tokugawa Period. Unpublished manuscript.

Pelzel, John
1979   Factory Life in Japan and China Today. In Japan: A Comparative View, Albert Craig, ed., pp. 371-432. Princeton: Princeton University Press.

Rohlen, Thomas P.
1974   For Harmony and Strength: Japanese White-Collar Organization in Anthropological Perspective. Berkeley and Los Angeles: University of California Press.
1979   "Permanent Employment" Faces Recession, Slow Growth, and an Aging Work Force. The Journal of Japanese Studies 4 (2): 235-272.

Rosaldo, Michelle Zimbalist
1974   Woman, Culture, and Society: A Theoretical Overview. In Woman, Culture, and Society, M. Z. Rosaldo and Louise Lamphere, eds., pp. 17-42. Stanford: Stanford University Press.

Roth, Julius A.
1963   Timetables: Structuring the Passage of Time in Hospital Treatment and Other Careers. Indianapolis: Bobbs-Merrill.

Wagatsuma Hiroshi
1975   Pencil Making in a Tokyo Ward. Revista International di Scienze Economiche e Commercial, 22 (4): 369-390.

Whitehill, Arthur M., Jr., and Shin-ichi Takezawa
1968   The Other Worker: A Comparative Study of Industrial Relations in the United States and Japan. Honolulu: East-West Center Press.

Wilensky, Harold
1968   Orderly Careers and Social Participation: The Impact of Work History On Social Integration in the Middle Mass. In Middle Age and Aging: A Reader in Social Psychology, Bernice L. Neugarten, ed. Chicago: University of Chicago Press.

Wimberly, Howard
1973   On Living with Our Past: Style and Structure among Contemporary Japanese Merchant Families: Economic Development and Cultural Change 21 (3): 423-428.

# Timetables and the Lifecourse in Post-Industrial Society

JULIUS A. ROTH

One of the questions I raised in the last chapter of my book *Timetables* (Roth 1963) concerned the culture-bound nature of structuring the passage of time in a linear fashion. It is a process commonly associated with Western industrialism, although it is also clearly a theme in other times and places.

How widespread is the linear organization of time? This is a question which can be approached by studying parts of the world other than Western industrial countries. Japan is not the best test of this issue since it has clearly adopted many of the forms of European and North American society. However, it is sufficiently removed to serve as at least a limited test. The answer I would give on the basis of some of the papers in this book is that the Japanese apply a linear concept of time — certainly in the occupational sphere — strikingly like that of Western Europeans and present-day North Americans.

Let us take, for example, the railroad workers described by Paul Noguchi in Chapter Four. These workers appear to structure career timetables in a way similar to that reported in the United States in the case of long-term careers within a given organization. The career is seen as a series of stages that one can be expected to move through up to a point, and there are norms about how long one may be expected to remain at each stage. Older platform workers (typically an early-career position) working with youthful colleagues are regarded as out of joint with common expectation. Those who spend significantly longer than the expected time in any one position are thought to be "running late," and they may stave off the feeling of relative failure only by constantly reinterpreting the career timetable.

248

If a large, complex organization has more than one promotion track, some workers may be uncertain about which one they are on. Also, some positions (combinations of job title and geographical location) are sometimes used to sidetrack workers who are not likely to be promoted further. This produces uncertainty of expectations, but it also more readily allows the explaining away of apparant failure. The higher organizational authorities themselves are aware of timetable expectations and feel the pressure of "too many" workers running late. Thus, when the exigencies of the development of the railroads in postwar Japan and the flood of returning war veterans required a great deal of hiring during a short time span, resulting in an oversupply of candidates at a later point in the promotional pyramid, more middle-management positions were created to absorb some of the excess aspirants.

Much of the same can be said for the somewhat more exalted career lines in the public corporation described by Kenneth Skinner in Chapter Three. The fact that many employees began their careers with the corporation as part of an entry cohort makes differential promotions among them more obvious. In this setting, job security and regular salary increases provide the orderly aspects of the career. It is the specific job assignments which are highly uncertain, an uncertainty increased by frequent shifting of managers. However, the Japanese employees, like their North American counterparts, do not accept the uncertainty as an inevitable fate, but constantly attempt to acquire and interpret information which will increase career predictability. They use any information gleaned from any source to try to understand the reason for a reassignment and to assess the effect it will have on their future career. They will use information about the reassignment of others to try to fathom managerial decision patterns that might be applied to their own career. They try to shape their reputation to influence future assignments, despite the fact that frequent changes of managers reduces the effect of personal reputation.

Over a historical period, career timetables may not only be slowed up, as in the case of railroad workers, but may be speeded up by changes in technology or the social structure. Jill Kleinberg's chapter on the cottage pottery industry (Chapter Ten) shows how special new skills acquired by a younger generation upset the traditional timetable of learning the craft and moving up the control hierarchy within a household. The newer skills plus accompanying economic demands for the resulting products place the younger members of a pottery household in a position where they can establish themselves on their own if their advancement within the household is not fast enough to please them. If the older members of the household wish to retain their younger member's services and loyalty, they must grant authority and rewards at an earlier stage of life. Traditional expectations of family organization are modified if necessary to keep the enterprise going. Thus the technology and the economic conditions of the broader society have a direct effect on the fabric of relationships, especially on patterns of relative authority, within an economically productive extended family.

One of the papers in this book, Theodore Cook's Chapter Seven, describes an extreme instance of complete career collapse — the position of military officers in a totally defeated and dismantled military service. It was a devasting event for all of them temporarily and for some permanently, the more so because the military had pervaded the entire lives of the incumbents to a much greater extent than do most occupations. However, the effect varied depending on the career stage at which surrender caught a given officer. Those still in early training could rather readily switch educational careers and enter another occupational field, usually a profession. Those who had spent years in the military and were most solidly established as officers found themselves treated as criminals and cut off from most lines of occupational activity. The affected men had to start over in different occupational spheres with varying degrees of success. Many of them initially turned to farming and small business because they were cut off from government, corporation, and university jobs.

It is remarkable, however, how many ex-officers appeared to be quite successful in a post-military career by the common-man tests of judging such success. Here is an indicator of the links of occupational life to other relationships, a theme I will refer to again. An occupation creates links to persons and social segments outside one's occupation. If one's occupational status is high, these links are likely to be with relatively powerful persons. At a time of adversity, such powerful links can be used to make a recovery in another line of work, frequently starting out at a rather high level. To switch career ladders, if one has the appropriate connections, one need not drop to the bottom of the new one in order to start climbing it. The change, however, was often experienced as a complete shift in occupational and civic timetables, spoken of by some of the ex-officers as a "rebirth."

One of the most interesting, important, and controversial concepts arising from the study of Japanese industry is that of lifetime employment. Some of the early writers (e.g., Abegglen 1958) pose lifetime employment as an important feature of Japanese industry that distinguishes it in a major way from Western capitalist enterprise. In more recent years the pervasiveness of lifetime employment has been questioned (Cole 1971; Dore 1973). Some of the papers in this book (especially Solomon Levine, Karen Holden, Kenneth Skinner, Samual Coleman) present still more data showing that lifetime employment does *not* characterize most of Japanese business enterprise.

The Levine and Skinner papers demonstrate that lifetime employment is limited almost entirely to large corporate enterprises and to certain levels of government employment. Levine points out in Chapter One that most workers are employed by small firms and these rarely provide lifetime employment for most of their employees. Thus, we have different career timetables for workers in large and in small firms. Many in the large corporations enter at an early age and move through a career line in a relatively predictable way. In small firms there is much turnover (one-fourth changing jobs each year), not very different from patterns found in the United States and the United Kingdom. Among those taking jobs, one-half are recruited from other jobs. Furthermore, workers seldom move from small to large firms, and so the career timetables are not readily convertible, one to the other. None of the authors focussed specifically on the long-term work lives of men whose entire careers (if that is the right word) involve small firms (or more likely, a series of small-scale employers), so we do not have a picture of how such persons attempt to structure their occupational patterns over the years. Like the auto workers described by Chinoy (1965) and Walker and Guest (1952), they may focus their attention on other aspects of their lives and regard the job as simply a way of financing more important and interesting activities while at the same time fantasizing about escaping the unattractive work routine. For such persons, the job search becomes a matter of seeking better and more secure forms of financing. But without more specific information about the Japanese worker without lifetime employment, this issue is too speculative to pursue.

One characteristic of lifetime employment is that there is typically a gradual increase in salary from the time one begins to the time of retirement, regardless of specific job assignments. In most lines of work the most productive level is likely to be reached well before retirement and thereafter may actually decrease significantly, but the salary continues to go up. In effect, workers are being paid later for work done earlier. (This is no different from many career lines in

251

the United States and elsewhere.) This arrangment makes the older employee less attractive to the employer and may be responsible in part for the early retirement age among those with lifetime employment in Japan.

Several of the papers in this book suggest that retirement careers are more important to the Japanese than to North Americans, perhaps because the usual retirement age gives them more years to pursue a career after retirement. The retirement jobs or careers are often tied to the pre-retirement status, so that the pre- and post-retirement position appears to be part of a single occupatinal timetable. The pottery-maker retires from the household and shop headship to pursue a speciality. Government ministry officials "retire" to high-level positions in private business or public corporations, often associated with their ministry responsibilities.

Lifetime employment cannot include most workers in a capitalist economy. To have all or most workers locked into a job would not allow business enterprise to respond flexibly to changes in market demands. The large proportion of workers who are not in life employment provide such flexibility. They work for small firms which subcontract with large firms when demand for a given product is high and readily reduce their work force when demand is low. Even the large firms have a segment of their work force without lifetime employment status. A major element in this segment are women workers.

We have in this book more information about women than about men without life employment (Holden, Coleman and James McLendon). When we examine the position of women workers in Japan, it becomes clear that lifetime employment rarely pertains to them. Thus, a large and constantly growing proportion of the labor force is omitted from this purportedly distinctive feature of Japanese enterprise. A commonly expected pattern of female labor is that they will take jobs immediately after completing their schooling, keep their eyes open for a potential husband (and the attraction of leading firms for young attractive cultured women is that they have the best husband material among their junior management employees), and after a successful catch and resulting marriage (certainly no later than their first child), they retire gracefully. The timetable of such a female employee is built around finding a suitable husband rather than improving her job situation. Here too there are norms about how long each stage should take, and a woman who has not been married and retired from work by 30 at the firm studied by McLendon (Chapter Eight) is deemed a failure in her quest. From an organizational point of view, the expectations of the young women workers means that the careers of the women do not have to be taken into account in setting organizational goals and practices. There is an expectation of a short working span with great turnover, little or no promotion, and early retirement without the need for retirement pay. Thus, the "problems" posed by lifetime employment male workers do not exist in the case of women. As Coleman puts it, in Chapter Nine the female labor force tends to be treated as auxiliary and temporary, concentrated in the less skilled jobs with few opportunities for advancement.

Some women *do* stay in the labor force over a long period of time, even in those large firms where long tenure for women is discouraged in a variety of formal and informal ways. In McLendon's portrayal, those who stayed past 30 are the "unsuccessful" ones; that is, those who did not land a suitable husband and are thus forced to continue working as an alternative. This poses a problem for some managements who have difficulty finding a suitable slot for such women in their organization. The obvious solution of having them supervise younger women is considered undesirable because they present an improper "role model" — managers do not want to give a young woman the notion that it is alright to stay single and keep working. So there is an effort to find specialized jobs where the women have some skill and where they are relatively isolated from the younger women workers.

Of course, there *are* women who continue to work as a matter of choice, sometimes even after marriage and children, and their number is increasing. In recent years, women have made up 40 percent of the labor force, with the greatest increase in the 35 to 64 age range that accounts for 45 percent of employed women. Seventy percent of employed women are in white-collar jobs as Holden shows in Chapter Two.

In any case, the occupational timetables for women are typically different from those of men in the same firm or line of work. The progression in terms of promotion or change in job assignment is different, the opportunities to express managerial or skill talents is different, and the degree of linking to other segments of life is different. Marriage for men and women is relatively late, but almost all marry, so the great majority of women over 35 in the labor force are married. Childlessness is rare, but children come early in marriage and are usually bunched close together. Whatever the rationale for such bunching may be, the effect is to leave women available to work outside the home for a relatively long period of time. The fact that women have almost all the responsibility for housework and child-rearing (is there any place in the world where this is *not* the case?) would reduce competition with men for the most desirable positions even if there were no perception of women as secondary workers.

Let us look more closely at the linking issue. This is seen most clearly in the household pottery industry (Kleinberg) where the manufacture of the product and the fabric of relationships within the extended families are intertwined. Marriage into a pottery household gives a man not only kin privileges, but a given position in the pottery-making hierarchy, a hierarchy through which he could be expected to rise over time. In fact, if a man has not been born into a pottery family, he can most readily accomplish entry into this industry through marriage to a pottery family daughter. We may wonder, in fact, which decision is the primary one, and indeed this may often not be clear to the participants. It is interesting that changes in career timetables in pottery making have affected related family positions. A man who moves up faster than previously was the case into control over the manufacture and sale of pottery is also likely to become head of household earlier than was usual. The "old man" must make way in both spheres at once. During a period of transition, such shifts in expectations are likely to result in frequent conflict as different participants vary in their acceptance of the changing timetables. Note too that women do not gain dominant positions in either the family or the occupational sphere. Their primary activity is the domestic operation of the household. In the shop they are assigned the more menial assisting task. Their dependent family status is accompanied by their assistant role in pottery-making. Their community status is largely dependent on the status of their father or husband.

Susan Long also presents, in Chapter Five, a picture of intertwining occupations and family, as well as consumer, civic, and hobby careers. Medical professionals with a private practice located in their home must select this home and arrange their working times in coordination with the needs of their family life, needs which change over the years at the same time that the professional practice is developing. The woman in this case also has an occupation, that of doctor's wife, which requires her to answer the telephone and respond to callers in a way which will assist her husband and maintain and improve his practice, while at the same time running the household and caring for her children. The type of medical career selected depends in part on family members and friends in medicine who may be able to offer a position at the "right time" — that is, at a time when a career shift is being considered, such as when a university doctor realizes he is not likely to obtain a permanent university professorship. The birth of his children or their reaching a given age (e.g., college entrance) may entail expenses which make some positions more desirable than others. His movement from one career timetable (e.g., hospital appointment) to another (e.g., private practice) may be dictated not only by the career contingencies of the occupation itself, but by the point in the life cycle of his parental and matrimonial families. It may also be linked to the careers of other people — for example, if a sponsor's university career is blocked, his follower also has to seek another career line. If a physician wants to pursue a civic career, he will be able to do so more easily in a private practice than in a university or hospital job. Long argues that such links are probably not unique to medical careers, but represent a pattern which could be widely detected if we were to focus the same kind of attention on persons in other lines of work.

The papers give evidence of other linked careers. Jack Lewis in Chapter Six shows that election to public office is closely associated with occupations with a combination of property and discretionary time, e.g., farming and private business. Among other things, a political career (whether one is elected or not) does not disrupt the occupational career of such persons. McLendon and Noguchi show a link between marriage and occupation for men as well as for women. Young corporate men are less likely to be promoted if they are not married, and their superiors will let them know this if they have not taken action on their own by a "reasonable age." The character of the marriage partner may also have an effect on their promotion chances. Among railroad workers we find instances of a reverse cause and effect — a young man's marriage chances are reduced if he fails to get expected early promotions.

## Conclusion

Taking off from the contributions of papers in this volume, what might we say about career timetables in modern societies?

First of all, the linear time structuring in Japan does not seem significantly different from that of modern North America and Europe. Is this because such time conceptions are widespread throughout humankind or because Japan is so thoroughly "Westernized"? This question cannot be answered on the basis of the information in this book. However, until we have contrary evidence, it seems reasonable to assume that this is a characteristic of industrial and post-industrial societies. It underlies the vast amount of planning, from individual to organizational to national, in an effort to predict and control the future. Not only does such planning project one's experiences forward in time (the very words assume a linear time flow), but criteria of successful outcome of planning are based in part on meeting a timetable of goals. I believe we may also assume that linear structuring of time is spreading as more parts of the world become "developed," that is, more like our Western European society. Thus, this mode of analysis of behavior becomes ever more universal.

Secondly, the Japanese materials point up the importance of timetable linkages. They can be thought of as two kinds. An individual intertwines the timetables of different aspects of his/her life. And two or more individuals or organizations possess timetable links that affect one another.

The links between occupational and family careers receive the most attention in this book. There are instances of men making career shifts in response to or as a consequence of getting married, the birth of children, or children entering advanced schooling. Women's occupational phases and changes are even more closely linked to family events. Although the evidence is even thinner, there are suggestions that civic activities, hobbies and recreation, and major consumer expenditures are also often linked to changing conditions of one's occupation and that occupational activities may be modified to accommodate other important areas of one's life (or vice versa). This book includes a few detailed case studies of such intertwining careers. When one looks for comparative cases in North America or Europe, there proves to be a dearth of such studies. Of course, one can readily think of anecdotal information to demonstrate the same points, but it is remarkable how little systematic study has been directed toward the interconnections of occupation, family, and other spheres of life.

In an unpublished study of ambulance services (with Dorothy J. Douglas), we found the industry dominated by small-scale companies, often family affairs. Jobs and positions in the companies were more dependent on relationships to the controlling family than on one's skills or credentials, much like the pottery households described by Kleinberg. Thus, in one case the son-in-law of the owner was made garage foreman, but when he and his wife separated, he was promptly fired from his job. This may appear to be an anachronistic footnote to modern American enterprise, but is it indeed all that rare? Our research focus on large-scale enterprise with bureaucratic procedures has caused us to miss the process of linked careers involving a substantial portion of the population whose occupational fate may be heavily dependent on their personal relationships, including their kinship position.

Then there is the sharp differential between women and men in the nature of their lifecourse. The analysis spawned by the women's movement in the West has demonstrated the differing cultural perspectives of the two sexes. Even when men and women work together, they measure their lives by different events and create different, although often interdependent, timetable norms. The assumption is often made that men (compared to women) have the greater power to make their career goals the primary ones in a family, especially with respect to holding a job or pursuing a career. Occupational status and mobility studies have focussed almost solely on male workers. The Japanese studies reported in this book show the women workers being treated as secondary and auxiliary in the large corporation as well as in the cottage industry. Such a model suggests that the lifecourse of a family is determined by the decisions and occupational needs of the male head, to which the wife adapts as best as she can.

Suppose, however, that we apply a different model, in which the wife has power equal to or greater than that of her husband, including her own source of income from work outside the home. If the lives and goals of the husband and wife are different in some important respects — and books such as that of Bernard (1972) show that this is almost universally the case — we would have the conditions for negotiated timetables. A study of such negotiations should tell us more about the nature of intertwining careers and how they influence one another and about how the feminist model of family life develops in practice. The latter goal is approached in recent works on the "dual career" family (Pepitone-Rockwell 1980; Rapoport and Rapoport 1971). For example, how are decisions made on geographical movement to promote the professional career of one or both of the partners? How does the division of household and child-rearing tasks affect the occupational career advancement of occupational activity? We must keep in mind, however, that the "dual career" concept has affected only a very small proportion of couples in the United States, mostly in a few professional fields of work. In the case of most "dual-job" couples, there is no effect to pursue a feminist ideal and indeed the wife may be working only out of economic necessity. In such cases the "negotiation" is frequently an arena of conflict in which goals and timetables repeatedly clash without resolution. (This situation is graphically depicted by Lillian Rubin in chapter 9 of *Worlds of Pain*.) Clearly, if we are to gain a broad understanding of woman/man negotiation over lifecourse timetables, we need studies at various points in the socioeconomic scale as well as differing cultural settings.

Remember too that the feminist movement does not speak with one voice. One aspect is the demand for equality in the race for status and material reward — women should have as good a start and as many opportunities as men in the competition for "successful" careers in the more desirable lines of work and other ac- tivites. This approach would focus on career timetables in much the same way that we have done in the past, except that women would be included as major contestants in the race. We already have some data to show that in an occupational race defined in this manner, the wife, the single woman, and indeed the single man is at a dis- advantage compared to the married man who, despite ideological statements, receives disproportionately large career support from his wife while making disproportionately small contributions to household and child-rearing activities.

Another feminist approach declares that the race itself is in- human — a male game to put women down and incidentally mak- ing the world a less pleasant place to live in. Proponents of this view would presumably support radically different goals for both women and men, and with them different occupational, family, and other lifecourse timetables. What would such a lifestyle look like? There are already people trying to live in close approximation of a non- competitive philosophy, but except for the communes of the late 1960's and early 70's, social scientists have paid little attention to them. Even though a noncompetitive lifestyle may never become a prominent feature of the post-industrial world, it could show how far people can modify the commonly accepted career patterns of their society.

## References

Abegglen, James C.
1958   The Japanese Factory. Glencoe, Ill.: Free Press.

Bernard, Jesse
1972   The Failure of Marriage. New York: Bantam.
Chinoy, Ely
1965   Automobile Workers and the American Dream. Boston: Beacon
       Press.
Cole, Robert E.
1971   Japanese Blue Collar. Berkeley and Los Angeles: University of
       California Press.
Dore, Ronald P.
1973   British Factory — Japanese Factory. Berkeley and Los Angeles:
       University of California Press.
Pepitone-Rockwell, Fran
1980   Dual-Career Couples. Beverley Hills, Calif.: Sage Publications.
Rapoport, Rhona, and Robert Rapoport
1971   Dual-Career Families. Baltimore: Penguin.
Roth, Julius A.
1963   Timetables. Indianapolis: Bobbs-Merrill.
Rubin, Lillian
1976   Worlds of Pain. New York: Basic Books.
Walker, Charles, and Robert Guest
1952   The Man on the Assembly Line. Cambridge, Mass.: Harvard
       University Press.

# Index